MW01378746

Constitution Day

*Reflections
by Respected Scholars*

Rhode Island Publications Society
Providence ∗ 2010

For information write:
The Rhode Island Publications Society
200 Allens Avenue
Providence, Rhode Island 02903
TEL: (401) 272-1776
FAX: (401) 273-1791
www.ripublications.org

Printed in the United States of America
ISBN 978-1-930483-05-7

Typeset in Adobe Caslon and Igino Marini's
IM Fell Great Primer, IM Fell Double Pica
and IM Fell English

Book design and composition by Clifford Garber
Cover photograph: Patrick T. Conley

Printed by Courier, Westford, Massachusetts

This Book is Dedicated

to

My Beautiful Wife

GAIL CAHALAN CONLEY

Hostess for Constitution Day

and

My Loyal and Patient Partner in Life

The dedication of the 7,000-volume Conley Library (shown here) on September 17, 2000, was the catalyst for the annual Constitution Day observance.

Acknowledgments

Constitution Day has had two aspects: it has been part scholarly exercise and part social spectacle. This book represents the former, and in its pages the learned contributors are duly acknowledged. Those who produced those pages for print include my secretary Linda Gallen, Rhode Island Publications Society editor Dr. Hilliard Beller, and designer Cliff Garber. They have transformed the efforts of an e-literate (me) into a finished product.

The social component of Constitution Day has involved many others, some of whom are depicted in the book's photos. The list of volunteers is longer. The Rhode Island Militia, most notably the Pawtuxet Rangers and the Bristol Train of Artillery, provided pageantry; the French Guard, led by Albert Raoul Beauparlant and Michael Dubois, handled many details, including those of a technical nature; my youngest daughter, Colleen Conley, marketed our books at each event; Professor Bob Poniatowski video-taped every lecture, and George Lincoln Sisson broadcast them for viewers on Full Channel TV and the statewide interconnect cable system; Father Joseph Lennon, O.P., gave eloquent invocations that were a regular reminder that we are "one nation, under God"; Professor Scott Molloy warmed up every audience with his lavish and original introductions; Professors Bob McCarthy, John Kaminski, and Gordon Wood assisted me in the selection and recruitment of speakers; my lifelong friend Dr. Stanley Gurnick, our accomplished Constitution Day pianist, traveled from his Chicago-area home to nearly every annual event and indirectly furnished much of the funding that allowed Gail and me to stage these elaborate celebrations; Linda Gallen, in addition to her critical role in producing the book, handled all correspondence, invitations, and preliminary arrangements involving the speakers and the attendees, with an assist from Anna Loiselle;

and my wife, Gail, the perfect hostess, made every Constitution Day at Gale Winds an exercise in elegance.

In Gail's words, Constitution Day "was like having a wedding at our home every year!" The final "wedding" occurs on September 12, 2010, when this book is presented to its creators and to those regular attendees who helped to make our Constitution Day a satisfying and memorable experience.

Foreword

ON SEPTEMBER 17, 2000—Constitution Day—I dedicated my new library building at "Gale Winds," a Narragansett Bay-front home I share with my wife Gail at the tip of Bristol Point in the historic port town of Bristol, Rhode Island. The Jeffersonian-style library, built from my design by contractor Harold Brown, is an octagon, twenty-two feet in diameter, consisting of a full basement and a main level with a fireplace and a twelve-foot domed ceiling. The intricate moldings and shelving were crafted by furniture-maker Joseph Voltas and carpenter Mark Giroux and finished by artisan James Marshall (no relation to Chief Justice John). The two-level structure was designed to house 7,000 volumes. As of this writing in 2010, it is bursting at the seams with 7,600 tomes, prompting my wife to remind me repeatedly that she advised me in 1999 to increase the diameter to thirty feet.

Because my scholarly specialty has been Rhode Island constitutional development, with a brief and enjoyable foray into the realm of federal constitutional history with Professor John Kaminski, I chose September 17, 2000, as the date to dedicate my library. I had just fully and systematically stocked it with the assistance of my son Thomas, who transported the books for me to shelve.

Having served as chairman of Rhode Island's bicentennial of independence observance (ri76) and its bicentennial of statehood, as well as the chairman of the United States Constitution Council, I had become accustomed to pageantry and formal observances. So I reasoned, "Why not make my new library, filled as it is with books on American and local history, constitutional development, and law, the object of a dedicatory event?"

Constitution Day 2000 was indeed an event—passed hors d'oeuvres, drinks at the gazebo, musical entertainment including singers, two pianists, and a bagpiper, and a splendid setting on a lawn, beach, and dock from which the 105 guests had an unobstructed view of the Newport Bridge, eleven miles southward down Narragansett Bay. Those guests were equally impressive — a majority of the state Supreme Court, several judges of the Superior Court, former and incumbent state and local officials, a U.S. congressman, generals and heads of local militia units, professors and administrators from nearby colleges, lawyers, authors, business leaders, and many of my former graduate students.

The pièce de résistance, however, was the speaking program which I emceed. It consisted of an erudite invocation by Father Joseph L. Lennon, O. P. (styled by some as Rhode Island's version of Fulton J. Sheen); eloquent introductory remarks by Rhode Island's chief justice Joseph R. Weisberger, and audience-engaging scholarly presentations by Pulitzer Prize-winning historian Gordon Wood of Brown University and noted eighteenth-century scholar Jack Greene of The Johns Hopkins University, the leading authority on Anglo-American history during our colonial era. Their presentations are published herein.

Constitution Day 2000 was such a success that many attendees suggested that my wife and I make this academic exercise an annual event. We did so with enthusiasm. For the remainder of the decade, I selected prominent scholars to be Constitution Day speakers. They appeared under the auspices of the Rhode Island Publications Society (which I also chair), with the coordination of my secretary Linda Gallen, who arranged all ten events. Most of these lecturers were provided with a stipend, travel expenses, and lodging at Gale Winds, if necessary, in return for an original lecture on a constitutional theme that would eventually be incorporated into a published anthology. After ten Constitution Days and twelve lectures, that time has come.

All of our annual events were memorable and were preserved on video taken and edited by Professor Bob Poniatowski for viewing on statewide cable TV through the intercession of the late George Sisson, the "father" of cable TV in Rhode Island. Among the more salient memories were the journey by auto of John Kaminski from Madison, Wisconsin to speak at Constitution Day No. 2 in the immediate aftermath of 9/11, when planes were grounded; the off-shore cannonading of our party at Constitution Day No. 4 by the crew of the continental sloop *Providence*, a replica of the first ship of the U. S. Navy; and the unveiling at Constitution Day No. 5 of a life-size statue of noted Rhode Island reformer Thomas Wilson Dorr, commissioned for the Heritage Harbor Museum by Gail and me and equisitely executed by sculptor Joseph Avarista.

On April Fool's Day 2004 — in retrospect a most appropriate time for us to start our Providence harborfront development venture — Gail and I began the renovation of a four-story industrial building on Allens Avenue. Eventually this 1899 Providence Gas Company "purification plant" (later transformed into a warehouse for the Fabre steamship line and then into a tire company) merited inclusion on the National Register of Historic Places. By September 2005, the building's top floor had been sufficiently completed as a conference and function center so that it could become the new site for Constitution Day. Unfortunately, the lavish and salubrious setting of Gale Winds seemed better suited for constitutional contemplation than the austere atmosphere of a converted manufacturing plant on Providence's still derelict harborfront. The attendance at Bristol, which had grown to 150, dwindled to less than one-third that number in the Conley's Wharf Building, even though participants were enticed by my one-hour narrated historic tour of Providence's harbor aboard our 49-passenger tour boat, *Providence Piers*.

Constitution Day was an enjoyable academic enterprise. It gained Gail and me acquaintance with some of America's foremost constitutional historians and cemented our relationships with those who were already friends, such as Gordon Wood, John

Kaminski, and Joe Weisberger. Sadly, say the pundits, all good things must end; but happily, in these published essays, Constitution Day lives on.

Preface

RHODE ISLAND, alone among the original thirteen states, refused to attend the Philadelphia Convention of 1787, but these dozen essays are not tributes to the twelve who did. Perhaps, because of the Rhode Island setting in which they were presented, one might consider these talks atonement for that historic boycott. Less facetiously, the reader might also regard them as serious and analytical attempts to shed small beams of light to augment Ben Franklin's "rising sun"—that Founding Father's oft-cited September 1787 metaphor suggesting how he viewed the just-completed Constitution.

There is no unifying theme to these essays, other than the Constitution itself, although many—perhaps to placate the hosts—contain allusions to Rhode Island's influence on or involvement with our nation's basic law.

These essays do not form a union (nor even a confederation). Together they constitute an old-fashioned *festschrift*, not to honor an individual but in honor of the secular document as amended, whose influence in America and upon the world has been greater than any other. English prime minister William E. Gladstone phrased it more eloquently on the occasion of the Constitution's centennial when he stated that he considered "that Constitution as the most remarkable work known to men in modern times to have been produced by the human intellect, at a single stroke (so to speak), in its application to political affairs."

Given their scholarly eminence (even historical star-power) the galaxy of writers in this anthology give it importance beyond its humble and somewhat unorthodox origins. Hopefully the reader will find illumination from their insights, speculations, and original research.

PATRICK T. CONLEY

About the Authors

GORDON S. WOOD is Alva O. Way University Professor Emeritus at Brown University, where he taught for forty years. He received his Ph.D. from Harvard University and taught there and at the University of Michigan before joining the faculty at Brown in 1969. His books include the Pulitzer Prize-winning *The Radicalism of the American Revolution* (1992); the Bancroft Prize-winning *The Creation of the American Republic, 1776–1787* (1969); *The Americanization of Benjamin Franklin* (2004); and *Empire of Liberty, A History of the Early Republic, 1789–1815* (2009), a volume in the Oxford History of the United States. He is a fellow of the American Academy of Arts and Sciences and the American Philosophical Society, and he writes frequently for the *New York Review of Books* and *The New Republic*.

JACK P. GREENE is a historian of the early modern British Empire who taught at Michigan State University, Western Reserve University, and the University of Michigan before joining the faculty of The Johns Hopkins University in 1966. He taught at Johns Hopkins for thirty-nine years until his retirement in 2005 as Andrew Mellon Professor in the Humanities Emeritus. Eighty-eight historians have taken doctorates under his direction at Western Reserve, Johns Hopkins, and the University of Virginia. He has published extensively in several different areas of his specialty. His most recent book is *Exclusionary Empire: British Liberty Overseas, 1600–1900* (2010).

JOHN P. KAMINSKI received his Ph.D. at the University of Wisconsin at Madison and became associate editor, then coeditor and director, of *The Documentary History of the Ratification of the Constitution*, a project he has worked on for forty-one years. In 1981 John started, and continues to direct, the Center for the Study of the American Constitution in the History Department at University of Wisconsin-Madison. He has published twenty-one volumes of the *Documentary History* and another twenty-one volumes on such topics as slavery, the Constitution, and the Bill of Rights, as well as quotation books and biographies. In 1990 he instituted a judicial education program that provides one-day seminars to federal, state, and international judges.

JAMES T. PATTERSON is Ford Foundation Professor of History Emeritus at Brown University and one of the most highly respected authorities on modern America. Jim received his doctorate from Harvard and taught at Indiana University for eight years before arriving at Brown in 1972. He has published ten books, including *Grand Expectations: The United States, 1945–1974* (1996), which won a Bancroft Prize; *Brown v. Board of Education: A Civil Rights Milestone and Its Troubled Legacy* (2001); and *Restless Giant: The United States from Watergate to Bush v. Gore* (2005). He is the only author to contribute two volumes to the prestigious *Oxford History of the United States*.

JACK N. RAKOVE is the William Robertson Coe Professor of History and American Studies and a professor of political science and (by courtesy) law at Stanford University, where he has taught since 1980. Jack earned his Ph.D. at Harvard University and taught at Colgate University for five years before coming to Stanford. He is the author of six books on the history of the Revolution and the Constitution, including *Original Meanings: Politics and Ideas in the Making of the Constitution*, which won the 1997 Pulitzer Prize in history, and, most recently, *Revolutionaries: A New History of the Invention of America*. He is a former president of the Society for the History of the Early American Republic.

CAROL RUTH BERKIN is Presidential Professor of History at Baruch College and the Graduate Center, City University of New York. She is the author of several books, including *First Generations: Women in Colonial America*; *A Brilliant Solution: Inventing the American Constitution*; and *Revolutionary Mothers: Women in the Struggle for America's Independence*. She is a frequent contributor to PBS and History Channel television documentaries on early American and Revolutionary-era history, and she serves on the boards of several professional organizations, including the Gilder Lehrman Institute of American History and the National Council for History Education.

PAULINE MAIER is the William Rand Kenan Jr. Professor of American History at MIT. Her writings on the Revolution include *From Resistance to Revolution: American Radicals and the Development of Intercolonial Opposition to Britain* (1972); *The Old Revolutionaries: Political Lives in the Age of Samuel Adams* (1980); and *American Scripture, Making the Declaration of Independence* (1997), which was on the *New York Times Book Review* editors' choice list of the eleven best books, fiction and nonfiction, of 1997. Her next book, a narrative history of the ratification of the Constitution, will be published by Simon and Schuster in the fall of 2010.

WILLIAM M. WIECEK teaches Constitutional Law, Property, and Federal Courts at Syracuse University College of Law, and he has taught as a visitor at Arizona State University, the University of California-Davis, and the University of Kentucky. He is a constitutional and legal historian who has written extensively on slavery and its abolition, republicanism, and the United States Supreme Court. His major work is *The Birth of the Modern Constitution, 1941–1953*, a volume in the Oliver Wendell Holmes Devise

History of the United States Supreme Court. He is a graduate of the Harvard Law School and earned his Ph.D. in history at the University of Wisconsin-Madison.

JOSEPH R. WEISBERGER has served in the Rhode Island judiciary for fifty-four years. He was appointed to the Superior Court in 1956 and became its presiding justice in 1972. He was elevated to the Supreme Court in 1978 and became chief justice in 1993. Retiring in 2001, he continues as an appellate mediator. Joe has been chairman of the American Bar Association's Trial Judges Conference and its Appellate Judges Conference. A graduate of Brown University and Harvard Law School, he served as a faculty member of the National Judicial College for thirty-three years and holds thirteen honorary degrees. He was appointed by Pope John Paul II to the rank of Knight Commander with Star of the Order of Saint Gregory. Like Gordon Wood and Patrick Conley, he is a member of the Rhode Island Heritage Hall of Fame.

CHRISTOPHER COLLIER is a professor of history emeritus at the University of Connecticut and a public historian. He was Connecticut's official State Historian for twenty years until his retirement in 2004, and he also served on the Connecticut Historical Commission. Kit has published a half-dozen scholarly works, including the Pulitzer Prize nominee *Roger Sherman's Connecticut: Yankee Politics and the American Revolution* (1971) and *All Politics Is Local: Family, Friends, and Provincial Interests in the Creation of the Constitution* (2002). He has coauthored thirty-two books with his brother James, including *Decision in Philadelphia: The Constitutional Convention of 1787* (1985) and many historical novels for middle schoolers, including the classic *My Brother Sam is Dead* (1974).

RONALD P. FORMISANO is the William T. Bryan Chair of American History at the University of Kentucky and a former president of the New England Historical Association. His latest book, *For the People: American Populist Movements from the Revolution to the 1850s* (2008), contains an extensive analysis of Rhode Island's Dorr War and the historical background from which it emerged. His books and articles have dealt with antebellum political culture as well as with contemporary forms of populism, both progressive and reactionary; the latter includes *Boston against Busing: Race, Class and Ethnicity in the 1960s and 1970s* (1991, 2004). Ron, a native Rhode Islander, received his doctorate in history from Clark University.

PATRICK T. CONLEY enjoys several careers. He was a professor of history and constitutional law at Providence College for thirty years, and he is a practicing attorney, a real estate developer, and a civic leader. Pat has written or edited twenty books and published numerous scholarly articles. He chaired the Rhode Island bicentennial celebrations of independence (1176) and statehood (1990) as well as the U.S. Constitution Council, and he founded the state's Heritage Commission and the Rhode Island Publications Society. Currently he is the president of the Heritage Harbor Museum project, the Fabre Line Club, the Rhode Island Senior Olympics, and the Rhode Island Heritage Hall of Fame, to which he was inducted in 1995.

CONTENTS

The Real Significance of *Marbury* v. *Madison*
Gordon S. Wood

T IS MY GREAT PLEASURE to speak this afternoon in honor of Pat Conley and the opening of his library. It is fitting that this occasion is being held on Constitution Day, September 17, the anniversary of the day the members of the Philadelphia Convention signed the Constitution and released it to the public. As you all know, Pat himself is a distinguished historian of the Constitution and its ratification, as well as being the leading scholar of Rhode Island's constitutional history. So this day has special meaning for him.

Pat asked me to talk briefly about some aspect of constitutional history. I have chosen for a subject many in this audience know a great deal about — the famous Supreme Court decision of 1803, *Marbury* v. *Madison*. We have all been told that this decision, written by Chief Justice John Marshall, was the one that established the practice of what came to be called judicial review. By judicial review we generally mean the authority of the Court to interpret the Constitution and to set aside acts of Congress and state legislatures that are in conflict with the Constitution. But the origins of this notion of judicial review are not what I want to talk about this afternoon. There are other things that are important about the *Marbury* decision.

Indeed, it may be that the *Marbury* decision is not really as important for the development of judicial review as we used to think. Some historians have claimed that the origins of the modern practice of judicial review can best be found not in the Marshall Court at all but only in the history of the last century or so. Apparently the term "judicial review" itself was only coined by constitutional scholar Edward Corwin in 1910. Certainly much of our image of Marshall as the originator of judicial review was a creation of the post-Civil War era—an image that culminated in the publication in 1916 of the four-volume biography of Marshall by Senator Albert Beverage.

Yet we cannot get away from the fact that the Marshall Court was crucially important in the development of the judiciary in America. Instead of focusing on Marshall's overturning of a statute, I want to emphasize something else that came out of the *Marbury* v. *Madison* decision—the idea of an independent judiciary that in fact made the development of judicial review possible.

Marshall is without question the most famous chief justice in our history and the longest-serving chief justice; he held office for thirty-five years and spanned the administrations of five presidents. Through most of this period he had more Republican than Federalist colleagues on the Court, yet he was still able to build a consensus and get the Court to speak with one voice. He had a robust and convivial personality and got along with people easily. "I love his laugh," Joseph Story, his colleague on the Court, said of him: "it is too hearty for an intriguer." The Court had a rule that the justices would not drink any wine during their deliberations unless it was raining. Marshall had the habit of going to the window and looking out and declaring that it must be raining somewhere in these United States.

In order to understand what a shrewd fellow Marshall was, perhaps I should remind you a bit about the nature of the *Marbury* case. Like Marshall himself, William Marbury was one of the Federalist "midnight judges" appointed in March 1801 by Federalist president John Adams in the waning hours of his term. Marbury was slated to be a justice of the peace for the District of Columbia. Adams, however, left office before Marbury's commission could be delivered, and when the Republican Thomas Jefferson became president, he refused to deliver it. Marbury then brought suit in the Supreme Court, seeking a writ of mandamus requiring Secretary of State Madison to deliver his commission. It looked to many that the Court might openly challenge the authority of the president. But the Marshall Court could only lose in a direct contest with the president: if the Court refused to order Jefferson to deliver the commission, Jefferson and the Republicans would win by default; if the Court did order the president to do so and he refused, the Court would be humiliated. The Court thus had to move in a very roundabout way to assert its authority.

The Court's opinion set forth in 1803 answered several key questions. Was Marbury entitled to his commission? And if so, did the law afford him a remedy? Yes, answered Marshall to both questions. Marbury had a vested right in the office for the term fixed by statute, and the law had to provide a remedy for a violation of a vested legal right. A collision with President Jefferson seemed imminent, but when Marshall asked and answered his third question, he wisely evaded such a collision. The question was this: Was the remedy for the violation of Marbury's right a writ of mandamus issued by the Supreme Court? No, said Marshall. The Supreme Court could not issue such writs because Section 13 of Congress's 1789 Judiciary Act authorizing that power was unconstitutional: Congress did not have the authority to alter the original jurisdiction of the Supreme Court contained in Article III, Section 2, of the Constitution. By posing the questions in this unusual order, Marshall was able to make his point without having to suffer the consequences of it. As Jefferson and other Republicans pointed out, the Court in its final question disclaimed all cognizance of the case, but in the first two questions it declared what its opinion would have been, if it had cognizance of it.[1]

Thus Marshall indirectly asserted the Court's role in overseeing the Constitution without the serious political repercussions that would have followed from a head-on collision with the Republicans. Indeed, because his decision was so indirect, few people understood what it meant. Although Marshall's decision in *Marbury* has since taken on immense historical significance as the first assertion by the Supreme Court of its right to declare acts of Congress unconstitutional, no one in 1803 saw its far-reaching implications. The Republicans actually liked the decision better than the Federalists. They thought that if Marshall wanted to circumscribe the original jurisdiction of his Court, then he had every right to do so. The decision thus seemed very limited and ambiguous. In fact, it was the only time in Marshall's long thirty-five-year tenure as chief justice in which the Supreme Court declared an act of Congress unconstitutional.

But Marshall's *Marbury* decision did contain some ideas that were relevant at the time, ideas that contributed to the development of judicial independence. I think that the idea of judicial independence was more important than judicial review; it was, in fact, a prerequisite for the development of judicial review. Establishing the judiciary as one of the three powers in a tripartite system of government, standing equally alongside the legislature and the executive, was a great achievement, and one that we historians haven't paid sufficient attention to.

By maintaining the Supreme Court's independence in a very hostile Republican climate, Marshall contributed to this achievement. He began in 1801 by immediately trying to escape from the partisan politics of the 1790s and to avoid any direct confrontation with the Republicans. In a series of decisions the Court retreated from the advanced positions the Federalists had tried to establish for the judiciary and federal law in the 1790s. The Marshall Court rejected the high-toned Federalist notion that the common law of crimes applied in the federal courts. And in the 1807 trial of Aaron Burr, Marshall set aside the broad definition of treason the Federalists had invoked in the 1790s and instead interpreted the Constitution's definition of treason very strictly and narrowly.

In a variety of ways Marshall sought to pull in the Federalist horns to save the judiciary from Republican efforts to reduce its authority, and his subtle and oblique *Marbury* decision was part of his policy of getting more out of less. Not only did he assert, however indirectly, the authority to the Court to set aside an act of Congress that contradicted the Constitution; he also set forth the idea that the courts in America had an important and exclusive role to play apart from politics. In seeking to justify the Court's assertion of authority to oversee the Constitution, he created two separate realms, a public one and a private one. Some matters, he said in the *Marbury* decision, belonged exclusively to the legislatures and executives. These were political matters; "they respect the nation, not individual rights," and thus were "only politically examinable." But questions involving the vested rights of individuals, he went on, were different; they were in their "nature, judicial, and must be tried by the judicial authority."[2]

This distinction was new and very significant. By drawing a line between politics and judicial activity and by turning all questions of individual rights into exclusively judicial issues, Marshall appropriated an enormous amount of distinct authority for the courts and helped to establish the independence of the judiciary.

In the colonial period there had existed no sharp distinction between politics and law, or between legislation and adjudication; indeed, the two had been hopelessly blurred. The colonial legislatures involved themselves in all sorts of judicial activity. They heard private petitions, which were usually only the complaints of one individual or group against another. They tried cases in equity, reversed court decisions, and often granted appeals, new trials, and other kinds of relief from lower court decisions. Indeed, they usually saw themselves as the highest court in their colonies, and one of them at least retained that title—the General Court of Massachusetts.

At the same time, the colonial judges were deeply involved in political activity. They were appointed to the courts because of their social and political rank and connections, not because of any legal expertise; many were not even legally trained. They were expected to exercise a broad, ill-defined magisterial authority befitting their social rank; they were considered members of the government and remained intimately involved in politics. In the colonial period Thomas Hutchinson of Massachusetts, for example, who was no lawyer, was chief justice of the superior court, lieutenant governor, a member of the Governor's Council, and judge of probate for Suffolk County, Massachusetts—all at the same time.

Since judges held their offices at the pleasure of the crown, many colonists tended to identify the judges—or magistrates, as they were often called—with the much-resented royal governors, or chief magistrates. The judiciary was far from being considered an independent entity or even a separate branch of government. Indeed, the colonial courts as magistracies were still essentially political bodies and often performed innumerable administrative and executive tasks.

The colonial courts in most colonies assessed taxes, granted licenses, oversaw poor relief, supervised road repairs, set prices, upheld moral standards, and all in all monitored the localities over which they presided.[3] Consequently it is not surprising that many Americans in 1776 concluded that there were really, as one writer put it, "no more than two powers in any government, that is, the power to make laws, and the power to execute them; for the judicial power is only a branch of the executive, the CHIEF of every county being the first magistrate."[4] The colonial judges therefore bore much of the opprobrium attached to the royal governors and were often circumscribed by the power of popular juries to an extent not found in England itself.

Even after the Revolution judges continued to be regarded as magistrates with political as well as judicial authority. In appointing men to the Supreme Court, President George Washington was much more interested in the political character of his appointees than he was in their judicial experience. Of the twenty-eight men who were appointed to the federal district courts in the 1790s, only eight had held high judicial office in their states, but nearly all of them had been prominent political figures, having served in notable state offices and in the Continental Congress. These judges saw their service on the court as simply an extension of their general political activity. Many of the judges even continued to exercise political influence while sitting on the bench. They wrote political articles for newspapers, approved Federalist patronage in their districts, and openly and vigorously harangued members of grand juries on the public's duty to support the Federalist party and oppose the Republicans.

During the 1790s the early Congresses assigned a surprisingly large number of nonjudicial duties to the federal judges, including conducting the census and serving on commissions to reduce the public debt. In nearly all cases the judges willingly accepted these administrative responsibilities.[5] In 1792 Congress, in its Invalid Pension Act, assigned the federal courts administrative and magisterial duties that were not strictly judicial and that were actually subject to review by the secretary of war and the Congress. John Jay and Oliver Ellsworth offered political advice to the Federalist administrations and undertook important diplomatic missions abroad while serving as chief justices of the United States. As Alexander Hamilton pointed out in 1802 in a summary of this traditional view, judges were ex officio conservators of the peace and were expected to do more than merely adjudicate. Their duties, he said, were twofold, "judicial and ministerial," and the ministerial duties were "performed out of Court and often without reference to it."[6]

But when Jefferson and the Republicans took control of the presidency and the Congress after 1800, this traditional view of the judiciary began to change. Since many of the more radical Republicans were bent on reducing the power of the judiciary—even if they had to impeach members of the Supreme Court to get them out of office — the Federalists and more moderate Republicans sought to defend the judiciary from these assaults. Judges did so by erecting fences between politics and adjudication, as Marshall did. They shed their traditional broad and ill-defined political and magisterial roles that had previously identified them with the executive branch and adopted roles that were much more exclusively legal. The practices of judges' politically haranguing juries from the bench and of justices' performing diplomatic missions while sitting on the Court ceased and were not duplicated. Separation of powers and the independence of the judiciary now took on enhanced meanings that they had not possessed earlier. From being the much-scorned appendages of crown authority, judges in America now became what the Federalists called one of "the three capital powers of Government." From minor magistrates identified with the colonial executives, they were now turned into an equal and independent part of a modern tripartite government. It was a remarkable transformation, taking place as it did in a relatively short period of time.

Judges now increasingly saw themselves as professional jurists, separated from politics, and they limited their activities to hearing cases and interpreting the law in the regular courts, which became increasingly professional and less burdened by popular juries. The Supreme Court refused to give extrajudicial opinions on matters relating to international law, neutrality, and treaties, and in fact declined to give any opinions that did not arise out of an actual litigation between parties (i.e., "a case and controversy"). In every way the Court sought to make itself into a more purely judicial body.[7]

After 1800 more and more judges tended to avoid partisan politics and to pride themselves on their judicial expertise. They supported the publishing of judicial opinions and the collecting of law reports. In 1798 Alexander J. Dallas published the first volume of cases decided by the Supreme Court of the United States, and in 1804 William Cranch began publication of his *Supreme Court Reports*. At the same time, states were busy publishing reports of their court decisions. By 1821 Justice Story estimated that more than 150 volumes of American reports had been published in the previous two decades, "containing," he said, "a mass of decisions which evince uncommon ambition to acquire the highest professional character."[8]

Everywhere jurists published treatises and promoted the emergence of law as a science known best by trained impartial experts. The more complicated the law, the more expertise that was needed. In *Federalist* No. 78 Hamilton had pointed out "that a voluminous code of laws is one of the inconveniences necessarily connected with the advantages of a free government." Since all these laws "demand long and laborious study to acquire a competent knowledge of them . . . there can be but few men in the society who will have sufficient skill in the laws to qualify them for the station of judges."

The states now sought to improve the quality of their attorneys by controlling entrance to the bar. New Hampshire required at least two years of practice before its Court of Common Pleas for admittance. In Delaware and Maryland three years of law study were needed, followed by examinations. Rhode Island required three years of apprenticeship or two years if the applicant had a college degree. Universities added professors of law to their faculties, and some jurists called for the establishment of separate law schools to teach the new science of law.[9]

As jurists became more professional and the law was increasingly regarded as a special science, the courts sought to withdraw from politics and to avoid the most explosive and partisan political issues. Certainly that was the secret of much of the success of the Marshall Court in these years. Even the Court's decision to issue a single anonymous "opinion of the Court" in place of the earlier practice of each justice delivering his own opinion tended to dampen controversy and to give the impression of more consensus than in fact existed.

Like Marshall in his *Marbury* decision, many other Federalists now argued that the laws of the land concerning individual rights belonged exclusively to the courts. And the reason they belonged exclusively to the courts was that they involved private matters, not public, and private matters concerning individual rights required adjudication, not legislation.[10]

Federalists and others who were worried about the chaotic and often unjust actions of popular legislatures sought to limit the authority of these legislatures by carving out an exclusively private sphere of individual rights that was the domain solely of judges. The state legislatures, declared a writer from Pennsylvania, should stick with their great public responsibilities, and not "take up private business, or interfere in disputes between contending parties" as the colonial assemblies had habitually done. The evils of such legislative meddling, the writer went on to say, were

> heightened when the society is divided among themselves; — one party praying the assembly for one thing, and opposite party for another thing. . . . In such circumstances, the assembly ought not to interfere by any exertion of legislative power, but leave the contending parties to apply to the proper tribunals [that is, to the judiciary] for a decision of their differences."[11]

These efforts to separate private issues from public ones, to remove some questions from legislative politics and transform them into contests of individual rights, contributed to the emergence of a powerful independent judiciary in the early Republic. Almost overnight the judiciary in America became not only the principal means by which popular legislatures were controlled and limited but also the most effective instrument for sorting out individual disputes within a private sphere that the other institutions of government were forbidden to enter. It was an extraordinary development, not duplicated anywhere else in the modern world. And John Marshall in his *Marbury* decision contributed to that development of judicial independence. That is the real significance of *Marbury* v. *Madison*.

NOTES

1. Dumas Malone, *Jefferson the President: First Term, 1801–1805* (Boston, 1970), 149.

2. *Marbury* v. *Madison* (1803), in William Cranch, ed., *U.S. Supreme Court Reports*, 166, 167.

3. William E. Nelson, *Americanization of the Common Law: The Impact of Legal Change on Massachusetts Society, 1760–1830* (Cambridge, Mass., 1975), 14–16; Hendrick Hartog, "The Public Law of a County Court: Judicial Government in Eighteenth-Century Massachusetts," *American Journal of Legal History* 20 (1976): 321–23.

4. *Four Letters on Interesting Subjects* (Philadelphia, 1776), 21.

5. *The Documentary History of the Supreme Court of the United States, 1789–1800*, ed. Maeva Marcus et al. (New York, 1992), 4:723–29.

6. Hamilton, "The Examination," Feb. 23, 1802, Harold C. Syrett et al., eds., *The Papers of Alexander Hamilton* (New York, 1977), 25:531–32.

7. Charles Warren, *The Supreme Court in United States History* (Boston, 1937), 1:52, 111.

8. Anton-Hermann Chroust, *The Rise of the Legal Profession in America* (Norman, Okla., 1965), 2:75–77.

9. Ibid., 2:36–37, 173–223.

10. William E. Nelson, "Changing Conceptions of Judicial Review," *University of Pennsylvania Law Review* 120 (1972): 1176. The courts left "to legislatures the resolution of conflicts between organized social groups," that is, conflicts of politics, and concentrated on protecting the rights of individuals.

11. *Pennsylvania Packet* (Philadelphia), Sept. 2, 1786.

A Rhode Island Reflection

Professor Wood's thesis is that the establishment of an independent judiciary emerged in America not only by providing a means "by which popular legislatures were controlled and limited" but also by proving itself "the most effective instrument for sorting out individual disputes within a private sphere that the other institutions of government were forbidden to enter."

In this latter respect, a case emanating from Rhode Island in 1792 was the first federal court decision asserting judicial review and the first to chastise a legislature for taking up private business and interfering in disputes between contending individuals. In February 1791 the Rhode Island General Assembly granted the petition of merchant Silas Casey by giving this prominent Warwick debtor a three-year exemption "from all arrests and attachments" arising from his substantial indebtedness. Two of Casey's English creditors—Alexander Champion and Thomas Dickason—filed suit in federal circuit court to set aside this state interference with the obligation of contracts, asserting that the Assembly's action was a violation of Article I, Section 10, of the new Constitution.

In June 1792 a three-judge panel, consisting of Chief Justice John Jay of the U.S. Supreme Court, Associate Justice William Cushing, and Rhode Island's federal district judge Henry Marchant, ruled for the Englishmen. Though no written opinion was filed, the local papers provided ample insight into the court's rationale. According to the *Providence Gazette*, the federal justices unanimously determined "that the legislature of a state have no right to make a law to exempt an individual from arrests and his estates from attachments, for his private debts, for any term of time, it being clearly a law impairing the obligation of contracts and, therefore, contrary to the Constitution of the United States."

In November another circuit tribunal, consisting of Marchant and Supreme Court associate justices James Wilson and James Iredell, heard rearguments in *Champion and Dickason* v. *Casey*. They reaffirmed the earlier decision—an opinion that ranks as the first instance in American history where a federal court employed the power of judicial review to strike down a state statute for violating the Constitution of the United States.

Rhode Island almost lost its judicial primacy. In two similar 1791 cases involving English creditors and American debtors, federal circuit courts sitting in Connecticut and Georgia invalidated debtor-relief statutes of those states, but not on constitutional grounds. These courts ruled that the challenged state laws infringed upon Article 4 of the 1783 Treaty of Paris, which ended the Revolutionary War. This provision stated that "Creditors on either side, shall meet with no lawful impediments to the Recovery of the full value in Sterling Money of all bona fide Debts heretofore contracted."

Nonetheless, these 1791 federal court rulings are important as the earliest assertions of national supremacy under the new Constitution and could well have been decided by invoking Article VI, Section 2, of that document. Certainly that National Supremacy Clause was implicit in these circuit court decisions, though not invoked unless in dicta. See Charles Warren, *The Supreme Court in United States History*, 3 vols. (Boston, 1922), 1:62–71; and Julius Goebel Jr., *Antecedents and Beginnings to 1801*, vol. 1 of *The Oliver Wendell Holmes Devise History of the Supreme Court of the United States* (New York, 1971), 589–96 (marred only by its reference to *Champion & Dickason* v. *Casey* as "Champion & Dickison v. Carey").

I suggested to my son and namesake, Patrick T. Conley Jr., that he study the *Casey* decision as part of his research regimen at the University of Connecticut Law School. He did so, and published its results as "The First Judicial Review of State Legislation: An Analysis of the Rhode Island Case of *Champion and Dickason* v. *Casey* (1792)," in the bicentennial issue of the *Rhode Island Bar Journal* 36 (October 1987): 5–9. I reprinted it with additional commentary in my *Liberty and Justice: A History of Law and Lawyers in Rhode Island*, *1636–1998* (Providence, 1998), 216–23.

An American Solution to an English Problem: Some Remarks on the Anglo-American Background to the Quest for an Independent Judiciary
Jack P. Greene

SHARE Professor Wood's gratitude at being invited to participate in this symposium marking both the completion of Dr. Conley's new library and the celebration of Constitution Day for the year 2000. Professor Wood's compelling and original reading of the contemporary significance of the case of *Marbury* v. *Madison* provides a superb example of the way a preoccupation with modern concerns can mislead the historian—and the jurist—about the contemporary meaning of specific developments. As Professor Wood persuasively argues, students of the national Constitution at the end of the nineteenth century and ever since, searching for the roots of the important modern constitutional practice of judicial review, have overlooked Chief Justice Marshall's main intent in his decision in *Marbury* v. *Madison*: to lay the intellectual and constitutional foundations for an independent judiciary. My task today is to talk, very briefly, about the historical background of the important development Professor Wood has so gracefully illuminated for us this afternoon.

As many of you may be aware, the creation of an independent judiciary represented, as Professor Wood explains, an American

Jack Greene delivered this talk on the same program as Gordon Wood. It was designed as a brief supplement so as not to tax the attention span of the attendees at the inaugural Constitution Day—hence its brevity as compared with the other lectures in this volume.

solution to an ancient English problem. For an English polity that took pride in the fact that (as Sir John Fortescue announced as early as 1453) its monarch was not, like the kings and princes of continental Europe, above the law but bound by it, the problem of how to implement this dictum had been an enduring one. As long as the monarch could appoint and remove judges at pleasure, how could judges, the interpreters of law, bring him within its bounds? How could they avoid following his will? And if the rights or interests of the subject came into conflict with those of the monarch, how could judges possibly be counted on to render impartial justice according to the rule of law?

The English juridical and legal communities' solution to this problem was to guarantee the impartiality of judges by making judicial tenure contingent not on the royal pleasure but on the judges' own good behavior. This device, English constitutional reformers hoped, would put judicial decisions beyond the possibility of royal or, for that matter, parliamentary interference. Yet it was a reform that proved long and difficult to implement. In the early seventeenth century Chief Justice Sir Edward Coke made the issue of judicial tenure into a major focus of public debate in his proclaimed struggle "to settle the contest between prerogative and liberty," to "ascertain the bounds of sovereign power, and to determine the rights of the subject." But James I dismissed Coke in 1616, and throughout the seventeenth century James and his successors stubbornly resisted all efforts to limit their control over the terms of judicial appointments. Indeed, during the late 1680s James II's flagrant removals of noncooperating judges, and their replacements with men whom he could bend to his will, became a significant component in the case for his own removal during the Glorious Revolution of 1688–89. Only in the wake of that revolutionary settlement did anti-royal forces gain their point. By stipulating that all judgeships should be held during good behavior rather than at the pleasure of the crown, the Act of Settlement of 1701 effectively guaranteed the independence of judges in England.

How far this stipulation extended beyond the bounds of England (and Wales), however, was an issue that continued to trouble the polity of the larger British Empire — what Benjamin Franklin would later call Great*er* Britain, principally consisting of Scotland, Ireland, and the numerous polities that English people had established in eastern North America and the West Indies. In the view of metropolitan officials, the requirement that judicial tenure continue during good behavior, like so many other components of the English revolutionary settlement, did not extend to British polities overseas, where all but a few colonial judges continued to hold their appointments during the pleasure of the monarch.

Nevertheless, the question of judicial tenure became a major issue in the American colonies only during the quarter century before the American Revolution. At the midpoint of the eighteenth century, a growing political consciousness among settler political cultures in most colonies, together with a new effort by the mother country to bring the quasi-republican political regimes of the colonies under closer crown supervision, produced among colonists a rising resentment about the many constitutional inequalities between the colonies and Britain and a revival of the ancient demand that Britons overseas have the same rights and constitutional protections that Britons enjoyed at home. One result was a series of efforts by colonial legislatures from Jamaica north to New York to pass statutes specifying that judicial tenure should continue during good behavior. The crown's adamant refusal, from 1750 to 1775, to allow any of these laws to stand, along with its efforts to grant judges salaries independent of the colonial legislatures in the northern royal colonies, effectively made judicial tenure and the independence of judges into an evocative constitutional issue. This issue found resonance in the Declaration of Independence with the charge that among George III's various acts of tyranny were his efforts to make "judges dependent upon his will alone for the tenure of their offices and the amount and payment of their salaries."

With American Independence, most of the new republican states took steps to insure the independence of judges by granting them tenure during good behavior. With the legislatures of these states paying their salaries, however, such tenure fell considerably short of the achievement of an independent judiciary sought by Chief Justice Marshall in *Marbury* v. *Madison*. As Professor Wood has so eloquently and succinctly argued this afternoon, Marshall's was a distinctive and enduring constitutional achievement, and one of the most important of the several innovative devices by which republican America improved on its inherited English constitutional traditions.

A Rhode Island Reflection

Professor Greene focuses upon the reform of tenure during "good be-havior" as a means of securing a more independent judiciary. Coincident with the first British-American colonial foundations in the early seven-teenth century, Sir Edward Coke made judicial tenure a major reform issue, but Rhode Island remained unmoved for three and a half centu-ries. Until the implementation of the Constitution of 1843, judges were elected annually by the General Assembly; from that date until 1994, judges of the state's Supreme Court were still elected by the two houses in grand committee, but each judge could hold office "until his place be declared vacant by a resolution of the General Assembly to that effect" at its organizational session, and the Supreme Court justices were to "receive a compensation for their services which shall not be dimin-ished during their continuance in office." Upon organizing in January 1935, the Assembly vacated the entire Supreme Court in a political coup known as the Bloodless Revolution.

Constitutional amendments in 1994 gave the governor the power to appoint Supreme Court justices "from a list submitted by an inde-pendent non-partisan judicial nominating commission," and the jus-tices were finally given the right "to hold office during good behavior," a measure of independence so long denied them.

The American Revolution: A Three-Act Drama

John P. Kaminski

EFORE I BEGIN my formal remarks, I want to offer Pat Conley a bit of advice. I have known Pat for about fifteen years, and I have been meaning to offer this advice for a while. We all know that Pat has had a troubled career. Yes, he had a little success teaching for thirty years at Providence College; and yes, he has written a book or two or maybe a few more; and yes, he has had some success in propagating Rhode Island history through the Rhode Island Publications Society; and yes, he has been successful in the law and in real estate. But I would feel remiss if I didn't offer Pat the same advice that Philadelphia physician Dr. Benjamin Rush—signer of the Declaration of Independence and delegate to the Pennsylvania Convention that adopted the U.S. Constitution—gave General Nathanael Greene, the greatest Rhode Islander of the Revolutionary generation. It is somewhat personal, so I must ask all of the rest of you not to listen (well, maybe you could listen, Gail).

As the Revolutionary War was winding down in 1782, Rush wrote Greene that "You must quit Rhode Island forever. It is too contracted a spot in its manners and government for a mind like yours to expand in. South Carolina will afford great escape in a few years for genius and virtue to display themselves to the greatest advantage. Human nature there is in a state of activity or, as we chemists express it, in a state of fermentation. In Rhode Island the mind of men has reached its ne plus ultra."[1] And we all know, when you reach perfection, declension is sure to follow.

I come to this second Constitution Day lecture as the fourth generation of the Wisconsin School of History. Let me explain what that means. It was two University of Wisconsin graduate students who led the way in looking at the American Revolution as an economic and social phenomenon, not merely as abused patriots rising up against a tyrannical British imperial government. In the 1890s Orin G. Libby argued in his pathbreaking dissertation, which he later published, that economics and social issues played critical roles in the Revolution and during the Confederation years.[2] Libby was followed by Carl Becker, who in his insightful study of the origins of political parties in New York coined the phrase that still resonates today — that the Revolution was to decide not merely the question of home rule but who should rule at home.[3]

These two pathbreakers greatly influenced Charles A. Beard, whose monumental book *An Economic Interpretation of the Constitution* dominated the historiography of the Constitution for over fifty years.[4] Beard's work, in turn, influenced my major professor, Merrill Jensen, whose study of the Articles of Confederation has informed the profession for sixty years.[5] Jensen encouraged his graduate students to look at the Confederation years as a period of success — not as the dismal failure so often ignored in history books. He also encouraged us to focus our studies at the state level. Jensen's first Ph.D. student, Jackson Turner Main, took Jensen's advice and examined political parties at the state level and the role played by Antifederalists, the opponents of the Constitution.[6] I too have followed Jensen's lead, first in writing about economic issues — such as the issuance of paper money by four northern states during the Confederation — and then in working day-to-day with him in editing *The Documentary History of the Ratification of the Constitution*, which I have continued to do since Jensen's death in 1980.[7]

Throughout that forty-year period I have written and spoken extensively about Rhode Island. In fact, I can say that Pat Conley and I are the only historians who have favorably written about

Rhode Island during the Confederation. I am therefore delighted to be back in Rhode Island, although frankly I must admit to being a little uneasy being here in Bristol, a Federalist bastion.

What I would like to speak about today is two things: how the debate from 1763 to 1776 over the coming of the Revolution influenced the debate over the ratification of the Constitution a decade later, and how Rhode Island — tiny little Rhode Island — fit into that picture in such an important way.

THE FIRST ACT

What caused the American Revolution? Historians have asked that question many times. None asked it so terrifyingly, however, as when Merrill Jensen put it to his graduate students at the beginning of one year. Now you have to understand how graduate students felt about their major professors during the 1960s. It was your major professor who admitted you into his seminar; without that admission you were not accepted into graduate school. Once invited to the seminar, your major professor determined whether or not you would receive financial support and whether you would be allowed to continue to earn the Ph.D. or be invited to leave, perhaps with a terminal master's degree. Then, once you got the Ph.D., he would in large part determine whether you got a job. The quite liberal University of Wisconsin History Department and its alumni situated at colleges and universities around the world were known collectively as "The Big Red Machine."

Thus you can imagine what a dozen young intimidated graduate students huddled in that smoke-filled seminar room felt like when Professor Jensen asked, "What caused the American Revolution?" No one volunteered an answer; no one wanted to make a fool of himself by giving a ridiculously simple answer to such a complicated problem. Finally, with no volunteer, Jensen called upon Father Terrance, a Jesuit priest, to answer the question. Father Terrance, head bowed, started to sweat—that flop sweat that happens when you know you're in deep trouble. Finally, Father Terrance looked Jensen right in the eye and said, "What caused the American Revolution? One damn thing after another!" That's the best answer to that question that I have ever heard.

Thomas Jefferson said as much both in his 1774 pamphlet *A Summary View of the Rights of British America*, and in the Declaration of Independence. In the pamphlet Jefferson wrote that

> Scarcely have our minds been able to emerge from the astonishment into which one stroke of parliamentary thunder has involved us, before another more heavy, and more alarming, is fallen on us. Single acts of tyranny may be ascribed to the accidental opinion of a day; but a series of oppressions, begun at a distinguished period, and pursued unalterably through every change of ministers, too plainly prove a deliberate and systematical plan of reducing us to slavery.[8]

The Declaration says that "when a long Train of Abuses and Usurpations, pursuing invariably the same Object, evinces a design to reduce [a people] under absolute Despotism, it is their Right, it is their Duty, to throw off such Government, and to provide new Guards for their future Security."

I will not bore you with a complete analysis of that litany, that "long Train of Abuses"; they fill every history book on the Revolution—the Proclamation Line and the Grenville Duties of 1763, the Sugar Act and Currency Act of 1764, the Stamp Act and Quartering Act of 1765, the Declaratory Act of 1766, the Townshend Duties of 1767, the Tea Act of 1773, the Intolerable Acts and the Quebec Act of 1774, and many others. Each one of these British measures demonstrated that Americans and Englishmen were operating on different planes—two entirely different levels of interpreting the English constitution. Both sides felt that constitutional and political right was on their side. Unless one side gave up its interpretation, constitutional crisis, and probably armed rebellion, were inevitable.

The key act in this "one damn thing after another," I believe, was the Declaratory Act. What did the Declaratory Act do? Parliament was astonished at the American responses to the new imperial policy instituted in 1763, especially the hostility of the American colonies to the Stamp Act. Because of such resolute and sometimes even violent opposition, Parliament gave in and repealed the Stamp Act. Seemingly to save face, on the same day that it repealed the Stamp Act Parliament passed the Declaratory Act, which said that despite all the American resolutions against parliamentary actions, the "colonies and plantations in America have been, are, and of right ought to be, subordinate unto, and dependent upon the imperial crown and Parliament of Great Britain" and that Parliament "had, have and of right ought to have, full power and authority to make laws and statutes of sufficient force and validity to bind the colonies and people of America . . . in all cases whatsoever." Furthermore, the act provided that all colonial "resolutions, votes, orders, and proceedings" questioning the laws and statutes of Parliament "are, and are hereby declared to be, utterly null and void to all intents and purposes whatsoever."[9]

Americans initially rejoiced with the repeal of the Stamp Act, thinking that the Declaratory Act was merely a rhetorical face-saving gesture. But when Parliament created a board of customs commissioners for America and enacted the Townshend Duties on a host of essential imports the following year, Americans sensed the danger.[10] Parliament really meant to exercise its sovereign superiority over the colonies and in the most objectionable fashion—by raising revenue from customs duties and earmarking some of this money to pay the salaries of royal officials in the colonies, thereby making these officials dependent on the crown and independent of colonial assemblies. No longer would colonial assemblies exclusively exercise the power of the purse in their annual jousting with royal governors. When these customs commissioners engaged in what one historian has termed "customs racketeering"—the use of technicalities in the law and arbitrary means to justify the seizure of American ships and cargoes—colonial self interest merged with the demand for self-government to generate a potent protest.

To the colonists' way of thinking, this was indeed a revolution overthrowing the English Constitution. According to Tom Paine, Parliament's declaration was "the loftiest stretch of arbitrary power that ever one set of men, or one country claimed over another."[11] "Even the expression [to bind us in all cases whatsoever]" was "impious, for so unlimited a power can belong only to God."[12] South Carolinian Henry Laurens declared that Americans preferred "poverty & Death to a tame Submission" to Britain's "diabolical measures."[13] According to "Connecticut Wit" Joel Barlow, "It was not the quantity of the tax" that the British levied, "it was the right of the demand, which was called in question. Upon this the people deliberated, this they discussed in a cool and dispassionate manner, and this they opposed, in every shape that an artful and systematic ministry could devise, for more than ten years, before they assumed the sword." American colonists reacted the only plausible way—with their own "declaratory Act of Independence, which gave being to an empire."[14]

The delegates to Congress knew the danger they faced by declaring independence. If the Revolution failed, these men surely would be executed as traitors. But the delegates also feared what might happen if independence was achieved. Thus, when Richard Henry Lee made the motion in Congress for independence, he also moved that a committee be appointed to draft articles of confederation that would unite the thirteen colonies in what the delegates hoped would be a perpetual league of friendship. It took Congress a year and a half to draft the Articles of Confederation and then another three and a half years to obtain the necessary unanimous ratification by the state legislatures.

At the same time that Congress drafted the Articles,

revolutionary leaders in eleven states (but not the corporate colonies of Connecticut and Rhode Island) drafted and adopted new state constitutions. Most of these constitutions either explicitly or indirectly repudiated Parliament's Declaratory Act. For example, the framers of the New York state constitution seized the initiative by stating in the very first article of their charter "that no authority shall on any pretence whatever be exercised over the people or members of this State, but such as shall be derived from and granted by them." This provision was a direct and categorical denial of the Declaratory Act. Thus the new American government would have to be a federal government—it would have only those powers over New Yorkers that New Yorkers themselves allowed.

The Revolutionary charters gave lip service to the doctrine of separation of powers, but in reality they vested virtually complete power in the state assemblies, which were usually elected annually by freemen. (In Rhode Island and Connecticut the freemen elected their assemblies every six months.) Congress had repudiated the concept of parliamentary supremacy, but the revolutionary state constitutions substituted in its place the legislative supremacy of state assemblies. Except in Massachusetts, governors had no veto power; judicial review was yet to develop; and state judges, even those who had tenure for good behavior, were dependent on the assemblies for their salaries and could be removed by address.[15]

Both the federal and state constitutions clearly demonstrated where Americans wanted to locate political power. The second article of the Articles of Confederation provided that the states retained their sovereignty, freedom, and independence and that Congress had only those powers expressly delegated to it by the Articles. Congress had no power to tax, to regulate commerce, or to enforce its measures; it could ask the states to supply their fair share of money to pay federal expenses or to provide men for the Continental army and navy, but if a state so desired, it could simply ignore the act or request, and Congress was helpless to coerce compliance. James Madison wrote that the states had the power "of rejecting or executing the acts of Congress . . . uncontroulable by the nominal sovereignty of Congress."[16] The states were clearly dominant in this new federal relationship.

All of the new state constitutions provided protection for the rights of their citizens either directly in the body of the constitution or in the form of a prefatory bill of rights. Some states confirmed rights adopted during their colonial experience. Such was the case with Connecticut, whose bill of rights of 1650 was reconfirmed on various occasions by the state legislature. Other state legislatures adopted new statutory bills of rights.[17] The Articles of Confederation contained no bill of rights because Congress was unable to act directly on the people; it could act only on states, and Congress could not force the states to do anything. Proposals to amend the Articles of Confederation came even before the federal charter was officially adopted. No amendment, however, obtained the necessary unanimous ratification of the state legislatures. Attempts in 1781 and 1783 to give Congress the power to levy a tariff that would have provided it with a revenue independent of the states failed when Rhode Island rejected the Impost of 1781 and when Congress found New York's ratification of the Impost of 1783 unacceptable. Thus the will of the majority was thwarted by the obstinacy of a small minority.

In adopting the Imposts of 1781 and 1783, the state legislatures were mindful of the dangerous powers they would be conferring on Congress. By giving Congress the power to collect a tariff, the states would tacitly be giving it the implied power to enact a variety of customs legislation, appoint customs officials, and create courts to punish those violating federal laws. Congress, in essence, would be given the same powers so vociferously and steadfastly denied Parliament during the pre-Revolutionary decade. Consequently, every state legislature that adopted the Impost of 1783 provided that their citizens were protected by the rights embodied in their constitutional documents; Congress could not violate state constitutions and bills of rights. The states, in essence, made Congress incorporate their constitutional protections.

New York went even further. In adopting the Impost of 1783, the state refused to give Congress the authority to collect a tariff. Instead, New York would collect the customs duties for Congress with its own collectors and then turn over the money to the central government. Congress would be given the revenue, but not the power to collect it. Without the power to collect a revenue, the federal authority would not be tempted to abuse its power, or so reasoned New Yorkers.

On January 26, 1787, the New York legislature passed "An Act concerning the Rights of the Citizens of this State." The first section of the act, which echoed the new state constitution, served as a declaratory act in favor of the state as the sole sovereign authority over its people: "That no authority shall, on any pretense whatsoever, be exercised over the Citizens of this State, but such as is or shall be derived from and granted by the People of this State." The penultimate section provided "That no tax, duty, or imposition whatsoever, shall be taken or levied within this State, without the grant and assent of the People of this State, by their Representatives in Senate and Assembly." Congress found New York's limitation unacceptable and rejected the state's ratification of the impost.[18]

THE SECOND ACT

The years immediately following the end of hostilities had brought America prosperity as never before. Surely Providence smiled on the new United States of America, which served as an example to the rest of the world that men could govern themselves. As he prepared to return to France, the Marquis de Lafayette addressed Congress in mid-December 1784. "May this immense temple of freedom ever stand a lesson to oppressors, an example to the oppressed, a sanctuary for the rights of mankind!"[19] But by mid-1786 the prayer of Lafayette had been shattered, and many Americans joined Noah Webster in decrying republicanism:

> I was once as strong a republican as any man in America. Now, a republic is among the last kinds of government I should choose. I should infinitely prefer a limited monarchy, for I would sooner be subject to the caprice of one man, than to the ignorance and passions of a multitude. I believe men as individuals enjoy more security, more peace and more real liberty under a limited monarch . . . than in republics, where people sometimes get furious and make laws destructive of all peace and liberty.[20]

What had changed Webster's mind? What had changed the thinking of so many Americans who agreed with Webster?

In 1785 and 1786 a severe postwar economic depression hit America. Much of the country's economy collapsed. Mechanics and artisans were thrown out of work, shipbuilding ceased, merchants went bankrupt, and farmers could not pay their taxes and debts. Foreclosures on farms became common. State and federal governments could not pay the interest and principal due on their wartime debts; holders of government securities were forced to sell to speculators for pennies on the dollar.

People demanded governmental assistance. Some state legislatures passed various relief measures postponing the collection of debts. Seven states issued paper money, some of which depreciated dramatically and was used to pay private debts and taxes. In states where relief did not come quickly enough, violence occurred. Mobs intimidated legislatures, incendiaries burned courthouses in backcountry and tidewater Virginia, and farmers, endangered by foreclosures, shut down the civil courts in western Massachusetts. Combustibles in every state were ready to be ignited by a single spark.

Rhode Island's response to the depression created fear throughout the country.[21] Debtors there resorted not to violence but to the ballot box. A revolution in government occurred in the spring 1786 elections as a new Country Party ran on the pledge "To Relieve the Distressed." With its candidates elected as governor and deputy governor and with sizable majorities in both houses of the legislature, the Country Party implemented the most radical economic program in American history. In May 1786 the legislature issued £100,000 in legal tender paper money to be loaned on real estate mortgages for fourteen years. Whenever a tender in paper was rejected, the debtor could lodge his money with a judge, who would advertise the lodgment in the newspapers for three weeks. If the creditor refused to claim the payment within three months, the debt was declared forever canceled and forfeited to the state, minus the fees to the judges and newspapers.

To counter the strong opposition of the state's mercantile party to the paper-money program, the legislature passed a Penalty Act in June 1786. Anyone convicted of refusing to accept the currency would be fined £100 for the first conviction; half the fine would go to the state; half to the informer. A second conviction produced the same fine, plus disenfranchisement. When mercantile opposition persisted, the legislature passed another Penalty Act in August, lowering the fines but providing that a special court would consider the cases with no jury trial and no right of appeal allowed. Retaliating against continued mercantile opposition, a group of rural Providence County towns met in mid-September 1786 and proposed a "state trade system"—a socialist plan that called for the state to own all ships, wharves, and stores, while a committee of the General Assembly would manage the economy.

When the General Assembly reconvened in October 1786, it did not implement the state trade system, but it considered the

Superior Court's handling of the case of *Trevett* v. *Weeden*. Under the second Penalty Act, this court, the state's highest tribunal, had ruled that it did not have cognizance in the case because it was not a special court; but the judges had agreed with Weeden's attorney, James Mitchell Varnum, that the Penalty Act's failure to provide for trial by jury made it unconstitutional. The legislature summoned the Superior Court judges and clerk to explain their actions. The General Assembly, which appointed all judicial officers and also served as a court of appeals and possessed the sole power to pardon and impeach, considered itself, like the British House of Lords, the highest judicial body in the state. The Assembly deemed the judges' response unsatisfactory, but it decided not to charge them with a crime. The four offending judges, however, were not reappointed the following year.[22]

The Assembly then proposed a Test Act, which required all Rhode Islanders to take an oath to support its paper money. Citizens who refused to take the oath would be disenfranchised, recalcitrant lawyers would be disbarred, merchants would be prevented from engaging in mercantile activities, and officeholders would be dismissed. Because of the controversy over this bill, it was sent to the towns for their consideration. When the legislature reconvened in December 1786, only three of the thirty towns endorsed the Test Act. A bill was then proposed calling for the abolition of all debts and the equal distribution of all property every thirteen years. (*Communism!*) This bill was reprinted in at least eleven newspapers throughout the country.

Americans were astonished at what was happening in Rhode Island. Could nothing be done to stop these radical measures? Rhode Island's government had been constitutionally elected, and no federal authority could intervene in the way that the King in Council could exercise an absolute veto power over all colonial acts before the Revolution. Fear shot through the country that Rhode Island's radical policies might be adopted by levelers in other states. According to the secretary of Congress, Charles Thomson, it seemed as if Rhode Island was "destined to be an example, and to warn the other states against the evils and mischiefs of pure democracy."[23]

Rhode Island was attacked in newspapers, in private correspondence, and in public assemblies during the late 1780s. The state was rebuked for rejecting the Impost of 1781 (the single most devastating act to kill the viability of the Confederation Congress), for violating property rights, for refusing to send delegates to the Constitutional Convention, and for repeatedly failing to call a state convention to consider the proposed Constitution.

It became common to blame Rhode Island for all of the country's problems, and the state was called one name after another — Rogue Island; Reedy Island; Fool Island; our apostate sister; our deluded Sister; that unhappy, fallen, lost sister; our little froward sister; that little nest of villains; that little detestable corner of the Continent; long-lost Rhoda; our stray sister; a disgrace to the human race; a plague to us; an outcast from Society; a Blank or rather a Blot in the Union; the stronghold of Satan; an absolute monarchy, subject to the Prince of Darkness; a System of Government which Beelzebub alone must rejoice at; that little insignificant, devoted spot of wickedness; a striking example of political madness and perverseness; a viper in our bosom; the little vaurien (that is, a good-for-nothing wretch, or a scamp); a certain Little pestiferous, pseudo island; that little trollop of a sister; the little Whore; a stench in the nostrils of the other States'; a Little speck in Creation; a kind of comet; a mole-hill in the neighbourhood of twelve important mountains; a filthy harlot; that shameless Prostitute; a foolish slut; and Cousin German to Gomorrah — just to mention a few. Suggestions were raised to obliterate the state as a political entity and to divide the land between Connecticut and Massachusetts.[24] John Trumbull, the painter, wrote from London that "As to Rhode Island if she continues troublesome, the new [federal] Government should crush her, & the sooner the better."[25]

THE THIRD ACT

What had happened to the glorious American experiment? Why were Americans so dissatisfied with their governments? Didn't Americans possess the virtue necessary to live under republican forms of government? Or were their governments themselves defective?

Whatever the cause of the difficult times of 1786, the states felt compelled to appoint delegates to a constitutional convention to strengthen Congress and to revise the Articles of Confederation. According to a Connecticut "landholder," the combination of "the rebellion of Shays [in Massachusetts] and the present measures of Rhode Island ought to convince us that a national legislature, judiciary, and executive must be united or the whole is but a name; and that we must be united or soon be hewers of wood and drawers of water for all other people."[26]

Americans looked to this Constitutional Convention as the last hope to preserve their freedom and to restore prosperity. In fact, many Americans thought that the convention was the last hope for mankind. Alexander Hamilton, in introducing *The Federalist* series, wrote that

> it seems to have been reserved to the people of this country, by their conduct and example, to decide the important question, whether societies of men are really capable or not, of establishing good governments from reflection and choice, or whether they are forever destined to depend, for their political constitutions, on accident and force. If there be any truth in the remark, the crisis, at which we are arrived, may with propriety be regarded as the era in which that decision is to be made.[27]

A mistake made by Americans would result in "the general misfortune of mankind." A correspondent in the *Massachusetts Centinel* fearfully predicted

> that unless an energetick, permanent continental government is speedily established, our liberties will be set afloat in the confusion that will inevitably ensue.—At present we ... are every day tottering on the brink of civil dissention. . . . It would be better to embrace almost any expedient rather than to remain where we are.[28]

Philadelphia physician and reformer Benjamin Rush addressed the "Freemen of the United States" under the pseudonym "Harrington" just five days after the Constitutional Convention had assembled.[29] He had previously addressed the people in 1774 and 1775 on "the interesting subject of the LIBERTIES of America." Now he wished to discuss the important subject of "GOVERNMENT." According to Harrington, it was "impossible to preserve freedom, without such constitutions and laws as are adapted to the circumstances and habits of our country."

The problems facing America, in Harrington's opinion, stemmed from the inadequacies of the country's constitution. The Articles of Confederation had been drafted by Congress "amidst the confusions of war, and in the infancy of our political knowledge." It was now clear that the Articles were "ineffectual to support public credit—to obtain alliances—to preserve treaties—to enforce taxes—[and] to prevent hostilities" between the states and insurrections among citizens.

Harrington warned Americans not to blithely accept the deficiencies of the Articles. "Mankind," he wrote, "insensibly glide into a stable government. The rich and the poor soon grow tired of anarchy. They prefer the order and tranquility of despotism to popular licentiousness." A circular theory of government was commonly held at the time. Anarchy would give rise to a benevolent dictator who would promise stability. Stability would indeed replace anarchy, but soon despotism would replace benevolence. Thus, Americans were told

> we have ... no choice left to us. We must either form an efficient government for ourselves, suited in every respect to our exigencies and interests, or we must submit to have one imposed upon us by accident or usurpation. . . . We are upon the brink of a precipice. Heavens! shall the citizens of America—shall the deposers of the power of George the third, and the conquerors of Britain in America—submit to receive law from a bold and successful demagogue, or a confederated body of usurpers?

The solution to the country's problems appeared simple to Harrington. The states should "throw their sovereignty at the feet of the convention," he admonished. "The more we abridge the states of their sovereignty, and the more supreme power we concenter in AN ASSEMBLY OF THE STATES (for by this new name let us call our federal government) the more safety, liberty and prosperity, will be enjoyed by each of the states." The alternatives seemed readily apparent. "Under the present weak, imperfect and distracted government of Congress, anarchy, poverty, infamy, and SLAVERY, await the United States. Under such a government as will probably be formed by the present convention, America may yet enjoy peace, safety, liberty and glory."

Americans like Rush believed that they had a special role to play. They knew that all of Europe was watching them—and many were hoping to see them falter. Europeans who had "extolled our success, and predicted our future greatness, now laugh at our folly—burlesque our policy, and contemn our dishonesty. They respect us for what we have been—admire us for what we might be, but despise us for what we are." Alexander J. Dallas, the editor of the *Pennsylvania Herald*, urged his readers on July 14, 1787, to "look forward to the happiness, to the power, and the dignity, which" Americans should bequeath to their posterity. It was, Dallas said, our responsibility "to provide the means for perpetuating the blessings we enjoy, and to expect with zeal and confidence, from the Foederal Convention, a system of government adequate to the security and preservation of those rights, which were promulged by the ever-memorable Declaration of Independency."[30] Dallas was deeply impressed with the uniqueness of what was then going on in Philadelphia: "Whatever measures may be recommended by the Foederal Convention, whether an addition to the old constitution, or the adoption of a new one, it will, in effect, be a revolution in government, accomplished by reasoning and deliberation; an event that has never occurred since the formation of society."

Most delegates came to the convention hoping to amend the Articles of Confederation in compliance with their commissions and with the resolution of Congress calling the convention. A handful of delegates, however, hoped for a far greater transformation, none more than James Madison. Seemingly addressing Rhode Island's radicalism, Madison wanted

> to arm the federal head with a negative *in all cases whatsoever* on the local Legislatures. Without this defensive power, experience and reflection have satisfied me that however ample the federal powers may be made, or however clearly their boundaries may be delineated on paper, they will be easily and continually baffled by the Legislative sovereignties of the States. The effects of this provision would be not only to guard the national rights and interests against invasion, but also to restrain the States from thwarting and molesting each other, and even from oppressing the minority within themselves by paper money and other unrighteous measures which favor the interest of the majority.[31]

"Let it [the new Constitution] have a negative *in all cases whatsoever* on the Legislative Acts of the States as the King of Great

Britain heretofore had," Madison wrote to Virginia governor Edmund Randolph. "This I conceive to be essential and the least possible abridgement of the State Sovereignties. . . . It will also give internal stability to the States. There has been no moment since the peace at which the federal assent would have been given to paper money, &c. &c."[32]

What, in fact, did the Constitutional Convention do? The delegates decided on their third day together to meet in secrecy. Within their first week they consciously violated their instructions—both from Congress and from their own state legislatures—when they voted to abandon, instead of to revise, the Articles of Confederation and to create an entirely new form of national government. They completed the abandonment of the Articles later when they totally scrapped its procedure for ratifying proposed amendments. At one point they even accepted Madison's proposal to give Congress a veto power over all state legislation, but they later substituted a clause providing that the Constitution, federal laws passed in pursuance thereof, and federal treaties "shall be the supreme law of the land."

The two most controversial provisions of the Constitution were an act of omission and one of commission. The lack of a bill of rights almost proved fatal to the new Constitution, while the "necessary and proper" clause—the "sweeping clause," as it was called—created fear and doubt among many people. To Antifederalists, this clause was in reality a reincarnation of Britain's Declaratory Act. After listing the delegated powers of Congress in Article I, Section 8, the controversial clause gives Congress the power "To make all Laws which shall be necessary and proper for carrying into Execution the foregoing Powers." Antifederalists believed the natural inference to be drawn was

> that the legislature will have an authority to make all laws which they shall judge necessary for the common safety, and to promote the general welfare. This amounts to a power to make

laws at discretion. No terms can be found more indefinite than these, and it is obvious, that the [national] legislature alone must judge what laws are proper and necessary for the purpose. . . . It is therefore evident, that the legislature under this Constitution may pass any law which they may think proper.[33]

"Brutus," an Antifederal spokesman, claimed that it was "utterly impossible to define this power. . . . If then the objects of this power cannot be comprehended, how is it possible to understand the extent of that power which can pass all laws which shall be necessary and proper for carrying it into execution? It is truly incomprehensible. A case cannot be conceived of, which is not included in this power."[34]

Antifederalists saw the Constitution as a counterrevolution. The Constitution, they said, defeated the intention of the Revolution, for nothing short of pure liberty was consistent with Revolutionary principles. Elbridge Gerry of Massachusetts, one of three delegates to the Constitutional Convention who refused to sign the completed form of government on September 17, thought the Constitution "neither consistent with the principles of the Revolution, or of the Constitutions of the several States." As sure as darkness brings the night, so the Constitution would bring the despotism of "foederal Chains."[35]

Samuel Adams, writing as "Helvidius Priscus," accused the Constitutional Convention of violating "the principles of the late glorious revolution,"[36] while "Philadelphiensis" (Benjamin Workman of the College of Philadelphia) warned Americans that

Every freeman, possessed of the smallest portion of patriotism and general philanthropy, ought, at this critical juncture, to think seriously, and determine cautiously. All that is dear to him, all that constitutes life, happy or miserable, is about to be unalterably fixed: The rivet of tyranny may now be clenched, that will bind forever the freedom of America in the indissoluble chains of cursed slavery. In the adoption of the new constitution in its present form, we will lose more than all we have fought for, and gained in a glorious and successful war of seven years.... In this act the bright orb of glorious liberty will go down under the horizon of cruel oppression, never never to illuminate our western hemisphere again! How much better, that she had never cast a ray upon Columbia, than thus to blaze for a moment, and then vanish forever![37]

A "Republican Federalist," writing in the *Massachusetts Centinel* on the very day the Massachusetts ratifying convention assembled, suggested that "The revolution which separated the United States from Great-Britain was not more important to the liberties of America than that which will result from the adoption of the new system. The *former freed us from a foreign subjugation*, and there is too much reason to apprehend that the *latter* will reduce us to a *federal domination*."[38]

Patrick Henry cautioned the Virginia ratifying convention "to be watchful, [and] jealous of your liberty; for instead of securing your rights you may lose them forever."[39] "Here," said Henry, "is a revolution as radical as that which separated us from Great Britain. It is as radical, if in this transition, our rights and privileges are endangered, and the sovereignty of the States be relinquished: And cannot we plainly see, that this is actually the case?"[40] Many Americans agreed with Thomas Treadwell of New York: The Constitution, he said, "departed widely from the principles and political faith of '76. . . . in this Constitution we have not only neglected,—we have done worse,—we have openly violated, our faith,—that is, our public faith."[41] "Who is so dimsighted," Philadelphiensis asked, "as to suppose that a constitution so essentially differing from the principles of the revolution, and from freedom, and opposed by so respectable a body of freemen, could be established in America?"[42]

"A Georgian" called upon his fellow citizens to recollect "our glorious Declaration of Independence, read it, and compare it with the Federal Constitution; what a degree of apostacy will you not then discover." He warned his readers to "guard against all encroachments upon your liberties so dearly purchased with the costly expense of blood and treasure."[43] Thomas Tudor Tucker, a South Carolina delegate to Congress, acknowledged the "very critical Period of American Politics." He confessed that he had begun to "doubt whether we have lavish'd the Blood & Substance of our Country for a good or bad Purpose."[44]

Some Antifederalists were astonished at what had occurred in America — it was an "incredible transition!" People who were willing to give up everything, including their lives, in order to obtain liberty were now "about to sacrifice that inestimable jewel, liberty, to the genius of despotism."[45] "How transitory," "Centinel" wrote, "are the blessings of this life. Scarcely have four years elapsed since the United States, [was] rescued from the domination of foreign despots . . . they are [now] about to fall a prey to the machinations of a profligate junto at home."[46]

Federalist Stephen Mix Mitchell, a Connecticut delegate to Congress, was less confident than Antifederalists that America would adopt the new Constitution.

> 'Tis doubtful in my mind whether those indomitable spirits, who have stood forth in the foremost ranks in this Revolution, will ever give up so much of their natural or acquired liberty as is absolutely necessary in order to form a strong and efficient federal government. Perhaps when this generation is passed away . . . something may easily and efficaciously be done in and for our new republic.[47]

Just as Antifederalists believed that the Constitution was a counterrevolution, so their opponents, the Federalists, believed that the Constitution was the fruition of the Declaration of Independence. In an address to the People of the United States, published in the nationally circulated *American Museum* in January 1787, Benjamin Rush wrote that

There is nothing more common than to confound the terms of the American Revolution with those of the late American war. The American war is over: but this is far from being the case with the American Revolution. On the contrary, nothing but the first act of the great drama is closed. It remains yet to establish and perfect our new forms of government; and to prepare the principles, morals, and manners of our citizens, for these forms of government, after they are established and brought to perfection.[48]

Joel Barlow, noted Connecticut poet and essayist, echoed Rush, arguing that

The revolution is but half completed. Independence and Government were the two objects contended for, and but one is yet obtained. . . . The present is justly considered an alarming crisis; perhaps the most alarming that America ever saw. We have contended with the most powerful nation and subdued the bravest and best appointed armies; but now we have to contend with ourselves, and encounter passions and prejudices more powerful than armies and more dangerous to our peace. It is not for glory, it is for existence that we contend.[49]

A correspondent in the *New Haven Gazette* on October 11, 1787, agreed with Rush and Barlow:

Our Revolution is yet but half completed; we have escaped the evils which threatened us from a foreign quarter, but we have not attained the positive blessings which we promised ourselves from the establishment of a free and independent empire. The truth is, such an empire is not yet established. In vain have we, for four years, pursued a phantom, a shadow without substance, an effect without a cause. . . . But this Revolution is still to be pushed—it must be perfected. . . . Until this is done, our object is but half attained; our hopes are but half fulfilled.[50]

According to a correspondent in the Boston *Massachusetts Centinel*, the new Constitution would, in fact, "usher into existence" that "empire of republican freedom" that would bring honor to the "individual states" and "happiness and glory [to] independent America."[51] "A Jerseyman," writing in the *Trenton Mercury* in early November 1787, maintained that the Declaration of Independence merely

> opened the door by which our entrance into national importance was first made ... it gave us only a chance for the establishment of our freedom. .... the most difficult and important task we have still to go through; it remains for us to convince our enemies that the liberty and independence which we had enterprise and bravery enough to acquire, we have wisdom and perseverance to secure. If this be effectually done, we shall reap the benefit of our labors while we live, and posterity will have cause to bless the memory of those who raised and completed so noble and magnificent a structure; but if the reverse of this picture should be forced upon the view of our citizens, how many and heavy would be the curses of all good men upon our heads.[52]

In Virginia, Alexander Donald gave his opinion to Thomas Jefferson that the adoption of the Constitution "will be the salvation of America, for at present there is hardly the semblance of Law or Government in any of the states, And For want of a Superintending Power over the whole, a dissolution [of the Confederation] seems to be impending."[53] Horatio Gates agreed. He wrote James Madison that

> every thing I hear, every thing I know, convinced me, that unless we have as Speedily as possible a Firm, Efficient, Federal Constitution established, all must go to Ruin, and Anarchy and Misrule, blast every Hope that so Glorious a Revolution entitled us to Expect.[54]

Madison realized that Americans in general, and Virginians in particular, were "tired of the vicissitudes, injustice and follies which have so much characterized public measures, and are impatient for some change which promises stability & repose."[55] Thus, according to Madison, the Constitutional Convention digested "a plan which in its operation would decide forever the fate of Republican Government." Every guard to liberty was provided for, but the delegates to the Convention were "equally careful to supply the defects [in government] which [their] own experience had particularly pointed out."

Another delegate to the Constitutional Convention, Hugh Williamson, explained the convention's motivation to his fellow townsmen of Edenton, North Carolina: "We imagined that we had been securing both liberty and property on a more stable foundation."[56] A correspondent in the *Connecticut Courant*, calling himself "The Republican," told his readers that "Our national hopes are fast approaching to their grand crisis; the friends of liberty throughout the world have their eyes fixed upon us; if we have not wisdom and virtue enough to unite *government* and *liberty*; the cause of liberty must be given up for lost."[57] According to "Peregrine," in the Winchester *Virginia Gazette*, the patriots who led America through the Revolution were the same patriots who drafted the Constitution; and the spirit of that Constitution was "calculated to support" the principles of the Revolution—by which he meant America's "strength and dignity as a nation" and the "peace and liberty" of its citizens.[58]

Although Federalists believed that the Constitution advanced the principles of the Declaration of Independence, they saw no inconsistency in admitting that a revolution had occurred—a "Revolution in the System of Government," directed against the Articles of Confederation. Federalists were particularly proud that their revolution was peaceful and accomplished "without the violent means which have uniformly been requisite for the like events elsewhere." It was a revolution "without bloodshed or violence," a revolution implemented "with the deliberate consent of the People."[59] This second American Revolution, as Jefferson called it, "promised to confer the greatest number of blessings, that could be rationally expected, attended with the fewest possible evils."

All Federalists agreed with one thing. Instead of guilt by association, they praised the Constitution by dissociation: the fact that Rhode Island opposed the Constitution and stayed out of the new Union for a year and a half meant that the Constitution surely must be good. Connecticut's Oliver Ellsworth, writing as "A Landholder," contended that "the little state of Rhode-Island was purposely left by Heaven to its present madness, for a general conviction in the other states, that such a system as is now proposed is our only preservation from ruin."[60]

In celebrating the ratification of the Constitution on the Fourth of July, 1788, James Wilson, a delegate to both the Constitutional Convention and the Pennsylvania ratifying convention, summarized what had just occurred:

> Delegates were *appointed* to deliberate and to propose. They *met*, and *performed* their delegated trust. The *result* of their deliberations was *laid before the people*. It was *discussed* and *scrutinized* in the *fullest, freest* and *severest* manner,—by *speaking*, by *writing* and by *printing*—by *individuals* and by *public bodies*,—by its friends and by its *enemies*. What was the *issue?* Most *favourable* and most *glorious* to the system. In *state* after *state*, at *time* after *time*, it was *ratified*—in some states *unanimously*—on the whole, by a large and very respectable *majority*.[61]

According to Wilson, the action of "A people, free and enlightened, *establishing* and *ratifying* a system of government, which they have previously *considered, examined* and *approved*," was "the most dignified" spectacle that had "yet appeared on our globe."[62]

James Madison realized that the country was dangerously split over the Constitution without a bill of rights. He and George Washington discussed the matter and agreed upon a strategy:

Washington would propose a bill of rights in his presidential inaugural address and Madison would introduce it and shepherd it through the U.S. House of Representatives, just as he had guided Jefferson's bill for religious freedom through the Virginia House of Delegates five years earlier.

Washington asked David Humphreys to write his inaugural address. Humphreys, one of a group of literati called the "Connecticut Wits," had been at Mount Vernon for a year and a half, working on a biography of the general. Washington's advisers recommended that Humphreys's draft be scrapped; it was far too long (two and a half hours) and too magisterial. Washington copied it over and realized how bad it was. He then asked Madison to write a new address with the recommendation of a bill of rights. Washington delivered Madison's speech in less than twelve minutes to a joint session of Congress.

Madison, serving in the House of Representatives, was appointed chairman of the committee to respond to the president's speech, and he said it was pretty good. Washington then asked Madison to respond to the House's response. Madison did, saying for the president that "Your very affectionate Address produces emotions which I know not how to express" (the president was almost speechless). And when the Senate's response to Washington's oratory arrived, Washington again asked Madison to draft his response to it. This time Madison had the president say that he looked forward to working with Congress "in the arduous but pleasing, task, of attempting to make a Nation happy."[63]

Now it was Madison's turn to implement the plan he and Washington had formulated. Against everyone's wishes, he introduced a bill of rights in the House on June 8, 1789, with one of the greatest speeches in American history.[64] But despite his best efforts, he knew he had failed to convince the two-thirds majority necessary to send the proposed amendments to the Senate. Thus Madison now turned to Washington for assistance, and the president obliged with a public letter endorsing Madison's amendments. With this support, Madison got a two-thirds vote for the amendments, which were sent to the Senate, modified, and then approved by a conference committee. On October 2, 1789, Washington sent the twelve amendments to the states, and in two years ten of the amendments were adopted by the necessary three-quarters of the states.[65]

Five years later, when Washington prepared to retire, he delivered his Farewell Address—this time with an assist from Alexander Hamilton.

> This government, the offspring of our own choice, uninfluenced and unawed, adopted upon full investigation & mature deliberation, completely free in its principles, in the distribution of its powers, uniting security with energy, and containing within itself a provision for its own amendment, has a just claim to your confidence and your support.—Respect for its authority, compliance with its Laws, acquiescence in its measures, are duties enjoined by the fundamental maxims of true Liberty.—The basis of our political systems is the right of the people to make and to alter their Constitutions of Government.—But the Constitution which at any time exists 'till changed by an explicit and authentic act of the whole People, is sacredly obligatory upon all.—The very idea of the power and the right of the People to establish Government presupposes the duty of every Individual to obey the established Government.[66]

As Washington proclaimed in his oft-quoted valedictory, the American Revolution had indeed ended.

NOTES

1. Benjamin Rush to Nathanael Greene, Philadelphia, April 15, 1782, L.H. Butterfield, ed., *The Papers of Benjamin Rush* (2 vols., Princeton, N.J., 1951), 1:268.

2. Orin G. Libby, *The Geographical Distribution of the Vote of the Thirteen States on the Federal Constitution, 1787–8* (Madison, Wis., 1894).

3. Carl Lotus Becker, *The History of Political Parties in the Province of New York, 1760–1776* (Madison, Wis., 1909).

4. Charles A. Beard, *An Economic Interpretation of the Constitution of the United States* (New York, 1913).

5. Merrill Jensen, *The Articles of Confederation: An Interpretation of the Socio-Constitutional History of the American Revolution, 1774–1781* (Madison, Wis., 1940), and *The New Nation: A History of the United States, 1781–1789* (New York, 1950).

6. Jackson Turner Main, *Political Parties before the Constitution* (New York, 1973), and *The Antifederalists: Critics of the Constitution, 1781–1788* (Chapel Hill, N.C., 1961).

7. John P. Kaminski, *Paper Politics: The Northern State Loan-Offices during the Confederation, 1783–1790* (New York, 1989); Merrill Jensen, John P. Kaminski, and Gaspare J. Saladino, eds., *The Documentary History of the Ratification of the Constitution* (21 vols. to date, Madison, Wis., 1976–), hereafter cited as DHRC. For the status of the historiography of the Constitution as of the date of its 1987 bicentennial, consult Patrick T. Conley, "Posterity Views the Founding," in Patrick T. Conley and John P. Kaminski, eds., *The Constitution and the States: The Role of the Original Thirteen in the Framing and Adoption of the Constitution* (Madison, Wis., 1988), 295–329.

8. Thomas Jefferson, *A Summary View of the Rights of British America* (Williamsburg, Va., 1774), 11.

9. 6 George III, c. 12, *The Statutes at Large*, ed. Danby Pickering (London, 1767), 27: 19–20.

10. John Adams to Dr. J. Morse, Quincy, January 1, 1816, *The Works of John Adams*, ed. by Charles Francis Adams (10 vols., Boston, 1850–1856), 10:197–98. Oliver M. Dickerson, *The Navigation Acts and the American Revolution* (Philadelphia, 1951), 195–96.

11. "The American Crisis" III, *Thomas Paine: Collected Writings* ed. by Eric Foner (New York, 1995), 118.

12. Paine, "The American Crisis" I, December 19, 1776, Foner, *Thomas Paine*, 91.

13. Laurens to William Manning, Charles Town, November 26, 1775, *The Papers of Henry Laurens*, ed. Philip M. Hamer et al. (16 vols., Columbia, S.C., 1968–2002), 10:521.

14. Joel Barlow, *An Oration, Delivered at the North Church in Hartford at the Meeting of the Connecticut Society of the Cincinnati, July 4th, 1787* (Hartford, 1787), 5–7.

15. Removal by address consisted of both houses of the legislature requesting the governor to remove the judge. The governor did not have to comply with the legislature's request.

16. Madison to Edmund Randolph, New York, April 8, 1787, Robert A. Rutland, ed., *The Papers of James Madison* (17 vols., Chicago and Charlottesville, Va., 1975–), 9:369–70.

17. New York's legislature passed "An Act concerning the Rights of the Citizens of this State" on January 26, 1787; *Laws of the State of New-York* (New York, 1787), 5–6. Rhode Island did not enact a statutory bill of rights until 1798. Its retained royal charter of 1663 contained no procedure for amendment.

18. Congress did not wish to trust the states to enforce federal customs duties. Jeremiah Olney, customs officer for Providence, R.I., described how state customs collectors handled their jobs during the 1780s. "The Merchants in General, in this District, were before strangers to an honorable punctuality and exactness, as they respected the collection and payment of the Duties imposed by the state Legislature; for it is a well known Truth, that the Merchants paid but little regard to the law when it clashed with their Interest; and that the officers of the Customs being annually chosen, were perfectly under their controul; hence they were permitted to make such Entries as they pleased (very seldom exceeding half the cargoes), to regard the law in other respects (particularly in *altering registers at their pleasure etc.*) so far only as it suited their own convenience." Jeremiah Olney to Alexander Hamilton, Providence, April 22, 1793, Harold C. Syrett, ed., *The Papers of Alexander Hamilton* (27 vols., New York, 1961–1987), 14:333.

19. Marquis de Lafayette: Address to Congress, Trenton, December 13, 1784, Worthington C. Ford et al., eds., *Journals of the Continental Congress, 1774–1789* (34 vols., Washington, D.C., 1904–1937), 27:684.

20. "Political Paragraphs," *Connecticut Courant*, November 26, 1786.

21. The account of Rhode Island's economic policy is taken from Kaminski, *Paper Politics*, 169–219.

22. Patrick T. Conley, *Democracy in Decline: Rhode Island's Constitutional Development, 1776–1841* (Providence, R.I., 1977), 90–101.

23. Thomson to William Ellery, New York, May 26, 1788, GLC 4847, Gilder Lehrman Collection, on deposit at the New-York Historical Society.

24. "Jonathan," *United States Chronicle*, May 25, 1786; Francis Dana to Elbridge Gerry, Newport, September 2, 1787, L. W. Smith Collection, Morristown National Historical Park; *United States Chronicle*, November 1, 1787; *Providence Gazette*, February 7, 1788; Hartford *American Mercury*, May 5, 1788.

25. John Trumbull to Jonathan Trumbull, London, September 3, 1788, Yale University Library.

26. "A Landholder" V, *Connecticut Courant*, December 3, 1787, DHRC, 14:338.

27. *The Federalist I*, New York *Independent Journal*, October 27, 1787, ibid., 13:494.

28. *Massachusetts Centinel*, June 30, 1787, ibid., 148–49.

29. *Pennsylvania Gazette*, May 30, 1787, ibid., 116–20.

30. Ibid., 165.

31. Madison to Thomas Jefferson, New York, March 19, 1787, Rutland, *Papers of James Madison*, 9:318. By "minority" Madison meant the wealthy, while the "majority" meant debtors or the propertyless class.

32. Madison to Edmund Randolph, New York, April 8, 1787, ibid. 370. See also Madison to George Washington, New York, April 16, 1787, ibid., 383–84.

33. "Brutus" V, *New York Journal*, December 13, 1787, DHRC, 14:423.

34. Ibid., 425.

35. Gerry to John Wendell, Cambridge, November 16, 1787, ibid., 4:251. The two others who refused to sign the completed Constitution were Virginians George Mason and Edmund Randolph.

36. Boston *Independent Chronicle*, December 27, 1787, ibid., 5:538.

37. "Philadelphiensis" II, Philadelphia *Freeman's Journal*, November 28, 1787, ibid., 14: 252.

38. "The Republican Federalist" III, *Massachusetts Centinel*, January 9, 1788, ibid., 5:661.

39. Patrick Henry Speech, June 4, 1788, ibid., 9:930.

40. Patrick Henry Speech, June 5, 1788, ibid., 951.

41. Thomas Treadwell Speech, July 2, 1788, ibid., 23:2555.

42. "Philadelphiensis" XI, Philadelphia *Independent Gazetteer*, March 8, 1788, ibid., 16: 365.

43. "A Georgian," *Gazette of the State of Georgia*, November 15, 1787, ibid., 3:243.

44. Tucker to St. George Tucker, Philadelphia, November 21, 1787, ibid., 14:167.

45. "Centinel" VI, *Pennsylvania Packet*, December 25, 1787, ibid., 15:98.

46. "Centinel" VII, Philadelphia *Independent Gazetteer*, December 29, 1787, ibid., 178.

47. Mitchell to William Samuel Johnson, Wethersfield, Conn., September 18, 1787, ibid., 3:347.

48. Ibid., 13:46.

49. Barlow, *Oration*, 1787, 8, 11.

50. "The People," *New Haven Gazette*, October 11, 1787, DHRC, 3:361–62.

51. *Massachusetts Centinel*, September 29, 1787, ibid., 4:24.

52. "A Jerseyman," "To the Citizens of New Jersey," *Trenton Mercury*, November 6, 1787, ibid., 3:146.

53. Donald to Jefferson, Richmond, November 12, 1787, ibid., 8:154.

54. Gates to Madison, Travellers Rest, Va., November 26, 1787, ibid., 8:175.

55. Madison to Thomas Jefferson, New York, December 9, 1787, ibid., 228.

56. Hugh Williamson Speech, November 8, 1787, ibid., 16:207.

57. "The Republican," "To the People," *Connecticut Courant*, January 7, 1788, ibid., 3:532.

58. "Peregrine," "To the Americans," Winchester *Virginia Gazette*, April 2, 1788, ibid., 9:640.

59. William Brown to William Cullen, Alexandria, Va., July 19, 1788, ibid., 18:273. See also Thomas Jefferson to Edward Rutledge, Paris, July 18, 1788, ibid., 272.

60. "A Landholder" V, *Connecticut Courant*, December 3, 1787, ibid., 14:338.

61. James Wilson Speech, July 4, 1788, ibid., 18:244–45.

62. Ibid., 244.

63. George Washington to the House of Representatives, New York, and George Washington to the U.S. Senate, New York, May 8 and 18, 1789, W. W. Abbot et al., eds. *The Papers of George Washington, Presidential Series* (Charlottesville, Va., 1987–), 2:232, 324.

64. James Madison's speech in the U.S. House of Representatives, June 8, 1789, Rutland, *Papers of James Madison*, 12:196–209.

65. The second proposed amendment, dealing with alterations in compensation for members of Congress, was adopted 203 years later in May 1992 as the Twenty-seventh Amendment.

66. John P. Kaminski and Jill Adair McCaughan, eds., *A Great and Good Man: George Washington in the Eyes of His Contemporaries* (Madison, Wis., 1989), 223.

A Rhode Island Reflection

Given Professor Kaminski's frequent allusions to Rhode Island and his shared belief in the merits of local Antifederalist arguments during the protracted ratification struggle, my commentary is brief. That litany of shame recited by John — as complete as any ever assembled — reinforced Antifederal opposition. In fact, one might state that Rhode Island's hostility toward the union was conditioned in part by the union's hostility to Rhode Island.

Since the days of Roger Williams, when Rhode Island was dubbed a moral sewer by her haughty Puritan neighbors, the state had been subjected to the slings and arrows of outraged "foreigners." In the decade of the 1780s, however, this abuse from without, as Professor Kaminski has recited, reached unprecedented proportions. Beginning with Rhode Island's initial rejection of the impost of 1781 and continuing through the paper-money era, the state and its citizens were subjected to an endless stream of invective. Rhode Island newspapers of the day were replete with verbal barbs reprinted from distant presses. The Confederation Congress attempted to unseat Rhode Island delegate David Howell for his strenuous opposition to the impost; later, after the paper-money issue, the state was caricatured as the "Quintessence of Villainy" and as an example of "democracy run rampant." Such harsh actions and words of condescending "foreign" critics were most distressing to Rhode Island Islanders.

During the Constitution-making process the Federalists took Rhode Island to task. For them the state symbolized the danger to order posed by popularly controlled state legislatures. From the outset, when the *Massachusetts Centinel* described Rhode Island's absence from the Grand Convention as a "joyous rather than a grievous" circumstance, to the end of the ratification struggle, when some proposed the state's dismemberment and absorption by the surrounding states, Rhode Island endured repeated insult. Even the temperate James Madison found Rhode Island exasperating. "Nothing can exceed the wickedness and folly which continue to rule there," he exclaimed. "All sense of character as well as of right have been obliterated."

The most eloquent censure of all came from Connecticut, from the pens of a foursome who later joined a group of literati known as the Connecticut Wits. Their contribution to Rhode Island's litany of shame was a long poetical satire entitled the "Anarchiad, 1786–1787," which included these lines:

> Hail! Realm of rogues, renown'd for fraud and guile,
> All Hail; ye knav'ries of yon little isle.
> There prowls the rascal, cloth'd with legal pow'r,
> To snare the orphan, and the poor devour;
> The crafty knave his creditor besets,
> And advertising paper pays his debts;
> Bankrupts their creditors with rage pursue,
> No stop, no mercy from the debtor crew.
> Arm'd with new tests, the licens'd villain bold,
> Presents his bills, and robs them of their gold;
> Their ears, though rogues and counterfeiters lose,
> No legal robber fears the gallows noose.
> Each weekly print new lists of cheats proclaims,
> Proud to enroll their knav'ries and their names;
> The wiser race, the snares of law to shun,
> Like Lot from Sodom, from Rhode Island run.

This cascade of castigation caused anger and resentment in Rhode Island, and it produced a banding together of the citizenry, especially in the country towns, against the outside agitators. The foreign Federalists won few friends in Rhode Island with their abusive tirades.

Legacies of *Brown* v. *Board of Education*
James T. Patterson

HEN RALPH ELLISON heard about the *Brown* v. *Board of Education* decision in May 1954, he wrote a friend, "What a wonderful world of possibilities for the children."

Other African American leaders were equally excited, in part because they had truly wondered, even as late as May 1954, what the Court might say: Roy Wilkins of the NAACP, in fact, had prepared two very different press releases to be given out following the Court's announcement, one of them lamenting the failure of the Court to knock down segregation. Among these other excited voices was Harlem's *Amsterdam News*, which editorialized, "The Supreme Court decision is the greatest victory for the Negro people since the Emancipation Proclamation." The *Chicago Defender* added, "This means the beginning of the end of the dual society in American life." Thurgood Marshall, chief litigator for black defendants in the case, recalled, "I was so happy, I was numb." At the time he estimated that state-mandated school segregation would be wiped out, nationwide, within five years.

I was so taken with Ellison's comment—about the "wonderful world of possibilities for the children"—that I wanted to use it as the title, or subtitle, for my book on the case. My publisher, however, demanded a title that would tell readers clearly what was in the book, which therefore has the wonderfully catchy and imaginative title of *Brown v. Board of Education: A Civil Rights Milestone and Its Troubled Legacy*.

Still, it is Ellison's high hopes—and those of many other African Americans in 1954—to which I return again and again in my book on the *Brown* case, and on which I wish to reflect today. To what extent may we say, nearly fifty years later, that these hopes have been realized?

There are any number of legacies of the case that can be examined, but let me focus on two questions:

First: How great an impact did the decision have on advancing the powerful civil rights movement that mushroomed thereafter, especially in the early 1960s?

Second: Has desegregation of schools made a significant difference in the academic and lifetime achievement of black students, or should we conclude—as many discouraged Americans (blacks as well as whites) have come to believe in recent years—that meaningful integration of schools is all but impossible, and that the Supreme Court might have done better in 1954 (and since) to focus on enforcing the *Plessy* decision of 1896—that is, on ensuring educational *equality* for blacks, instead of demanding desegregation?

So, to the first question: Did *Brown* do much to promote an intensification of the civil rights movement after 1954?

When the movement gained force in the 1960s, the answer to this question seemed to be an obvious yes. Americans had only to look at the chronology of events following *Brown*—events that suggested that the decision was indeed the first strong link in a chain of causation leading to the great acceleration of the civil rights movement in the 1960s. Only one and a half years after *Brown* came the memorable boycott of buses in Montgomery, Alabama. In 1957 President Eisenhower sent in federal troops to maintain token desegregation of Central High School in Little Rock. (This would not have happened, of course, without *Brown*). And then, in the 1960s, the movement swelled, ultimately forcing Congress to pass the historic Civil Rights Act of 1964 and the Voting Rights Act of 1965.

There are also events in this chain that seem to link directly to the *Brown* decision. For instance, Martin Luther King Jr. staged a Prayer Pilgrimage to Washington in 1957 on May 17, the third anniversary of *Brown*. The first group of 1961 Freedom Riders, organized by CORE, announced that they intended to reach their final destination, New Orleans, on May 17.

William Chafe's excellent book concerning Greensboro, North Carolina, *Civilities and Civil Rights*, made this apparent causal connection—between *Brown* and the Movement of the 1960s—especially clear. The day after *Brown* the city's school board indicated that it would desegregate the city's schools. But when white opposition quickly mounted, the board betrayed its promise. Nothing of substance changed in the racial composition of the city's schools. Finally, four black college students staged their historic sit-in at Woolworth's in February 1960. Three of them had grown up in Greensboro and had had to attend all-black segregated schools. Their anger at noncompliance with *Brown*, Chafe argued, spilled forth into the decision to sit in. The rest, as we say, is "history," because the Greensboro sit-ins touched off the huge explosion of civil rights activity that followed in the next few years.

In hindsight, however, I think we may be justified in wondering—as scholars have done in recent years—how vital the *Brown* decision was as a stimulant to the civil rights activism that really took off only in the 1960s. Martin Luther King, for instance, necessarily turned for help to the federal courts; indeed, the Supreme Court ultimately backed the Montgomery boycott, thereby giving King and his fellow protesters a victory in December 1956. But King and most other young militants had relatively little faith in slow-moving, case-by-case legal strategies. Indeed, they deplored the Court's decision in the so-called *Brown II* ruling of 1955, which failed to set a deadline for compliance with *Brown*, stating mysteriously that desegregation should proceed with "all deliberate speed." (Marshall later said he finally understood what this phrase meant: "s-l-o-w.") Supporters of segregation were generally delighted with *Brown II*; Florida's legislators, following a reading of it, stood up and cheered.

The *Brown* decision was obviously well known, and welcome, to King and to other young activists, but for years it made little difference in the schools, which remained segregated. Discouraged, blacks did relatively little demonstrating between 1954 and 1960: in 1955, 1957, and 1959 there were in fact fewer civil rights protests in the United States than there had been in 1943, 1946, 1947, and 1948. We can surely agree that the *Brown* decision had some visible effects — for instance, in encouraging nonsouthern states to enact civil rights laws against discrimination in employment and public accommodations. Eight western states did so between May 1954 and June 1955. We can also see modest progress, following *Brown*, against school segregation in predominantly white areas of the border states. And we can agree that *Brown* had symbolic value both to civil rights activists and to African Americans throughout the nation; after all, the "law" was finally on their side. More generally, *Brown* encouraged Marshall and other black lawyers to "rally the troops," as Marshall put it, in selected local southern communities, helping thereby to lessen feelings of despair and helplessness among black people. Still, it remains debatable whether the symbolic value spurred a great deal of real change at the time.

We should also remember that the direct action phase of the movement that accelerated after 1960 surprised and, at least for a while, alarmed Thurgood Marshall and some of his associates. A few of these attorneys were cool at first to the urgent pleas from protestors for financial and legal assistance. Marshall was later reported by a young aide to have reacted emotionally to the trouble caused by the activists, "storming around the room proclaiming . . . [that] he was not going to represent a bunch of crazy colored students who violate the sacred property rights of white folks by going in their stores and lunch counters and refusing to leave when ordered to do so." Although Marshall and the Legal Defense Fund did soon help the militants, his initial reaction indicates that the movement had taken turns in 1960 that he had not anticipated or welcomed. Only reluctantly and belatedly did he recognize that neither the *Brown* decision nor subsequent litigation was in itself sufficient to upend racial segregation in the United States.

The nearly fifteen-year success of massive resistance to *Brown*—which confined 99 percent of Deep South black public school children to all-black schools as late as 1964 (ten years after *Brown*)—then and later has led many liberal scholars to lament what they regard as the timidity of the Court in 1954. Chief Justice Earl Warren and his fellow justices, they point out, failed to denounce racism or de facto segregation; they shied away from ruling against segregation or racial discrimination (including state laws banning racial intermarriage) outside of public schools; they set no timetable for compliance with the decision; and they supplied no criteria for determining what should be the educational effectiveness of desegregation. I think that these criticisms, while understandable in hindsight, reflect widespread gloom about progress in civil rights since the 1960s. They tend to forget that asserting the unconstitutionality of de jure segregation in public schools was at that time a historic step that American elected officials refused to take. Still, these criticisms do remind us that much more needed to be done than *Brown* demanded in 1954.

Other scholars have offered variants of what has become known as a "backlash thesis" concerning the origins of the civil rights movement that flourished in the early 1960s. This thesis also holds that *Brown* did relatively little to promote more liberal race relations, at least in the short run. On the contrary, this argument continues, successful litigation such as that which resulted in *Brown* caused liberals to have excessive faith in what turned out to be protracted and sometimes inconclusive legal strategies, thus delaying the rise of all-important direct action militancy that finally promoted effective legislation, such as the Civil Rights Act of 1964 and the Voting Rights Act of 1965.

Other critics even wonder if *Brown* might have made matters worse, for blacks, again in the short run, because it aroused a backlash among southern whites, who were fearful above all about desegregation of the *schools*, and who therefore turned to massive resistance. This resistance, it is also claimed, impeded ongoing progress — slow though this was — toward desegregation of transportation and public facilities, and of higher education and college sports in the Upper South. *Brown,* in short, further racialized southern politics and isolated southern white liberals. Moreover, the successes of massive resistance exposed the impotence of the Court as an agent of rapid social change. Only indirectly and in entirely unintended ways, these critics conclude, may *Brown* be said to have promoted much change: that is, it stimulated a volatile white backlash that in turn (after 1960) sparked greater black militancy, a "counter-backlash." Then, and only then, six years after *Brown,* did militants manage to form a politically potent civil rights movement. Thus, it was ironically the *limits* of the effects of *Brown* that several years later led to progressive changes in American race relations.

Those who question the impact of *Brown* also argue, finally, that many larger socioeconomic and educational forces existing independently of the decision were probably more important stimulants of the civil rights movement. These forces included massive South-to-North migrations of blacks, rising economic and educational levels (of whites as well as blacks), struggles against colonialism in Africa, and the Cold War. How could America claim to be the leader of the so-called Free World if it denied basic rights to its African American population? The thrust of some of these forces, notably the Cold War, was apparent in the thinking of some of the justices in 1954, and it became increasingly strong by the 1960s. As Philip Elman, a liberal Justice Department official, observed, "In *Brown* nothing the lawyers said made a difference. Thurgood Marshall could have stood up and recited 'Mary had a little lamb,' and the result would have been exactly the same." Jack Greenberg, a top associate of Thurgood Marshall, offered a similar judgment years later. "There was a current of history," he said, "and the Court became part of it."

I am personally skeptical of some versions of the "backlash" approach, for it seems to me that most southern whites would have resorted — indeed, did resort — to massive resistance against virtually all challenges, not just litigation aimed at desegregation of the schools. We should not, therefore, see *Brown* as an event that made southern race relations much worse, nor — given the racial attitudes of most white southerners at the time — is it easy to imagine any wholly peaceful or gradual way that racial segregation could have been dismantled. Still, it is clear that *Brown* was an insufficient spark for the dramatic expansion of the civil rights movement that raced ahead so strongly in the 1960s. We should think twice before assigning it some sort of iconic status.

I should say here, as an aside, that this conclusion is not what I had expected in 1996 when I signed the contract for my book, which is the first in a new series by my publishers, a series labeled "Pivotal Moments in American History." The case was indeed important, especially as a constitutional precedent that decisions in the late 1950s could build upon (concerning not only public schools but also public buses, parks, playgrounds, and beaches). Since 1980 the case has also been cited by plaintiffs seeking equalization of educational resources for predominantly black schools. But whether the case was "pivotal" for the civil rights movement — of that, I am not so sure.

Now, my second question: To what extent has desegregation of the schools — once *Brown* was finally implemented (mostly after 1968) — promoted academic achievement among blacks?

In 1954 Thurgood Marshall and most other foes of segregation did not think very deeply about that question. It was self-evident to them that Jim Crow in schools meant unequal education for blacks; inevitably, they thought, desegregation would result in better schooling for black children. But there already existed a few nonracist voices that had expressed doubts about large hopes concerning the educational benefits of school desegregation. America's most prominent black intellectual, W. E. B. Du Bois, had articulated these doubts in a controversial essay published in 1935. "A Negro school," he wrote, "where children are treated like human beings, trained by teachers of their own race, who know what it means to be black . . . is infinitely better than making our boys and girls doormats to be spit and trampled upon and lied to by ignorant social climbers, whose sole claim to superiority is ability to kick 'niggers' when they are down."

Zora Neale Hurston, a well-known black writer (and a conservative in her politics) was even more skeptical than Du Bois about the educational virtues of desegregated schools. Criticizing the reasoning behind the *Brown* decision in 1955, she wrote, "The whole matter revolves around the self-respect of my people. How much satisfaction can I get from a court order for somebody to associate with me who does not wish me near them? The American Indian has never been spoken of as a minority and chiefly because there is no whine in the Indian. Certainly he fought, and valiantly, for his lands, and rightfully so, but it is inconceivable of an Indian to seek forcible association with anyone. His well-known pride and self-respect would save him from that. I take the Indian position."

Since the 1960s, of course, many other African Americans have echoed such doubts about school desegregation. Derrick Bell, the well-known law professor, wrote in 1994, "The insistence on integrating every public school that is black perpetuates the racially demeaning and unproven assumption that blacks must have a majority white presence in order to either teach or learn effectively." More recently, Bell has said that in 1954 the Court should have focused on enforcement of educational equality, not on desegregation. In effect, he endorses the *Plessy* v. *Ferguson* standard, rendered by the Court in 1896, that called for "separate but equal" in matters regarding race.

As you know, many black parents have also developed doubts about school desegregation. One commented in 1992, "I'm from the segregation time, back in the '50s and '60s, so coming from that background I felt that my children would have a better opportunity to interact socially in an integrated situation. That's where it turned out to be a mirage. It proved to me that educationally and socially your children can learn just as much in a predominantly black situation as opposed to an integrated situation."

Perhaps the most striking recent example of thinking along these lines came from Supreme Court Justice Clarence Thomas in the case of *Missouri* v. *Jenkins*. Supporting a 1995 majority decision (of five justices) that placed important aspects of a school desegregation plan of Kansas City in jeopardy, Thomas strongly rejected a central psychological theory underlying *Brown*: that children in all-black schools developed feelings of inferiority and had low motivation. Thomas countered, "The theory that black students suffer an unspecified psychological harm from segregation that retards their mental and educational development . . . not only relies upon questionable social science research rather than constitutional principle, but it also rests on an assumption of black inferiority."

As the statements of Bell and Thomas indicate, views such as these cut across the ideological spectrum, and in our own times they also expose profound discouragement about the so-called White/Black Test Score Gap. The scores of blacks on key academic achievement tests had increased slowly but encouragingly between the early 1970s, when desegregation at last advanced in the South, and the early 1990s, thereby narrowing the black-white gap. But the gap still remains huge. In 1994, reading scores for seventeen-year-old blacks were 3.9 grade levels below those for whites, and most of the gaps have persisted, even rising slightly, since then.

Why these gaps persist remains debated, but they clearly have not narrowed as much as people like Ellison and Marshall might have anticipated in the 1950s and 1960s. This is of course a very serious matter, for it means that blacks on the average have great difficulty gaining admission to selective colleges and universities, in staying in colleges when they do secure admission, and in finding well-paying employment when they graduate. Widespread popular awareness of the gaps, moreover, has had the effect in many communities of lessening the support of parents—black as well as white—for strategies to promote desegregation. Among the results of such feelings are not only "White Flight" to white suburbs, but also "Bright Flight"—of some black as well as white parents. In the early 1960s Thurgood Marshall sent his young children to mostly white private schools in New York City. When criticized by integrationists, he replied, "I think my children should have the best education that I can afford."

For all these reasons, research into the sources of these gaps—and action to narrow them—are imperative if racial desegregation of the schools is to move ahead in the future. The sociologist Christopher Jencks, a careful student of the test-score problem, has concluded that fighting the gaps "would do more to move America toward racial equality than any politically possible alternative."

Let me ask one final question: What can we conclude concerning the broader impact of *Brown* on race relations generally since 1954? At the risk of repeating myself, I would stress several things.

First, it is historically inaccurate to be nostalgic—as some blacks have become—about black schools in the segregation era. It is true that some black schools, as in Washington, D.C., were excellent; that many black schools stimulated great pride, loyalty, and solidarity among the students who attended them; and that networks of black teachers, parents, and administrators served as key building blocks in struggles for civil rights thereafter. The closing of many of these black schools in the desegregation era has been bittersweet to black people in the South. But we cannot claim much for the educational quality of those Jim Crow schools; while a handful of such schools offered students a challenging academic curriculum, the vast majority of them were badly funded, inferior institutions that seriously damaged the opportunities of black people. One such school in the District of Columbia had only a Bunsen burner and a goldfish bowl in its science lab. Most black children who go to significantly nonsegregated schools today receive much better supported schooling than they did in the truly bad old days. Contrary to the doom-and-gloom rhetoric of many commentators today, some things have become better over time.

Second, nonsegregated schools, where they exist, do not yet seem to have promoted significantly greater interracial understanding in American life, let alone to have helped us to achieve the kind of broader racial integration dreamed of by hopeful people like Ralph Ellison and Martin Luther King Jr. More often than not, we find racially obvious "tracking" in these schools, and relatively little social interaction between black and white children.

Many people have therefore grown despondent. Linda Brown-Thompson, whose father was the Brown of *Brown* v. *Board*, reflected in 1994, "Sometimes I wonder if we really did the children and the nation a favor by taking this case to the Supreme Court. I knew it was the right thing for my father and mother to do then. But after nearly forty years we find the Court's ruling unfulfilled." Elizabeth Eckford, one of the "Little Rock Nine" of 1957, had even greater doubts. "There was a time when I thought integration was one of the most desired things," she said. But now "I appreciate blackness more than I did then."

Yet to single out unhappy survivors such as Eckford is to slight another, brighter picture: the other eight among the Little

Rock Nine, for instance, proclaimed themselves glad, in retrospect, that they had challenged Jim Crow. All went on to colleges or universities. Other black adults, too, have looked back positively on their experiences in nonsegregated schools, insisting that their experiences were beneficial in many ways: proving to them, for instance, that whites are not necessarily smarter, and offering them exposure to the all-important social and economic networks of a larger multicultural world than predominantly black schools could normally have provided. Some white people, too, maintain that going to school with blacks has helped to dispel or weaken ugly stereotypes.

Moreover, to expect nonsegregated schools to promote wonderful advances such as those perhaps dreamed of by Ellison or Martin Luther King is to erect very high goals that no human society, alas, has come very close to achieving. Measuring the impact of *Brown* according to more modest criteria of "success," I agree with Richard Kluger (the author of *Simple Justice,* a magisterial book on the *Brown* decision) that the unanimous ruling of 1954 helped to further a "re-consecration of American ideals"—ideals that were more luminous than other contemporary quests, such as anticommunism or the furthering of material abundance. And so these ideals remain.

For these reasons, I believe that greater desegregation of schools remains a worthy social and educational goal. Many Americans also understand that to tolerate resegregation in public schools (which has been slowly developing, especially in urban areas, since the late 1980s) is to risk the greater resegregation of society at large, along class as well as racial lines, and therefore to heighten racial isolation and denial of equal opportunity. As Jencks has put it, "The more you let society pull itself apart, the less commitment the haves have to the have-nots."

Finally, the contested history of *Brown* since 1954 reveals that courts must normally have large popular backing and sustained political support if they hope to promote significant change, at least in the short run. This support, of course, the Supreme Court did not receive in the late 1950s, either from the white American public (which showed little interest in civil rights at the time) or from President Eisenhower, who refused to endorse the *Brown* decision or (until 1959) to state that segregation was immoral. As Jack Greenberg, a top attorney with Marshall, put it in 1994, "Altogether school desegregation has been a story of conspicuous achievements, flawed by marked failures, the causes of which lie beyond the capacity of lawyers to correct. Lawyers can do right, they can do good, but they have their limits. The rest of the job is up to society."

A Rhode Island Reflection

Rhode Island was the leading participant among the thirteen colonies in the nefarious Atlantic slave trade. Consequently, on the eve of the American Revolution, it had the largest percentage of slaves to its total population of any New England state.

Inspired by the liberating spirit of the War for Independence and the urging of the state's large Quaker community, Rhode Island passed a gradual manumission act in 1784. Three years later its General Assembly enacted a ban against participation in the slave trade by Rhode Islanders, and in the contest to ratify the Constitution, Rhode Island proposed an amendment to delete the twenty-year protection that document afforded to the foreign slave trade and ban it immediately. Rhode Island was the only state to suggest such an amendment during the ratification debate — perhaps to atone for past sins.

Rhode Island's free, landowning black males could vote until stripped of the franchise in 1822. That privilege was regained in the state Constitution of 1843, a document that also banned slavery outright. Such generosity by the ultraconservative drafters of that document stemmed from the assistance provided by blacks to the Charter, or Law and Order, faction in suppressing the Dorr Rebellion.

The next racial injustice to be addressed was segregation in Rhode Island's public schools. Here black businessman George T. Downing (1819–1903), a New York native and Hamilton College graduate, played a major role. In 1846 Downing moved to Newport, bought a house, and opened a restaurant. Four years later he acquired a catering business and a residence in Providence, and in the summer of 1855, with capital borrowed from his father, Downing built a luxury hotel in Newport called Sea Girt House, which attracted a distinguished and rich white clientele.

In the 1850s Downing's efforts turned not only towards abolitionism but also towards civil rights for freed blacks. An 1855 Massachusetts statute banning racially segregated public schools served as the catalyst for Downing's unrelenting efforts to secure a similar law in Rhode Island that would prevent this common practice. For the next decade

Downing appeared before school committees in the offending communities, repeatedly petitioned the General Assembly, testified before legislative committees, wrote and published addresses, and tried to mobilize the black vote on behalf of his great cause, but to no avail. Then, in 1866, the legislature finally heeded Downing's plea; prompted by a temporary spurt of war-born idealism, it passed a statute outlawing racial segregation in public schools throughout the state of Rhode Island, eighty-eight years before *Brown* v. *Board of Education*.

Inventing a Constitution
Jack Rakove

I WOULD LIKE TO THANK my old friend and Harvard classmate Bob McCarthy, now a Providence College professor of history, for his generous introduction, which, I must confess, I also happened to write myself. I was worried that Bob might reminisce about what I was really like as a young graduate student of twenty-two, just starting out in the field but feeling my oats even then. Mercifully, he is going to keep that a secret.

My task is to provide the serious, educational part of this afternoon's festivities. I will do my best to make the learning both light and informative. But at the outset I want to insist that just as the occasion we are celebrating is itself a serious one, so is the subject I propose to discuss. It will begin with a simple and straightforward question. But to give that question the answer it deserves involves explaining just how the American revolutionaries and constitution-makers of the 1770s and 1780s took the critical innovation that has distinguished our constitutional tradition ever since.

That innovation depends upon a simple definition. When Americans talk about a constitution of government (or our Constitution), we define it in these terms: It is a document which operates as supreme, fundamental law, a document which has to be adopted at a known moment of historical time by a special set of procedures that clearly distinguishes it from all other legal enactments, and which thereafter regulates everything that the institutions it creates can (and cannot) do in its name. This definition is so much a matter a common sense to us, so essential to our political identity as a people and a nation, something we take so much for granted, that it is difficult to overlook what a remarkable and striking innovation its original acceptance represented in the history of constitutionalism, and how much creative thinking and political entrepreneurship went into its realization.

The simple question I propose to consider, then, is this: How was this distinctive American definition created, and what made this definition the compelling one that Americans generally accepted over the course of their first decade of independent self-government — that is, between the adoption of the first state constitutions in 1776 and the drafting and ratification of the Federal Constitution in 1787–1788? It is a story whose significance I did not fully grasp when I began working on the project that became my book *Original Meanings*, and which also made the single chapter I devoted to telling it perhaps the most difficult one I had to write. In this story, you will be pleased to learn, the tiny state of Rhode Island played a critical, if somewhat perverse, role; but so did your great neighbor to the north and east, Massachusetts.

The story has three main parts or chapters. It begins with the revolutionary controversy that commenced with the Stamp Act dispute of 1765–1766 and culminated in the American movement for independence during the two years that followed Parliament's passage of the Coercive Acts in 1774. The second phase, or chapter, begins with that decision for independence, which also required the new American states (other than the so-called corporate provinces of Rhode Island and Connecticut) to adopt new constitutions of government in order to replace the old colonial regimes that had effectively collapsed. This second phase extends to 1780, when Massachusetts adopted its constitution under the new procedures that clarified the distinction between ordinary legislation and the special form of law that a written constitution was now understood to embody. The third and concluding chapter requires flashing forward to the events of 1787–1789 and understanding how the innovations developed within the states (and again, particularly in Massachusetts [*crowd noise: Boo! Hiss!*

Say it ain't so, professor!] were transposed to the project of federal constitutional reform.

We can tell the first part of this story fairly quickly. The American Revolution, like all great political upheavals, may have had many causes, but at its heart the controversy between Britain and its mainland colonies was essentially constitutional in nature. This controversy began, of course, with the passage by the British Parliament of the Stamp Act of 1765, imposing what was then called a direct or internal tax on the American colonists in the form of duties on newspapers, legal documents, and the like. Americans quickly protested, arguing that they were not bound to pay taxes levied by a distant Parliament in which they did not enjoy the basic right of representation. The British initially answered these protests with the counterclaim that the colonists were *virtually* represented in the House of Commons, even though they sent no members to Westminster, but this argument had little traction in North America, where Americans were habituated to political practices that closely tied lawmakers and their constituents. The argument not only enjoyed almost no traction in America; it was subjected to ridicule even in Britain, and the debate quickly shifted, or escalated, to a different argument.

This was an argument about sovereignty, not representation, and it posed theoretical challenges that the colonists found more difficult to rebut. Ever since the Glorious Revolution of 1688, when the Protestant couple William and Mary replaced the deposed Catholic King James II, it was generally recognized that Parliament (of which the king was a member) was the supreme, sovereign source of law within the realm of Great Britain. By its very nature, sovereignty was a unitary, absolute, ultimate power, and by definition it could never be divided or parceled out. There was no question that Parliament was the obvious repository, or locale, of sovereignty within the British polity, and if the colonies were part of that polity, which they seemingly must be, then it followed that they had to be ultimately subject to its jurisdiction. Attractive as their arguments about representation must be, those claims ultimately had to yield before the even more potent doctrine which said that there had to be some final, ultimate source of legal authority in every regime.

Americans found this argument a difficult one to counter, but they insisted that their claims based on representation were still strong enough to spare them from being governed by a distant legislature in which they did not enjoy, and by nature could never truly exercise, the great right of representation. From their perspective, that was a sufficient basis for rejecting the Stamp Act and all the other measures that Parliament subsequently enacted over the next decade. But from our perspective, thinking historically about the claims and counterclaims of the two "countries," what is striking is the extent to which both arguments were deeply rooted in, and validated by, a common constitutional tradition. Both positions — the colonists' appeal to representation, the British appeal to unitary sovereignty — were legitimate; both were deeply anchored in a common tradition; and neither could wholly vanquish the other.

That was the heart of the impasse that ultimately led to American independence in 1776. For two obvious reasons, there proved to be no way to bridge the gap that opened when these two theories of political obligation were pitted in direct conflict with each other. The first reason, quite simply, is that there was no common document to which the contending parties could point or appeal to resolve their quarrel. The British constitution that everyone admired in the eighteenth century was not distilled in a single text but scattered among many, and it also embraced a set of traditions and conventions of governance. Anyone could describe the traditions and norms of constitutional governance, and many texts (from Magna Carta to the parliamentary Bill of Rights of 1689) could be cited as evidence of what that constitution embraced. But there was no one document to whose authority the parties could appeal. Nor, in the second place, was there any institution capable of playing the same adjudicatory or mediating role that we now commonly ascribe to our Supreme Court. From the colonial vantage point, Parliament could hardly be an impartial arbiter of its own claims to supreme authority; when viewed from London, could such august bodies as the separate legislatures that met in modest provincial towns like Newport or Annapolis or Williamsburg possibly vie for authority with the mother of parliaments in Westminster?

The crisis on which the British empire in North America foundered, then, was a distinctly constitutional one. By 1774 there were two rival and irreconcilable views of the extent of Parliament's authority over the American colonies, one resting on the colonists' views of representation, the other on British views of parliamentary sovereignty. Within their common Anglo-American tradition, both views were valid, in the sense that they appealed to deep and genuine currents of constitutional thought and practice. Absent an authoritative constitution to which the sides could appeal and an impartial institution to adjudicate their dispute, there was no way to accommodate or resolve the controversy. In 1774 Parliament responded to the Boston Tea Party with a raft of punitive laws directed against Massachusetts, and these Coercive, or Intolerable, Acts, as we call them, amounted to a definitive expression of the idea that Parliament could legislate for Americans "in all cases whatsoever." The other colonies rallied to Massachusetts's defense, and the result was the event we call the American Revolution.

That brings us to the second chapter of the story — the point at which Americans begin to depart from that common tradition and to define constitutions in new and more specific terms. In most of the colonies, legal government, especially at the provincial level, collapsed, or at least was sharply circumscribed, with the crisis that broke across America in the late spring and summer of 1774. The two principal exceptions to this statement were, of course, the adjoining corporate colonies of Rhode Island and Connecticut, which elected or appointed all of their officers, and from which royal and imperial authorities were effectively absent (save for some odd customs officers who were in no position to execute their duties). Everywhere else, however, legal government virtually collapsed, primarily because royal governors were hardly prepared to allow colonial legislatures to continue to meet when these institutions were preparing to resist imperial authority and instead accept the political guidance of the Continental Congress.

Even in colonies where the legislatures did continue to meet, real power flowed inexorably to the surrogate, extralegal apparatus of committees and conventions that first appeared during the summer of 1774, and that also looked to Congress for political direction. Historians like Pauline Maier (who I am happy to say is with us today from her nearby farm in Little Compton) have rightly described these surrogate institutions as being "extralegal" in nature, meaning that even though not authorized by law, they enjoyed enough support from the community and public opinion to be recognized as legitimate sources of authority. More than that, royal officials and loyalists were impressed by the degree of popular support these entities commanded, recognizing that they were no less effective or authoritative than the legal institutions they had supplanted.

After 1774, colonists understood that they were living in a situation not so different from the condition that John Locke had described, almost a century earlier, as a "dissolution of government." This was a situation in which a tyrannical government had lost its legal capacity and its moral capacity to rule, and in which the people were therefore free to exercise their natural right to create new governments more consistent with their principles, rights, and interests. Perhaps the colonists could have accepted a more practical and perhaps efficient option, allowing their new apparatus of extralegal committees and conventions to retain their authority, the better to prosecute the revolutionary struggle without worrying too much about the finer points of legality. That was an option in theory, but it could never surmount one overarching objection. The management of daily affairs in America depended on the effective operation of courts, and whatever other functions the extralegal bodies might fulfill, they could not pretend to supplant the essential operations of the judicial system. Moreover, given a choice between revolutionary expediency and a restoration of lawful government, ordinary Americans would always favor lawful government. Steeped as they were in a deeply legalistic culture that was the legacy of their inheritance of English liberty, they could tolerate no other choice. Once it became clear that the break with Britain was permanent, that there were no serious prospects for reconciliation, Americans would want to restore legal government as quickly as circumstances allowed.

There was a catch, however. The old governments could not be restored, in the strict sense of the term, because (Rhode Island and Connecticut again excepted) they all contained significant royal elements in the form of governors and councilors whose commissions and powers flowed directly from the crown. Moreover, colonists caught up in revolutionary fervor wanted to new-model their governments, making them more consistent with the republican values that John Adams and other writers celebrated in publishing their *Thoughts on Government* (the title of Adams's influential tract on the subject of constitution making).

These new governments would therefore differ in at least some respects from their colonial antecedents. To reach agreement on these differences, the provincial conventions first had to deliberate, not on general principles but on the specifics of the new governments they proposed to create. In practice, in most of the new states and commonwealths, the provincial conventions that were sitting as surrogate legislatures delegated the task of constitution making to small committees of well-qualified individuals. But the work of these individuals still needed the collective approval of the larger bodies. And of course the draft constitutions also had to be discussed clause by clause, or article by article. Most important, for our purposes, there was no way these conventions could proceed without reducing their work to writing.

Thus was born, simply by circumstance, the idea that a constitution, properly defined, should be a written document, framed and adopted at a known moment of historical time, and not simply a collection of traditions and conventions of governance. In a sense, this invention was an accident—a byproduct of the fact that legal government had dissolved, that independence had become inevitable, and that the restoration of the rule of law required designing and installing new governments. One part of the new American definition was thus in place by the end of 1776; but a crucial part of that definition was still missing. This was the critical idea that a constitution should also be supreme, fundamental law, superior in authority to everything else that government would do under its authority.

The story of how this additional element of the definition emerged is primarily (but not solely) a Massachusetts story. Thanks to the Coercive Acts, Massachusetts was the colony where the transfer of authority from legal to extralegal institutions first took place, and it was also the first province where a semblance of lawful government was restored. But that was a literal restoration of the royal charter of 1691, with the elected council replacing the royal governor, and it did not involve creating a new constitution. In 1776 and again in 1778, the General Court tried to promulgate a new constitution under its own authority, but its efforts were greeted with vocal opposition from a number of towns, which protested that it was wrong for a sitting legislature to draft the charter of government under which it would, in turn, exercise its lawmaking authority. Though these protests came only from a minority of towns, originally led by Concord, their arguments were telling enough to compel the General Court to back down. In 1779 it agreed to follow a new tack: to call a special convention that would assemble for the sole purpose of framing a constitution, and then to submit their work to the town meetings for debate and approval.

Why did Massachusetts follow this course, and what does its innovation reveal about the character of American constitutional thinking? We could say that the protests of the dissenting towns were early expressions of that populist distrust of elite authority which has so often figured in our politics, and so, to some extent, they must have been. But in fact the argument that the General Court could not unilaterally frame and approve a constitution on its own sole authority was also grounded in a powerful legal doctrine that was destined to play a critical role in American constitutional thinking. This is the doctrine captured in the legal maxim *leges posteriores priores contrarias abrogant.* I know an audience this distinguished has no need for a translation from the original Latin into English (or whatever dialect of English is spoken here on Narragansett Bay); but just in case I mangled the pronunciation, here's a serviceable translation: *Later laws, contradicting earlier ones, abrogate them.* Imagine a conflict between two statutes, dealing in some way with similar subject matter: to which one should an interpreter give greater authority? The short answer is that the more recent statute trumps the earlier one, because the later one must be closer to the will of the current lawgiver than the prior one.

This seems like a very technical argument, obviously appropriate for lawyers but something ordinary citizens might not be expected to grasp. The evidence from Massachusetts suggests otherwise. Here is the dilemma that the protests from the towns rightly identified: Because the provincial conventions that drafted the other state constitutions of 1776, like the General Court of Massachusetts itself, were simultaneously acting as legislative bodies, doing the ordinary business of government even amid the extraordinary circumstances of revolution, any constitution they drafted had to be regarded as being essentially legislative in nature. That is to say, a constitution or frame of government—whatever you called it—had no greater legal authority than a statute, and as such it could be altered or even violated at any time by a subsequent meeting of the same legislature, which necessarily had the same power as its predecessor. In this sense, a constitution framed legislatively could not be a constitution in the sense in which we now use that term—a supreme fundamental law, unalterable by mere legislative will. Thomas Jefferson addressed this point in a revealing passage from his *Notes on the State of Virginia*, which was published in the mid-1780s, but the plain-spoken citizens of the great state of Massachusetts were arguably the real conceptual pioneers on this issue.

Massachusetts solved the problem—which was both narrowly legal and powerfully constitutional—with the novel procedures it invented. A constitution framed by a specially appointed convention would not be a legislative enactment, and a constitution submitted to the people, gathered in the towns, for ratification would enjoy the greatest seal of approval possible: the endorsement of a popular sovereign. Such a document could therefore claim to have greater legal authority than ordinary legislation, and it would thereby escape the *leges posteriores* problem.

This was the great precedent on which James Madison and his colleagues built when the time came to replace the Articles of Confederation, the nation's first federal charter, with the new Constitution that was drafted at Philadelphia in the summer of 1787. This brings us to the third chapter in the story—a chapter in which Rhode Island played an important, if somewhat perverse, role.

Like the original state constitutions, the Articles of Confederation was also drafted in conjunction with independence, but unlike the pre-Massachusetts constitutions, it was submitted to a form of ratification—by the state legislatures. That procedure made it vulnerable, at least in theory, to the same complaint: a federal charter that had gained no higher approval than that of ordinary state legislatures could be legitimately violated or transgressed against by any subsequent session of the same legislative body (or bodies). Because the Articles took the form of a compact among all the states, there was a more than three-year lag between the time Congress proposed it to the states in November 1777 and its final ratification by the last holdout state, Maryland, in February 1781. By the time the Articles took effect on March 1, 1781, many national leaders believed that the Confederation, as drafted, was already deficient in terms of the inadequacy of the powers it vested in its Congress. Accordingly, Congress launched its first effort to amend the Articles just as it began operating under its new (if already outdated) constitution.

Rhode Island was the state that doomed the first such amendment, the 5 percent impost on foreign goods which Congress sent to the states in February 1781. As Rhode Island fell firmly under the control of the pro-paper-money faction of the mid-1780s, it became increasingly identified as the premier antifederal state in the Union. The fact that it occupied a minuscule amount of territory clinging precariously to the New England coast, with a population that would barely be noticed in populous Virginia or Pennsylvania, came increasingly to highlight the absurdity of the rule which required amendments to the Articles to muster the same unanimous approval by all thirteen state legislatures as did the original Confederation. Rhode Island was not the sole culprit, of course, in the failure of any of the amendments that Congress proposed in 1781, 1783, and 1784 to secure ratification, but its renegade status in the Union made it an easy target for proto-Federalist opprobrium.

More important, Rhode Island's roguish stance on federal

issues ultimately proved to have an enormously liberating effect on the constitutional deliberations and decisions of 1787–1788. In the months after the abortive Annapolis Convention of September 1786 gave rise to the calling of the grand Federal Convention of 1787, Rhode Island clung to its antifederal positions, making itself the one state to refuse even to send a delegation to Philadelphia. A state that would not deign to attend a convention was unlikely to approve anything the convention proposed, indicating that anything the convention offered the American people seemed doomed to fall short of the unanimity rule of the Confederation. Far from discouraging or deterring the delegates at Philadelphia, however, the simple fact of Rhode Island's obduracy freed them to abandon that rule entirely. Something less than unanimity would have to suffice, and in the end the Framers opted for approval by nine states—the same number the Confederation required for Congress to reach decisions on major issues, such as treaties.

But who could speak for the states? Under the *leges posteriores* rule, and with the Massachusetts precedent in mind, it seemed both sensible and necessary to submit the proposed Constitution not to the state legislatures but to some other body: a special ratification convention, to be called for the sole purpose of constitutional deliberation. Rhode Island cannot be held accountable for this mechanism of ratification, which tapped the greater changes in constitutional thinking that had been developing since 1776, but it was still incidentally useful to the Federalist cause and strategy. After all, once the Confederation had been violated in one respect, what need was there to abide by it in others? Having forced the convention to abandon the rule of thirteen, Rhode Island freed the delegates to similarly ignore the mandate for legislative approval.

That left, however, one other major question to be resolved. By appealing to the authority of a sovereign people, by treating the decision on a new constitution as an expression of their natural right to alter and abolish governments, the Constitution created a juridical basis for distinguishing the extraordinary, superior authority of a written charter of government from the ordinary authority of lesser acts of state. But there remained the difficult question of exactly how the will of the people was to be expressed.

The Massachusetts precedent had not wholly solved that problem. When that state's constitutional convention of 1779 sent its handiwork to the towns for their discussion and approval, it did not explain exactly how the towns were to reply. The convention did not provide them with a handy check-off form, indicating whether the constitution was being approved or rejected in its entirety or approved in some parts while pending satisfactory revisions in others. When the convention gathered to review the "returns" of the towns the next spring, it discovered that the towns had not acted in any uniform, easily aggregated way. All kinds of responses were returned, not reducible to one simple tally. In the end, the Massachusetts convention effectively threw up its hands and decided that the constitution had been ratified.

The Framers of the federal Constitution and their Federalist supporters escaped this potential obstacle to a satisfactory decision on ratification, and they did so with a degree of ingenuity that combined powerful considerations of constitutional theory with adroit calculations of political expediency. By subjecting the Constitution to a form of popular ratification, they grounded its authority on a pure expression of the sovereignty of the people. Yet when the people spoke, with their loud and clear voice, they would only be allowed to utter one of two words, or take one of two actions: yes or no, up or down, on the Constitution *in toto*. That is, there could be no conditional form of ratification, no promise to agree later if certain changes were made in the meantime. The people, acting through their delegates in the separate state conventions, were free to accept or reject the Constitution, and free, too, to propose as many amendments for *future* consideration as they wished. What they were not allowed to do, by dint of Federalist persistence on this point, was to ratify the Constitution *conditionally*, in anticipation of amendments yet unknown, or to revisit their original decision should their expectations be disappointed.

The result of this careful management of both the concept and process of how one should go about ratifying the Constitution should not be underestimated or undervalued. It took a process that could have easily been criticized as more an assault on the existing Union than an effort to correct it, or which could easily have devolved into an unseemly cacophony of rival proposals and counterproposals, and made it a successful exercise in collective decision making for which there was no historical precedent. It kept that decision-making process carefully bounded, so that even its harshest critics were soon willing to accept its essential legitimacy. This in turn guaranteed that when Americans began disagreeing over what their Constitution, in its numerous details, meant — as they very quickly began to do — their disagreements were limited to the meaning of the clauses in question, not to the validity or legality or authoritative supremacy of the document itself.

This remains a remarkable achievement in the annals of recorded history, as impressive now as it was unprecedented then; and the more one studies it, the more impressive it becomes. Perhaps it could not quite have happened in the way it did had not Rhode Island, this tiny piece of real estate clinging to the New England coast, played the perverse role that providence (if not Providence) had destined for it. The rest of the states could not have done it without you — even if you sat out the real work!

A Rhode Island Reflection

It pains me to hear Jack's use of Rhode Island as a negative reference. Under the circumstances existing in the late 1780s, the absence of Rhode Island from the Grand Convention is inexcusable. Rhode Island's criticism of the proposed basic law, however, is more defensible, even though I realize it is easier to critique that document than it was to create it.

Does this tiny state's specific objections to the Constitution possess any merit? I would answer a resounding yes! In view of Rhode Island's resistance to an overweening and unrestrained central government, concern for the sovereignty and integrity of the states in the spirit of true federalism, solicitude for individual liberty (especially religious freedom), opposition to slavery and the incidents of servitude, and concern for direct democratic participation in the constitution-making process—features we now take for granted, but ones that the original Constitution lacked—perhaps Americans might ask not why it took "Rogues' Island" so long to join the Union but rather why it took the Union so long to join Rhode Island!

One other aspect of Jack's perceptive analysis might be expanded. He, John Kaminski, and I all agree that the basic, irreconcilable constitutional issue dividing Americans from the mother country was the locus of sovereignty. England insisted its empire was unitary, with indivisible sovereignty possessed by the King in Parliament. Americans gradually formulated a theory of divided sovereignty. Rhode Islanders Stephen Hopkins and Silas Downer were among the first colonials to develop and promulgate new constitutional conceptions of empire in the decade prior to the War for Independence.

Late in 1764 Hopkins, while governor of the colony, penned an elaborate analysis of imperial relations, one that shifted from a purely economical defense of colonial rights to a political and constitutional conception of the British Empire. In his pamphlet *The Rights of Colonies Examined*, Hopkins repeatedly referred not merely to the economic interests of Rhode Islanders, or of the northern colonists (as in his earlier essays), but rather to the broad rights of "Americans." This treatise is notable in that it suggests a federal theory of empire, with Parliament legislating on matters of imperial concern — war, trade, international relations — but with colonial assemblies possessing sovereignty in local affairs, including taxation. In 1766 this bold tract was published in London under the title *The Grievances of the American Colonists Candidly Examined*. Hopkins later became one of two Rhode Island signers of the Declaration of Independence.

In 1768 Providence lawyer Silas Downer — colleague, friend, and protégé of Hopkins — delivered a pathbreaking public discourse at the local "liberty tree," repudiating the recently passed Declaratory Act and going beyond the federal theory of Hopkins to deny the authority of Parliament to make laws of any kind to bind the colonies. This professed "Son of Liberty" went through the whole list of Parliamentary legislation, denouncing these statutes as "infractions on the natural rights of man," and therefore void. Downer expounded an embryonic theory of dominion or commonwealth wherein the American colonies gave allegiance to the sovereign while insisting upon self-government. He believed that "our distant situation from Great Britain and other attendant circumstances made it impossible for us to be represented in the parliament of that country, or to be governed from thence."

Professor Carl Bridenbaugh, late of Brown University, subtitled his biography of Downer "Forgotten Patriot" and asserted that this Providence attorney and scrivener was one of the first Americans to publicly deny the power of Parliament over the colonies. "We must be governed by our own parliaments, in which we can be in person, or by representation," exclaimed Downer at the local liberty tree. In 1774 Hopkins took attorney Downer to the First Continental Congress to serve as secretary to the Rhode Island delegation, which was headed by Hopkins and his former rival Samuel Ward.

Like Rodney Dangerfield, poor little Rhode Island gets no respect. If America's insistence on divided sovereignty (i.e., federal theory) was both the constitutional root of rebellion and a basic (if sometimes ignored) theory underlying our present constitutional system, where are Hopkins and Downer in the pantheon of our Revolutionary political theorists?

"A Good Canvas in Need of Retouching": Thomas Jefferson and the American Constitution

Carol Berkin

O N May 30, 1787, George Washington set down his thoughts to a friend on the Constitutional Convention, just beginning its sessions in the humid, fly-infested city of Philadelphia: "The business of this convention is as yet too much in embryo to form any opinion of the result. Much is expected from it by some, but little by others, and nothing by a few. That something is necessary, all will agree, for the situation of the General Government (if it can be called a government) is shaken to its foundations. . . . In a word, it is at an end, and unless a remedy is soon applied, anarchy and confusion will inevitably ensue." This letter, filled with General Washington's sense of urgency and impending crisis, was addressed to Thomas Jefferson.

It is almost a shock to realize that as political leaders from every state, save Rhode Island, gathered to consider the future of the republic, Thomas Jefferson was not present. Few significant political events in the long process toward independence and the creation of a republic seemed to occur without him. And yet he played no role in the constitutional convention; he was not among the "demigods" he later declared had sat in the East Room of Independence Hall. The explanation for his absence is a simple one: Thomas Jefferson was abroad, serving as minister to France.

While Jefferson may well have been missed, as was John Adams and John Jay, the convention did not lack for men of talent, genius, and political experience. Not all were demigods, of course; not a few, in fact, were men of ordinary intelligence, enriched by wealth, good education, and long political experience. At least one was a drunkard and one a snuff addict; one was simply a dandy, prouder of his elegant suits and gold buttons than his political record. Yet among the delegates were some of the most distinguished and brilliant men of the Revolution. Here was John Dickinson, the "penman of the Revolution," now emaciated, wracked by illness, but eager to join in replacing an ineffective government that he had originally drafted. Here too was the Pennsylvania lawyer James Wilson, tall, neatly dressed, his thick spectacles making him appear even sterner than his true nature; and here was Elbridge Gerry of Massachusetts, small and thin, whose slight stutter had never deterred him from voicing his razor-sharp criticisms of his colleagues and their political arguments. At the New Jersey table sat tiny, mild-mannered, modest William Paterson, who would emerge as the champion of the small states' interests, along with Connecticut's tall, ungainly Roger Sherman, a man who Thomas Jefferson declared had never said a foolish thing in his life.

Nearby at the Pennsylvania table sat Gouveneur Morris, whose brilliance, erudition, ironic wit, and remarkable literary style almost made the more moralistic members of the convention overlook his scandalous romantic adventures. Joining him was the financial wizard of the Revolution, Robert Morris, and when his gout and kidney stones permitted, the ineffable Ben Franklin was there too, America's true renaissance man, diplomat, scientist, politician, and shrewd judge of men's character.

South Carolina had sent the two Charles Pinckneys, Colonel Charles Cotesworth and his much younger, much more ambitious and impetuous relative Charles, whose high opinion of himself was almost entirely deserved. New York's delegation included the remarkable Alexander Hamilton, whose political genius was both admired and feared by those who knew him; "little Mars" they called him, for despite a face like Adonis, he had the war god's aggressive character.

Like Pennsylvania, Virginia had sent many of its most distinguished leaders: George Mason, author of the Virginia Declaration of Rights; George Wythe, legal mentor of Thomas Jefferson; as well as Governor Edmund Randolph and James Madison. Although Hamilton had orchestrated the call for the convention, it was Virginia's James Madison, who arrived in Philadelphia with a plan for a new government, who would earn the title "Architect of the Constitution."

Jefferson's absence then, while not a tragedy, perhaps became an opportunity—an opportunity for us to see the outcome of that summer in Philadelphia from a slightly different perspective. For if Jefferson was not a complete outsider, he was—for this moment in his life—physically removed not only from the center of decision making but from America itself. His correspondence during 1787 and 1788 offers us a chance to see how the Constitution looked to a Founding Father who was not a "Framer."

It is important to realize, as we begin to follow Jefferson's comments and queries on the convention and its outcome, that news traveled poorly in the late eighteenth century, and sometimes traveled not at all. Letters were lost or went astray; delays of months were not uncommon between the writing of a note and its reading. The exchange of information could not be synchronized. Like some poorly choreographed ballet, questions were sent off even as letters containing the answers were on their way. There is a disjointedness to eighteenth-century correspondence that is jarring to the modern reader: Madison, for example, wrote a long letter to Jefferson detailing the debates over the president's term of office months before Jefferson sent a letter to Madison, complaining that no thought was given to the implications of presidential terms. While we are outraged when e-mail does not open immediately or the cable goes out on our TV for a few minutes and we miss the nightly weather report, eighteenth-century men and women accepted the problems of erratic and unpredictable communication—not to mention slow, hazardous, and uncomfortable transportation—with considerable grace. These Americans patiently repeated themselves in follow-up letters, copying over, by hand, long commentaries or accounts of business or travel or family news, in hopes that their correspondent would receive one of several letters sent.

For Jefferson, as for everyone outside the locked doors and shuttered windows of Independence Hall's East Room where the convention met, there was the added frustration and complication of secrecy. As Madison apologetically explained on June 6, all he could provide Jefferson was a list of the delegates. "In furnishing you with this list of names, I have exhausted all the means which I can make use of for gratifying your curiosity. It was thought expedient in order to secure unbiassed discussion within doors, and to prevent misconceptions and misconstructions without, to establish some rules of caution which will for no short time restrain even a confidential communication of our proceedings." In other words, the delegates had pledged total secrecy, and even Madison, anxious to provide his father and his friends with blow-by-blow descriptions of his victories and defeats on the floor of the convention, honored this pledge.

We do not know whether Jefferson received Madison's explanation for secrecy before he learned that the proceedings would be secret. A letter dated June 9 to Jefferson from Edward Carrington, sitting in the Confederation Congress in New York, also mentioned the "profound secrecy" of the proceedings, but Carrington offered no justification for the delegates' decision. Jefferson's response was immediate and critical. In no uncertain terms Jefferson declared to John Adams, his counterpart in Great Britain, that the "tying up the tongues of the members" was an "abominable precedent."

Jefferson's condemnation of the clandestine convention may have stemmed from his frustration at being not only far from the scene but also left totally in the dark. But more was at work here than simple pique. For almost three years Jefferson had been abroad, observing and interacting with the French monarchy and the national rivalries and alliances that marked European politics of the era, and secret deliberations were common in pre-Revolutionary Paris. Writing to William Carmichael that August, Jefferson admitted that his information on much of the political maneuvering and strategies by factions within the French government was based on his "knowledge of some minute and particular circumstances" rather than from "authenticated facts." In short, he was an American awash in the intrigue, secrecy, and conspiracy of a powerful but troubled European monarchy; small wonder that he was sensitive to any tactic or action taken by his countrymen that smacked of European political conduct.

Indeed, three years in Paris had convinced Jefferson that monarchies, benevolent or cruel, were abominations and that aristocracies were like vampires, feeding on the blood of the people. His letters were peppered with criticism of European rivalries and territorial aggression. For Jefferson, the domestic corruption—the excessive power in the hands of kings, emperors, and decadent aristocrats—was linked inevitably to acts of aggression, such as the current invasion of Turkish lands by the Russians. In such an environment his devotion to his own struggling republic seemed to grow each day; even the faulty Articles of Confederation seemed to him so much more admirable than even the British constitution that he feared too much tinkering with it might open a Pandora's box for republicanism.

Jefferson, of course, was not naïve about the Confederation's failings. He had experienced firsthand the contempt in which European governments held the Confederation. The American government's failure to honor its debts and the "want of tone and energy" displayed by Congress had, in his words, "annihilated" all respect for the United States "on this side of the water." He thus fervently hoped that the Confederation, or the convention meeting to reform it, would act to correct its diplomatic flaws. We must be "one nation as to foreign concerns," he admonished Madison even before the convention began.

The need to reform the government was evident; the dangers of reforming it were just as clear to an American "on this side of the water." "I confess," he wrote to Edward Carrington early that August, "I do not go as far in the reforms thought necessary as some of my correspondents in America; but if the Convention should adopt such propositions I shall suppose them necessary. My general plan would be to make the states one as to everything connected with foreign nations, and several as to every thing purely domestic." Jefferson advocated effective centralized authority in foreign affairs and states' rights in domestic matters. He continued, "But with all the imperfections of our present government, it is without comparison the best existing or that ever did exist."

That same day he wrote another American correspondent: "I look up with you to the Federal Convention for an amendment of our federal affairs. Yet I do not view them in so disadvantageous a light at present as some do." He was "amazed, and saddened," he added, to hear that some at home were considering an American king. "If all the ills which can arise among us from the republican form of our government from this day to the day of judgment could be put into a scale against which this country [i.e., France] suffers from its monarchial form in a week, or England in a month, the latter would preponderate."

Throughout the summer Jefferson could discover little more about the decisions of the convention than he could about the deliberations of the French parliamentary junta. Rumor and supposition flew back and forth across the Atlantic. On July 31 Jefferson wrote to Adams, who was of course equally in the dark about the convention, that the "leading Principles or great Outlines" of a new constitution had been settled. In all likelihood Jefferson was referring to the compromise that produced a bicameral Congress.

But he could not have known that an extended discussion — and many impasses — remained ahead for the convention as it tackled for the second time the question of the executive branch.

Not knowing what had been decided, or when — or perhaps more important, what had been considered and rejected during the course of the convention — Jefferson could only forge ahead, sending suggestions to delegate friends. On August 14 Jefferson sent a long letter to Washington. "I remain in hopes of great and good effects from the decisions of the assembly over which you are presiding." He once again expressed his support for empowering the central government in order to deal effectively with foreign affairs, and he expressed his opposition to granting greater powers over domestic matters to that government. He endorsed a separation of powers: the creation of an executive, a legislative, and a judicial branch. He opposed any additional radical changes: the Articles was a good republican document, and with all its defects "the inconveniences resulting from them are so light in comparison with those existing in every other government on earth, that our citizens may certainly be considered as in the happiest political situation which exists."

At last, on September 6, Madison — clearly about to explode from keeping in all the news of the convention — broke his vow of silence and sent Jefferson a letter detailing many of the delegates' decisions. He provided Jefferson with the broad outlines of the powers and duties of the three branches of government and a brief explanation of the basis for selection of members in the Senate and the House. Two days later John Jay wrote from New York, informing Jefferson that the convention was likely to adjourn the following week. Finally, in a long letter begun on October 24 and completed on November 1, Madison sent his friend in Paris a fuller account of the convention's deliberations. Having taken copious notes during the entire proceedings, Madison was able to reproduce for Jefferson the arguments, pro and con, on most major issues. He took special care to describe the reasoning behind the decision to provide a four-year term for the president, with eligibility for reelection.

Jefferson had perhaps already gotten a copy of the Constitution, or at least an accurate report of its contents, before he received this letter. On November 10 John Adams wrote that he had forwarded to Jefferson a copy of the Constitution that had been sent to him by Elbridge Gerry. "How doe you like our new constitution?" Jefferson wrote to Adams on November 13. He then launched into his own objections. "I confess there are things in it which stagger all my disposition to subscribe to what such an Assembly has proposed." He doubted, he told Adams, that a Senate composed of two men from each state would be adequate to manage either foreign or domestic affairs. Far worse, however, was the description of the presidency. "Their President," he declared, "seems a bad edition of a Polish King. He may be elected from four years to four years, for life. Reason and experience prove to us that a chief magistrate, so continuable, is an office for life. . . . Once in office, possessing the military force of the Union, without the aid or check of a council, he would not be easily dethroned, even if the people could be induced to withdraw their votes from him. I wish that at the end of the four years, they had made him forever ineligible for a second time."

More than anything else, Jefferson's letter to Adams conveyed a sense that the convention had gone too far; it had too radically altered what might have been simply amended. "I think all the good of this new constitution might have been couched in three or four new articles, to be added to the good, old and venerable fabric, which should have been preserved even as a religious relique." In essence, Thomas Jefferson was voicing the view of many who would become Antifederalists in the months ahead.

Adams, too, had his objections to the new constitution, but he disagreed wholeheartedly with Jefferson on the matter of presidential rotation. Writing on December 6, Adams expressed his views in what, for him, seems a lighthearted, jesting tone:

> You are afraid of the one — I, of the few. . . . You are Apprehensive of Monarchy; I, of Aristocracy. I would therefore have given more Power to the President and less to the Senate. . . . You are apprehensive the President, when once chosen, will be chosen again and again as long as he lives. So much the better as it appears to me. You are apprehensive of foreign Interference, Intrigue, Influence. So am I. But, as often as Elections happen, the danger of foreign Influence recurs. The less frequently they happen the less danger. . . . Elections, my dear sir, Elections to offices which are great objects of Ambitions, I look at with terror.

Neither Adams nor Jefferson were aware how much their debate echoed long debates in the convention itself, nor were they aware that the same fear — or, rather, the anxiety — about the dangers of investing power in any individual or any branch of government was a major leitmotif of the convention. Indeed, fear of the tyranny of the one, or the tyranny of the few, was a virtual obsession among the delegates in their debates.

In the months of reading and rereading the records of the convention for my book, *A Brilliant Solution*, I came to the conclusion that Cecelia Kenyon was wrong: the Antifederalists were not the only "men of little faith"; the delegates to the constitutional convention, from Benjamin Franklin to Gunning Bedford Jr. to Madison himself, took a dim view of men's innate character and believed that power was capable of corrupting even the most noble patriot. The Herculean task the delegates saw before them was this: how to empower a man, or a group of men, or a whole government of men, in order for their nation to survive and prosper without allowing their power to grow unrestrained and unchecked. Like the good lawyers most of them were, they labored to find every loophole in the restrictions they placed on each branch of government, and they strove to eradicate them.

Adams and Jefferson, like the rest of the American public, were not privy to the long hours of debate over issues of power. The finished product they saw did not reveal the days of discussion over incipient dangers or the alternative solutions and alternative structures that were considered. In the end, secrecy had its price; while it allowed free-ranging debate on the floor of the convention, it also allowed men like Jefferson to entertain the thought that the decision to allow a president to run for reelection was made without consideration of its consequences.

On December 20, having by then received Madison's long letter composed in October and November, Jefferson sat down to write his friend "Jemmy" Madison. He began with a list of changes in government that he supported, including the separation of powers, the popular election of the House, and the stipulation that votes within the Congress be by individual senators or representatives rather than by a collective state vote. He then moved quickly and bluntly to a statement of his objections: "I will now tell you what I do not like." He strongly objected to the absence of a bill of rights, for such a bill "is what the people are entitled to against every government on earth . . . and [which] no just government should refuse or rest on inference." Like the Antifederalist leaders George Mason of Virginia and Elbridge Gerry of Massachusetts, Jefferson would return to this point again and again. A frame of government without such guarantees to the people as freedom of speech, press, and religion could not be called a republican document.

The second feature that Jefferson professed to "dislike, and strongly dislike" was the abandonment, as he put it, of rotation in office for the presidency. Here Jefferson was virtually alone in his complaint, as soon he would reluctantly acknowledge. Jefferson ended his commentary on the new Constitution with this admission: "I own I am not a friend to a very energetic government. It is always oppressive." Yet his democratic principles trumped his strong opposition. "It is my principle that the will of the Majority should always prevail. If they approve the proposed Constitution in all its parts, I shall concur in it cheerfully, in hopes that they will amend it whenever they shall find it works wrong."

Jefferson continued to state his two main objections to the Constitution to many of his correspondents during the winter months and into the spring. Drawing from his December 20 letter to Madison, he in fact created a document that detailed his objections and added it as an enclosure with letters to friends. He also continued to muse on why no one except his friend the Marquis de Lafayette seemed concerned about the rotation issue. It was not until May 1788 that Jefferson settled upon an answer: the public's lack of concern over the presidential term was intimately related to the man everyone assumed would be the first president. Writing to Edward Carrington on May 27, Jefferson observed that the universal admiration for and trust in George Washington "put to sleep" all fear of tyranny. Yet there was only one Washington. "After him," Jefferson predicted, "inferior characters may perhaps succeed, and awaken us to the danger which his merit has led us into."

If the admiration and trust elicited by George Washington explained the absence of any public outcry against the abandonment of rotation in the office of president, Jefferson could find no reasonable excuse for what he believed was a popular apathy over the missing bill of rights. "I own it astonishes me," he declared to William Smith in early February 1788, "to find such a change wrought in the opinions of our countrymen since I left them, as that threefourths of them should be contented to live under a system which leaves to their governors the power of taking from them the trial by jury in civil cases, freedom of religion, freedom of the press, freedom of commerce, the habeas corpus laws, and of yoking them with a standing army." This, he told Smith, "is a degeneracy in the principles of liberty to which I had given four centuries instead of four years."

By now Jefferson had also begun to articulate his own unique strategy for the ratification process. He did not want to see the Constitution fail of adoption; yet he did not want it to begin its life with an overwhelming mandate. His solution: "I would advocate [ratification] warmly till nine states have adopted, and then as warmly take the other side to convince the remaining four that they ought not to come into it till the declaration of rights is annexed." He shared his wish for this scenario with everyone from Smith to James Madison. "I sincerely wish that the 9 first conventions may receive, and the 4 last reject it," he bluntly told Madison. Rhode Island, especially, would take Jefferson seriously!

Jefferson withdrew his game plan for ratification after learning that Massachusetts had a superior, more direct solution. That state's ratifying convention had approved the Constitution, but it stipulated that a bill of rights be added. Nevertheless, his widespread dissemination of his criticisms of the new government and his equally widespread dissemination of his ratification strategy had wreaked considerable political damage back home. In the summer of 1788 the battle over ratification was both fierce and close in Jefferson's native state of Virginia, and the Antifederalists had no compunctions against using Jefferson's criticisms to their advantage.

On July 24 Madison wrote his friend in Paris, chiding him for his indiscretion and explaining the damage control he had been forced to engage in as the head of Virginia's proratification forces. Both Patrick Henry and George Mason had quoted Jefferson's demand for a bill of rights, and, as Virginia was one of the last four states to vote on the Constitution, Henry made full—and brilliant—use of Jefferson's now abandoned game plan. "This illustrious citizen," Henry told the Virginia convention, "advises you to reject the government till it be amended. . . . At a great distance from us he remembers and studies our happiness. . . . he thinks yet of bills of rights." "In this situation," Madison concluded to Jefferson, "I . . . took the liberty to state some of your opinions on the favorable side." In other words, Madison too had used Jefferson's personal correspondence in order to counteract the damage done to the cause of ratification by the clever tactic of Henry and Mason.

Not yet aware of the problem he had caused the Federalists in Virginia, Jefferson sent Madison a congratulatory note that same month, having at last learned that nine states had ratified. "I sincerely rejoice at the acceptance of our new constitution by nine states. It is a good canvas, on which some strokes only want retouching."

Jefferson was not an Antifederalist, although his outrage over the missing bill of rights was that faction's strongest objection as well. He was, however, an American far from home, in the midst of a monarchical state which was making desperate efforts to democratize. The daily injustices of monarchies and aristocracies that he saw firsthand as minister to France impressed him deeply, and his affection for the Articles of Confederation, a frame of government born of the American Revolution and reflecting its commitment to republicanism, deepened in the process. Yet his diplomatic experiences drove home to him, more sharply perhaps than to those who remained in America, the costs of a government unable to act honorably and with healthy self-interest in its foreign affairs. He knew there must be change. What he feared was sweeping changes that discarded the positive features of the Confederation — its inability to interfere too much in domestic or internal matters — as readily as they corrected that government's genuine failings. He was, and would remain — despite many later actions that seemed to deny it — an opponent of (as he put it) "too energetic a government in domestic matters."

Jefferson's diplomatic assignment isolated him from the great grueling discussions and debates engaged in by the delegates to the convention during almost four months of continuous sessions. He could not know, or could not be certain, that they were considering every danger, every consequence of the changes they proposed. Sworn to secrecy, Madison could not assure him that the prevention of tyranny was indeed as much the convention's goal as the creation of an effective national government. To Gouveneur Morris's credit, this remarkable stylist transformed a bulky, disorderly document — the product of endless compromises, firm desires, and deep-seated fears — into an elegantly presented frame of government called the Constitution. In doing so, however, Morris, and the convention that endorsed the document, may have given the impression that the design was settled too easily, with too little attention to the dangers of conspiracies, overweening ambitions, and a decline into tyranny.

Nothing could be farther from the truth, but Jefferson, across the water, could not know this. The delegates had dismissed the notion of a bill of rights, introduced in the last weeks of the convention, not out of callousness but out of a conviction that the states had already secured these in every instance — and, no doubt, out of an exhaustion and a desire to adjourn without another lengthy discussion. They looked at the presidency — its powers, the mode of election, the term of office, even the number of men it should comprise — repeatedly and from every angle. Jefferson could know none of this. This is not to say, of course, that even if Jefferson had been a delegate, he would have been any less disturbed by the omission of a bill of rights or by the issue of presidential rotation. It is only to suggest the context in which he formed his objections, far away in Paris.

It might be interesting to compare Jefferson's sustained concern over the structure and the form of the new Constitution with the reaction of Alexander Hamilton. Hamilton had been the driving force behind the call for the convention, but when it finally met, he was as marginalized as Jefferson. True, he was a member of the New York delegation; yet with the exception of one long — and negatively received — speech on the floor of the convention, Hamilton said little and absented himself frequently.

It was not difficult to find the cause of his limited participation. He was hampered—in fact, hamstrung—by two factors: the antinationalist composition of the New York delegation and his own radical vision of the shape the new government should take.

At every turn, Robert Yates and John Lansing, spokesmen for the powerful Antifederalist governor of New York George Clinton, canceled out Hamilton's influence on the convention floor, because voting on issues was not individual but by state delegations. Hamilton could not bargain for concessions if he could not offer New York's vote as payment or reward; he could not influence tight votes by throwing his state's vote into the aye or nay column as long as Yates and Lansing were there. And when his two adversaries departed in protest against the convention's trajectory in early July, Hamilton became a rump delegation. This was an embarrassment and a frustration he felt to the core.

But the composition of the New York delegation was not the only factor, nor perhaps even the main one, in marginalizing Hamilton. The truth was that Alexander Hamilton's views on the structure of a new government were out of sync with the views of most of the delegates. The men gathered in Philadelphia were ill at ease with his advocacy of life terms for elected legislators (imagine Jefferson's reaction to this suggestion!), and their republican principles were offended by his call for an executive officer who did, indeed, bear a close resemblance to a benevolent monarch. But most disturbing of all was Hamilton's complete and utter disregard for state sovereignty and his willingness—indeed, his eagerness—to see the states reduced to little more than functional departments in a national political structure. In short, Hamilton thought too continentally for his colleagues, and he was far too perceptive not to realize it.

Yet Hamilton was surprisingly philosophical about the gap between his preferences and those of the delegates. He registered little protest; he engaged in no letter-writing campaign to rouse support for his views. Why? Because what Hamilton wanted, above all, was the creation of a national government with sufficient powers to serve as the basis for future greatness. As long as the convention produced a government with the power of the purse — that is, taxing powers — Hamilton felt confident that much of what he desired, much of what he envisioned for the young nation, would follow. Unlike Madison and Jefferson, Hamilton saw the Constitution as a shell, a foundation upon which men could build, not by amendment but by policymaking. Programs and policies would complete the edifice that the convention had begun to build. And he, of course, meant to have a major role in setting those policies and creating those programs.

More perhaps than any other political leader of the era, Hamilton considered the Constitution a beginning rather than a completion. Consider how far from Jefferson's notions this was: Jefferson spoke in the end of the Constitution as a canvas in need of some retouching; Hamilton viewed the Constitution as a shell in need of policy and programs to give it direction, purpose, and life. Small wonder that in the 1790s they would became bitter combatants in a struggle to define the future of the republic.

A Rhode Island Reflection

With Jefferson in Paris as American minister and Rhode Island defiantly absent from the Philadelphia Convention, it is difficult to draw a Rhode Island nexus to the theme of this essay other than to assess the immediate impact of Jefferson's constitutional thought — and that of Hamilton — on party development in Rhode Island during the first years of statehood.

The agrarian-based Country Party under Jonathan Hazard and Joseph Stanton — both of whom resided in rural Charlestown — had delayed Rhode Island's ratification by raising such valid and defensible Antifederalist issues as debtor relief, anti-slavery, state sovereignty, and protection of individual rights. In 1790 this faction reached a modus vivendi with the victorious Federalists. Stanton was elected to the U.S. Senate in tandem with Federalist leader Theodore Foster of Providence, but the more volatile Hazard was bypassed, the victim of political expediency. Benjamin Bourne of Bristol and Providence, an ardent advocate of adoption, became the state's lone U. S. congressman. Both sides acquiesced in the election of Arthur Fenner of Providence as governor. He served from 1790 until his death in 1805, becoming a nominal Democratic-Republican as the two-party system emerged.

In the first five presidential elections Rhode Island displayed no rigorous, ideological partisanship. It did not participate in Washington's first election, and like every state, supported him in 1792. In 1796, Rhode Island's electors (now four in number) cast four votes each for their sectional neighbors — John Adams of Massachusetts and Oliver Ellsworth of Connecticut. In the tumultuous election of 1800, Rhode Island's four electors were chosen at-large by popular vote for the first time. Federalist electors polled 1,941 votes and Democratic-Republicans 1,694, so the state cast four votes for John Adams (Fed.), three votes for Charles C. Pinckney (Fed.), and one vote for John Jay (Fed.). In the runoff election between Jefferson and Burr (each of whom had garnered 73 electoral votes), Rhode Island's two U. S. representatives voted consistently for Burr on all thirty-six House ballots. However, when Jefferson ran for reelection in 1804, without a New England opponent, he received

Rhode Island's four electoral votes. Jefferson's unpopular embargo ensured Madison's rejection by Rhode Island in 1808.

Given these inconclusive indicators of partisan allegiance during an era that my mentor, Marshall Smelser, described politically as "an age of passion," what can one discern from such balance and ambivalence? Certainly Rhode Island had long espoused such Jeffersonian views as the importance of individual liberty, especially in the realm of religion, and its citizens shared Jefferson's concern for state sovereignty and his fear of an overreaching central government.

Conversely, Rhode Island had a strong commercial tradition, and its emerging industrialization embraced the Hamiltonian goal of national economic self-sufficiency. Starting with Samuel Slater's water-powered textile mill in 1790, Rhode Island made the transformation from a primarily agrarian economy to one with an industrial base, and it made that transformation before any other American state. With that accomplishment came the related developments of urbanization and immigration, both hallmarks of modern American life. Here in Rhode Island, Hamilton's vision of a new economic order reached its earliest fulfilment on a statewide basis. How ironic that the last of the original thirteen to join the new Union should be the first to capitalize upon the economic advantages afforded by its new constitutional system!

Clearly Rhode Island's agrarians favored the party of Jefferson, and merchant-industrialists were Federalists. Yet, as my former student Joseph Norton concluded in his doctoral study of Rhode Island Federalists: "Commercial expansion was possible only with the acquiescence of the more numerous agrarians, and the Federalists adopted a policy of political conciliation with them. . . . They were not anti-agrarian since they knew that . . . their commercial prosperity depended on the agrarians' ability to furnish trading commodities." Enlightened self-interest rather than divisive ideology characterized Rhode Island's fledgling party system.

In sum, Rhode Island's early years of statehood under the federal Constitution exhibit a theme that blended the views of these two architects of nationhood—the espousal of Hamiltonian goals without relinquishing adherence to Jeffersonian ideals.

"Take This or Nothing":
Did the "Antifederalists" Have a Case?
Pauline Maier

AM DELIGHTED to be the speaker at an occasion that has celebrated "Constitution Day" for many years. Most Americans, I suspect, never heard of that "holiday" until Congress decided to make all institutions receiving federal money do something to recall the anniversary of the day the Philadelphia convention adjourned.

This talk is based on research for a book I am in the process of writing, and it comes with a disclaimer: I retain the right to change my mind on anything I say sometime between now and when the book sees print. Consider what I say an "interim report," a statement of my thoughts at this point in time, September 2005, which remains early in the project's development.

My book is on the ratification of the Constitution, that is, the process of debating and deciding whether or not to enact the Constitution, a debate which occurred within the states between September 17, 1787, and July 26, 1788, when the eleventh state—New York—voted to ratify. The last two states, North Carolina and Rhode Island, ratified only after the new national government had begun, and the book will include that story as well as the First Federal Congress's decision to attach to the Constitution those amendments that we call the Bill of Rights. (Whether people at the time used that term remains for me an open question.) The ratification controversy was a raucous, widespread, knock-down, drag-out fight, played out in the press, in conventions, and no doubt in taverns and across dinner tables. At times it looked as though the Constitution might not be ratified. Not many Americans know the story.

Or so my editor at Simon and Schuster, Robert Bender, must have suspected when he could find no book dedicated to telling the story of the Constitution's ratification and went out to find an author to write such a book. He found me. Actually, he contacted my agent, who asked if I had any ideas who might write the book for Bender. It took me twenty seconds to volunteer. There were several reasons I was so ready to sign up. For one thing, I knew that a group of expert historians at the State Historical Society of Wisconsin were publishing a multivolume *Documentary History of the Ratification of the Constitution* (DHRC). They were collecting more documents than any scholar knew existed, and new documents often lead to new interpretations of historical subjects. I also thought it would be interesting to test a rule of narrative history that I once, long ago, heard Barbara Tuchman describe. She said writers can build up tension even if their readers know the outcome of a story if the writers just don't mention how it will come out until they get to that part of the story. ("You're planning to write a thriller *on the ratification of the Constitution?*" someone once asked in total disbelief. Yes. I'm not sure my writing skills are up to that, but the ambition seems worthy.)

Finally, I realized the subject could have juridical significance today, given the interest in the Founders' understanding of the Constitution. James Madison once said the meaning of the Constitution "beyond the face of the instrument" should be sought in the state ratifying conventions that breathed "life and validity" into the document, not the convention that proposed it.[1]

Jurists have not in general followed that maxim, since the Federal Convention's records are easier to consult than the scattered documents on state ratification conventions. Even pulling those documents together in the twenty-odd volumes of the DHRC has not solved the problem. But a book on ratification might—just might—have an influence on the way living Americans understand the Constitution.

I should make clear that historians have not neglected the subject of ratification. There are books on ratification in the various states, and even two fine books with essays by different authors on ratification in each of the states. We also have an abundance of books and articles that explore questions about ratification—whether the divisions were fundamentally economic, whether the "Antifederalists" were more democratic than their opponents, and so on.

And there are a small handful of books that come close to offering a general account of ratification and so might be cited against Bender's conclusion that no such book exists. The best known is Robert A. Rutland's *Ordeal of the Constitution,* which was originally published in 1965. However, its subtitle— *The Antifederalists and the Ratification Struggle of 1787–88*—suggests that even Rutland aspired to something less than a comprehensive account of the ratification process. As he said in the book's preface, he hoped "to tell readers something of the Antifederalists' personalities, their problems, and their hopes." I should also mention a book on both the Federal Convention and the ratification process by the German historian Jürgen Heideking, *Die Verfassung vor dem Richterstuhl: Vorgeschichte und Ratifizierung der Amerikakischen Verfassung, 1787–1791* (Berlin, 1988),[2] which has not been published in translation, and so has had, so far as I can tell, little or no observable impact on American scholarship.

It is not hard to understand why historians have been reluctant to write a general history of the Constitution's ratification. The documentation is so extensive and scattered that it was beyond the capacity of any single scholar to collect and master—until the editors of DHRC did the collecting and arranging for us. But, as I have discovered, not even that series makes telling the story of ratification easy. It includes a mass of documents as well as chronologies, introductions, and explanatory footnotes; but it remains the historian's job to figure what story they're part of, that is, what was going on and why. And my understanding of a story is like that of the historian David McCullough, who once said the statement that "the king died and the queen died" does not tell a story; but, McCullough went on to say, "the king died and the queen died of grief" does. Stories trace not just events but their causes and consequences, the way one event leads to another with human emotions and, sometimes, learned convictions or personal interests interceding that explain why the events happened as they did. And strangely, as I try to tease out the story of ratification from the masses of documents now so readily available, I have become more and more suspicious of the historical truisms that I have taught for the better part of forty years.

Above all else, I have come to realize how much our understanding of the period is pro-Federalist. Indeed, the story historians tell—even some of those who focus on the "Antifederalists"—is pretty much the story as the Federalists saw it. The Federalists, we like to think, were both intellectuals on the cutting edge of political science and magnificently effective politicians. By contrast, those who worked against ratification in the way demanded by the Federalists were men compulsively suspicious of federal power, narrow-minded local politicians protecting their turf, and often uneducated backwoods bigots who said stupid things.

Those generalizations are not entirely wrong. The Federalists were, by and large, better educated and more articulate than their opponents, and they did make critical contributions to the science of politics. Indeed, over the course of the ratification debate they made theoretical sense of a Constitution that at first seemed to them an incoherent jumble of compromises, and in that process they convinced themselves that it was a greater achievement than they at first recognized. Moreover, the Federalists won: in the end, the Constitution was ratified, and it's hard to quarrel with success. Finally, after more than two centuries under the Constitution, it is sometimes difficult to imagine how anyone could have opposed its ratification.

There is, however, yet another reason why our view of ratification tends to be Federalist. The Federalists controlled the documentary history of the ratification controversy on which historians depend. Indeed, they took managing the news to an entirely new level. At the beginning of the controversy, in particular, they tried desperately to keep criticisms of the Constitution out of circulation. They wanted to convey the impression that nobody was doing anything but throwing his hat in the air and shouting "huzzah." For example, in debates on the Constitution in both the Continental Congress in late September 1787 and again in the Pennsylvania ratifying convention, which met from mid-November to mid-December 1787, critics of the Constitution proposed amendments to it that the Federalist majority refused to include in the meetings' published journals. They thought it would be harmful for the public to know about efforts to change the Constitution. Even more surprising, the published debates of the Pennsylvania convention include only the speeches of Federalists. You would think nobody else was there, except that one delegate on the other side made a short intervention that appeared in the published debates.

Fortunately, Alexander Dallas, editor of the *Pennsylvania Herald*, printed full texts of speeches by both sides for a few days in late November and on December 12, when the convention voted to ratify. Unfortunately, his accounts suggested—correctly—that the "Antifederalists" got the better of some exchanges, and perhaps even won converts to their position; and so the Federalists cancelled their subscriptions and the *Herald*'s owner fired Dallas. That ended his verbatim publication of convention speeches. As a result, aside from brief newspaper summaries, the only record we have of what "Antifederalists" said in the last part of the convention, when they were apparently particularly eloquent, is the notes of their opponents.[3]

One challenge in rethinking the controversy over the Constitution, then, is to overcome the Federalist bias in the documents. The place to start is, I propose, in the last week of the Philadelphia convention, when divisions over the Constitution first emerged. On September 10, 1787, the delegates received a polished version of the Constitution prepared by a "Committee of Style." They had been in session with only one short break since May, and they were anxious to go home. The convention had already gone over the parts of the document several times; now, while giving the document one last going-over, the delegates made or rejected proposed changes with very little discussion.

Viewed in retrospect, those hasty debates are awesome. The delegates threw out one proposal after another that might have made ratification a lot easier. Twice, for example, the delegates rejected proposals to increase the size of the first House of Representatives, which was to consist of only sixty-five members, a fraction of the size of many state legislatures and far too few, the Constitution's critics would say, to constitute an adequate representation of the people. And on September 12 George Mason of Virginia proposed that the delegates add a bill of rights to the Constitution. Such a document, he said, "would give great quiet to the people; and with the aid of the State declarations, a bill might be prepared in a few hours." Massachusetts's Elbridge Gerry made a motion to that effect, and Mason seconded it. Only one delegate offered an objection, which Mason answered. And yet not one state delegation voted for Gerry's motion, and the Constitution went out to the country without a bill of rights—which caused the uneasiness Mason predicted.[4]

The exchange that gave me the title of this talk occurred, however, on September 15, two days before the convention adjourned. Governor Edmund Randolph of Virginia, a strong advocate of

The Reverend Dr. Joseph L. Lennon, O.P. (left), who would eloquently deliver most of the Constitution Day invocations, is shown in 2000 as he, hostess Gail Conley, and Pat Conley prepare to greet the guests at the entrance to Gale Winds.

The lecturers at the first Constitution Day, Jack Greene (left), of The Johns Hopkins University, and Gordon Wood, of Brown, pose on the lawn of Gale Winds with Pat Conley and Chief Justice Joseph Weisberger (right), who was a regular attendee at Constitution Day and its 2007 speaker.

At Constitution Day 2001, held just after 9/11, the speaker, John Kaminski (left), and Pat Conley autograph their jointly edited books on the ratification of the Constitution and the origins of the Bill of Rights. Orchestrating the signing is Colleen Conley, office manager of the Rhode Island Publications Society. The bearded gentlemen awaiting signatures is Henry Brown of the famous Brown family of Providence. With all planes grounded, Kaminski drove from Madison, Wisconsin, to deliver his talk, accompanied by Constitution Day pianist Dr. Stan Gurnick, who hooked up with Kaminski in Chicago's northwest suburbs and shared the driving.

Militiamen of the Pawtuxet Rangers, under Colonel Fred Holst, and the Bristol Train of Artillery, under the direction of General Everett Francis (left), prepare to fire on the Continental sloop *Providence* from the lawn of Gale Winds on Constitution Day 2002. For the purposes of this reenactment, the Providence portrayed the notorious HMS *Rose*, a British vessel commanded by Captain James Wallace that patrolled Narragansett Bay and terrorized Rhode Islanders in the mid-1770s.

The modern *Providence*, under the gun of a Pawtuxet Ranger, is an authentic replica of the ship that was one of the first two U. S. naval vessels and the first command of John Paul Jones. The sloop, originally named *Katy*, belonged to John Brown, one of Providence's leading eighteenth century merchants. In this encounter, the *Providence*, a/k/a *Rose*, bombarded not only our Rhode Island militia batteries but also the Constitution Day attendees, almost eclipsing the drama of Professor Jack Rakove's lecture. The reenactors claim that this deafening mock battle was the first local ship-to-shore engagement involving reciprocal shelling.

Pulitzer Prize-winning historian Jack Rakove delivered the 2003 Constitution Day address. Listening intently in the background is Dr. Bob McCarthy, Rakove's former classmate at Harvard and Pat Conley's former student. McCarthy took Pat's position at PC in 1988 when Conley retired from the faculty and relinquished his tenure to devote more time to his legal practice and real estate development.

Sculptor Joseph Avarista, of Jamestown, Rhode Island, speaks at the 2004 unveiling of his statue of noted Rhode Island constitutional reformer Thomas Wilson Dorr. Avarista carved the life-sized Dorr—holding the *Commentaries* of his mentor, James Kent, in his left hand and the People's Constitution in his right—from a single block of basswood. The sculpture was commissioned by Pat and Gail Conley to be one of the focal points of the long-awaited Heritage Harbor Museum of Rhode Island History. Carol Berkin was the lecturer on this Constitution Day and shared the spotlight with Tom Dorr.

For Pat Conley, a major feature of Constitution Day was his reunion with his graduate students. Shown here are the authors of the six doctoral dissertations Professor Conley directed at Providence College. Left to right: Catherine Osborne DeCesare, Scott Molloy, John Fredericksen, Professor Conley, Bill Jennings, Father Robert Hayman, and Donna McCaffery.

This was a typical social scene at Gale Winds on Constitution Day. The gazebo, where drinks were served, was always a focal point of the observance. Spirits were not solely patriotic.

This was a scene from the balcony of the Conference Center in the Conley's Wharf Building on the Providence waterfront, a structure then on its way to completion and selection for inclusion on the National Register of Historic Places. Pauline Maier, the building's first Constitution Day speaker, was followed by Bill Wiecek, Joe Weisberger, Kit Collier, Ron Formisano, and Pat Conley. In this photo, Professor Scott Molloy, of the University of Rhode Island, fulfills his usual Constitution Day role of introducing the program.

Professor Pauline Maier addressed the first Constitution Day audience at Conley's Wharf in 2005. In the background is a framed poster from the Fabre Steamship Line based in Marseilles, France. This line made Providence its American terminus in 1911 and transported approximately 84,000 immigrants from the Mediterranean, the Black Sea area, and Portugal to Providence's State Pier No. 1, before its visitations ceased in 1934.

Because State Pier No. 1 is adjacent to the Conley's Wharf Building, which served briefly as a warehouse servicing the line, the Conleys created the Fabre Line Club in 2007 as a d/b/a of the Rhode Island Publications Society. The club is devoted to educational and cultural pursuits. By the end of 2009 it had 324 members, including every Constitution Day speaker, and it had hosted fifteen book signings and over sixty cultural events.

From 2005 onward, Constitution Day attendees were treated to a narrated cruise in historic Providence harbor aboard the *Providence Piers*, a 49-passenger tour boat owned by the Conleys. The vessel is shown docked in the Providence River near the downtown, with the unfinished building of the Heritage Harbor Museum of Rhode Island History in the background. Conley assumed the presidency of the museum project's board of directors in 2008.

All good things must end. With Professor Bob Poniatowski rolling the video, as he had done since 2000, Pat Conley delivered one of the two final Constitution Day lectures in September 2009. The beer and wine glasses on the conference table are indicative of the leisurely, relaxed, and convivial atmosphere that marked every Constitution Day.

the convention who had presented the "Virginia Plan" in its opening days, said he had some serious objections to the Constitution, above all with "the indefinite and dangerous power given by the Constitution to Congress." He didn't want to differ with the convention's majority and hoped to find a way to "relieve him from his embarrassments." He therefore moved that state ratifying conventions be allowed to propose amendments to the Constitution, and that those amendments would be considered by "another general Convention" before the Constitution went into effect.[5]

Mason agreed; the Federal Convention had written the Constitution "without the knowledge or idea of the people." Only after a broad public debate could the "sense of the people" be known and the Constitution adjusted so it fit the people's preferences more exactly. "It was improper," Mason said, "to say to the people, take this or nothing."

Charles Pinckney of South Carolina objected. Delegates to a second convention, he said, would be so tightly bound by instructions from their home state protecting local interests that they could never come to any agreement, and the resulting "general confusion" would ultimately be settled "by the sword."

Then Elbridge Gerry of Massachusetts gave what has to be one of the most unfortunate speeches in the history of American politics. He liked the idea of a second convention, he said, because he, too, had objections to the Constitution, which he proceeded to list. As Gerry criticized everything from the allocation of three-fifths representation for slaves through the length of senators' terms, Congress's power over commerce, and the new government's power to tax and raise an army, delegates no doubt saw the real possibility that all their hard-won compromises would dissolve into nothing. Or were they more concerned with Gerry's charge that Massachusetts had been given too few representatives? If the states started fighting for their particular interests in that way, what chance was there that the Constitution would be improved by the process Mason, Randolph, and Gerry supported? Gerry, in short, seemed to prove Pinckney's point. Not one state delegation voted in favor of Randolph's motion for a second convention.

Because Randolph, Mason, and Gerry refused to sign the Constitution, they effectively forfeited the honor of being remembered as "Founders" of the nation. But there was a lot to say for Mason's position that it was improper to tell the people "take this or nothing." The Constitution, we all know, begins "We the people . . . do ordain and establish this Constitution for the United States of America." That formula was taken from the Massachusetts constitution of 1780, a landmark document in the history of American constitutionalism. Earlier state constitutions had been written and ratified by state legislatures or their functional equivalents, which then changed their constitutions at will or, worse yet, ignored them whenever their provisions interfered with something the legislators wanted to do. How could Americans make a constitution that was different from other laws, a *fundamental* law that bound and limited all parts of government, including the legislatures?

The answer came from ordinary townsmen in places like Concord or Pittsfield, Massachusetts, who said the people should elect a special convention to draft a constitution that would then be submitted to the state's democratic town meetings for ratification or rejection. A law ratified in that way would be a direct act of legislation by the sovereign people. By the late 1780s constitutional scholars such as James Madison came to see ratification by the people as essential to any constitution.

The Federal Convention did not follow the Massachusetts precedent exactly. Its delegates were chosen by state legislatures, not elected by popular vote; and most people expected the convention to propose amendments to the Articles of Confederation, not an entirely new form of government. Moreover, the convention met in secret, so the public had no idea what it was doing until after it adjourned. The delegates then sent the Constitution to the Continental Congress, together with a resolution asking it to forward the Constitution to the state legislatures with a request that they convene specially elected conventions within their states to decide on the document. The Constitution would go into effect after nine state conventions voted to ratify (although, of course, it would go into effect only for those nine).

That was different from the process for amending the Articles of Confederation, which required the unanimous consent of all thirteen state legislatures. By taking the decision on ratification away from the legislatures, which had the most to lose, the new procedure made ratification more likely. It would bring enormous pressure on any state holdouts, which would have to decide not how much they liked the Constitution but whether they would remain part of a union that was going to exist with or without their participation. Popular ratification also justified the assertion that "we the people" ordained and established the Constitution, endowing it with powers delegated from the people's residual sovereignty. It was therefore both politically helpful and ideologically consistent. But could the people do anything besides ratify or refuse to ratify the Constitution in the precise form the Philadelphia convention proposed?

Those who had serious reservations about the Constitution were more likely to support the possibility of amendments, and George Mason had a whole list of "objections" to the document that he scribbled on the back of a committee report before the convention ended. Elbridge Gerry copied the list and showed it to some like-minded people in New York on his way home to Massachusetts. Mason also showed it to Robert Whitehill, a leading Pennsylvania critic of the Constitution, who was interested enough to copy the list; and the day after the convention adjourned, Mason sent a copy of his objections to Richard Henry

Lee. A Virginia delegate in the Continental Congress, Lee proposed a series of amendments to the Constitution that were designed to "fix" the problems Mason mentioned and a few that Lee thought up on his own.

These men were not alone in finding fault with the proposed Constitution; virtually every leading Federalist considered the Constitution imperfect in the early fall of 1787. George Washington, Henry Knox, Gouverneur Morris, Alexander Hamilton, James Madison, and James Wilson all thought some parts of the Constitution were mistakes. Madison even wrote Jefferson that it included flaws so serious that they would keep it from achieving its purpose. On the final day of the Federal Convention, Benjamin Franklin confessed that he, too, disliked some parts of the document, although he understood that, with time, his reservations might seem misplaced. He consented to the Constitution, he said, "because I expect no better, and because I am not sure that it is not the best."[6]

In some measure those mixed feelings were a natural result of the compromises the convention had made: a good compromise leaves all parties to it somewhat dissatisfied. If some provisions of the Constitution caused real problems when put into effect, the Federalists said, they could be fixed through the process of amendment described in the Constitution itself. First, however, the Constitution had to be ratified. Their position was like that of a shopkeeper who let customers alter a suit of clothes only after they paid for it.

But was a procedure that made some sense in buying a suit of clothes appropriate in adopting a constitution that would affect the freedom and welfare of the American people far into the future? The demand for amendments was perhaps more like insisting that the seller of a used car fix the faulty brakes before the purchaser puts his money down and drives it away. In any case, if the people thought some changes would improve the Constitution, shouldn't they be able to get them before committing themselves and their children to its terms? Was it right, as Mason put it, to tell the people to "take this or nothing"? Shouldn't the sovereign people have some greater say in the definition of their government?

To insist that the Constitution go to the country as it was, without amendments, Richard Henry Lee told the Continental Congress, was "like presenting a hungry man 50 dishes and insisting he should eat all or none." Amendments, moreover, would make ratification *more* likely, "as capital objections will probably be removed." The idea that the Constitution had to be agreed to "or nothing else" supposed that "all wisdom centers in the Convention," and that nobody outside the convention had anything to contribute but a quiet nod of approval.[7] Lee got nowhere in the Continental Congress, which refused even to debate his amendments — and then excised them from its journal.

This suggests that contenders in the ratification controversy did not differ over the need to strengthen the federal government. The Confederation was in such dire straits that virtually everyone recognized the need of giving it more power, and many who found fault with parts of the Constitution nonetheless recognized that it was a step in the right direction. Mason, for example, wrote Washington that his "objections" were "not numerous" and could easily have been removed by "a little Moderation & Temper, in the latter End of the Convention."[8] And Richard Henry Lee seemed to see the Constitution as an improvement over the Confederation, though it seriously needed a few fixes.

To that extent, the Constitution's critics were not "Antifederalists," a term the Federalists had invented for persons who opposed strengthening the Confederation long before the Federal Convention met. Those they called "Antifederalists" never liked the name, but they failed to come up with a better one — in part because the Federalists had co-opted the one that fit their views best. Opponents of the Constitution wanted to assure that both the states and the federal government would continue on into the future, and therefore that the new central government would not absorb all of the states' powers.

To be sure, some critics of the Constitution were more extreme than Mason and Lee. Maryland's Luther Martin preferred to strengthen rather than replace the Confederation, and the Antifederalist writer "Centinel" wanted a second convention not to amend the Constitution then on the table, which he described as a "first try," but to write a better one. However, not even Martin and Centinel were "Antifederalists" if the term referred to persons who denied the importance of a viable central government able to defend the collective interests of the American people in general. Only when the Federalists continued to insist that the people "take this or nothing" did many critics of the Constitution oppose ratification of the document as written (or, in the language of the day, "as it now stands"). They hoped to amend the Constitution before it went into effect or, in a few cases, to get a stronger national government in some other way.

For purposes of argument, let me propose a counterfactual scenario. Suppose the Continental Congress had "fixed" the Constitution by adopting Lee's amendments before sending it out for ratification. Lee proposed adding to the Constitution a bill of rights "to restrain and regulate the exercise of the great powers necessarily given to Rulers." It would include provisions protecting the rights of conscience, the press, petition, and assembly, trial by jury in both civil and criminal cases, the independency of judges, and free election of legislators; it would outlaw excessive bail or fines and cruel and unusual punishments, and it would require a two-thirds vote of both houses of the legislature before permitting "standing Armies in time of peace," which were "dangerous to liberty." Lee also wanted to enhance the separation of powers by taking the task of providing "advice and consent" from the Senate and giving it to a special "Privy Council" tucked neatly into the executive branch. He proposed to eliminate the vice president, who had nothing to do (as many future vice presidents have complained) except preside over the Senate, and to let the Senate choose its own presiding officer. Lee wanted the Constitution to avoid the "vexations and oppressive calling of Citizens" to courts distant from their homes by restricting the jurisdiction of federal courts in cases over property when the dispute was between citizens of different states or citizens and foreigners. He proposed to increase the size of the House of Representatives as well as the number of votes necessary to pass new laws or amend old ones. Finally, he suggested changing the provision on representation in the Senate so it stood "on the same ground that it is placed in the House of Delegates [Representatives], thereby securing equality of representation in the Legislature so essentially necessary for good government."[9]

The last provision would have been a killer: members of Congress who had served in the Convention knew how painfully it had arrived at the "great compromise" on representation. On the other hand, some Federalists—including Madison—thought that equal state representation in the Senate violated republican principles. Like many critics of the Constitution, Madison considered the initial size of the House of Representatives—sixty-five members—far too small. A full and fair representation of the people was for him a necessary prerequisite of giving substantial power to Congress.[10] And so, ironically, Lee's amendment on representation would have better fitted the Constitution to Madison's preferences and saved him from having to defend parts of the Constitution with which he personally disagreed. That amendment would also have affected the allocation of presidential electors among the states, ending the weighting of individual votes in small states over those in more populous ones, and so make the presidential electoral system a less flagrant violation of democratic principles. But if the provision on equal state representation in the

Senate was to be changed, that had to be done *before* the Constitution was ratified, and therefore before the enactment of a provision in Article V that said "no state, without its Consent, shall be deprived of it's [*sic*] equal Suffrage in the Senate."

Lee failed to mention another amendment that several states later demanded and that he himself would advocate—an amendment to give state legislatures the first option on raising direct taxes. If the states refused or failed to raise their portion of the general levy, and only then, the federal government could raise that portion itself, plus interest from the time the requisition was first filed. Federalists said that the national government would generally rely on indirect taxes—duties on imports perhaps supplemented by excise taxes—but might need direct taxes in a national emergency. A provision allowing the nation to raise direct taxes without going through the states in cases of war or the threat of war might have been added to the provision if amendments had been seriously considered.

Would ratification have been easier, as Lee suggested, if amendments such as these were adopted right away? Delaware and New Jersey would certainly have been angry: in the convention they fought hard for equal state representation in the Senate. But if their victory was taken away, would they have refused to ratify the Constitution—and risked having to continue paying New York's tax on imports, as they did under the Confederation?

Eighteenth-century forms of direct taxation—poll taxes and levies on real estate—have never been a major source of federal revenue, in part because the apportionment provision in the Constitution is clumsy and arguably unjust, having required that direct taxes be divided among the states in proportion to their free population and three-fifths of all others (i.e., slaves), without consideration of their relative wealth.[11] During the Civil War, Congress saw the problem and moved instead toward novel "indirect" forms of taxation, including an income tax, but in 1895 the

Supreme Court called the income tax a "direct" tax. The Sixteenth Amendment—ratified in 1913, 125 years after ratification of the Constitution—solved the problem by allowing Congress "to lay and collect taxes on incomes . . . without apportionment among the several States."

Would the amendment on direct taxes proposed in 1787 and 1788 have undermined the federal government's credit with lenders in the 1790s, when it most needed to reestablish its financial viability, or would it have threatened in some other way the government's long-term strength? Those possibilities, too, seem doubtful, given how rapidly Secretary of the Treasury Alexander Hamilton was able to establish national credit without levying direct taxes.

Lee's proposed amendment requiring a two-thirds vote of Congress to raise a "standing army in time of peace" would have made it more difficult to maintain a large peacetime army. It is more difficult to predict what difference would have been made by the adoption of his restrictions on federal court jurisdiction or his demand for larger congressional majorities to pass or amend legislative acts. If those provisions proved troublesome, they could of course have been eliminated through the process of amendment. But the enactment of a proper bill of rights, not the watered-down amendments tacked onto the Constitution by a reluctant first federal Congress—amendments that did little to protect Americans from violations of their rights by the state governments until the 1920s—might well have given significant protection to basic rights from the very beginning.

Historians tend to accept the Federalist position that amendments would have caused chaos and indecision because the various states would insist upon provisions that served their particular interests, and so conflicted with the demands of other states. In fact, there was substantial agreement on which changes were most urgently needed;[12] no critic of the Constitution had the illusion that individual states could impose changes without the agreement of the others. Could the Constitution have been ratified with less division and less rancor, based—like independence had been—on a broad national consensus? If the Constitution had been amended as Lee proposed, with the provision on direct taxes added to his list, would the United States have become a less "respectable nation," unable to claim an "equal place" in the community of nations? Or would the long-term result have been much the same—or perhaps better?

There's no doubt we needed the Constitution. But did we need the Constitution we got?

NOTES

1. Madison in the U.S. House of Representatives, April 6, 1796, in Max Farrand, ed., *The Records of the Federal Convention of 1787*, vol. 3 (1911; reprint ed., New Haven, Conn., 1966), 374.

2. The title, roughly translated, is *The Constitution before the Seat of Judgment: the Prehistory and Ratification of the American Constitution, 1787–1791.*

3. See the discussion of sources in Merrill Jensen, ed., *The Documentary History of the Ratification of the Constitution* (hereafter DHRC), vol. 1, *Constitutional Documents and Records, 1776–1787* (Madison, Wis., 1976), 323, on congressional debates on the Constitution and the excision of amendments proposed by Richard Henry Lee from the official minutes after another congressmen said they "would do injury by coming on the Journal"; on the documentary records of the Pennsylvania ratifying convention, ibid., vol. 2, *Ratification by the States: Pennsylvania* (Madison, Wis., 1976), 39–43. The Federalist position was explicit in a letter from Ebenezer Bowman to Timothy Pickering, Wilkes-Barre, Pennsylvania, November 12, 1787, ibid., 257. Pickering had sent Bowman, a local Federalist leader, a collection of Federalist essays to distribute among the people, but Bowman protested. He had, he said, "carefully avoided letting them [the people] know that any objections were made to the Constitution as I knew they were so prone to opposition that they would readily join in any to prevent that excellent plan [the Constitution] from taking place." Although the essays Pickering had sent contained "sufficient to convince any rational mind of the excellence of the proposed Constitution, yet as they discover [reveal] that some persons oppose it, I thought they would do more harm than good in this place." In short, by answering criticisms of the Constitution, the Federalist writers let the cat out of the bag: there were people who found fault with the proposed document.

4. For the exchange on September 12, see Farrand, *Records of the Federal Convention*, vol. 2, 587–588.

5. This and the following exchanges on September 15 are in ibid., 631–33.

6. Ibid., 641–42.

7. Jensen, DHRC, vol. 1, 336.

8. Mason to Washington, October 7, 1787, Merrill Jensen, ed., DHRC, vol. 13 (Madison, Wis., 1981), 348.

9. Ibid, vol. 1, 337–39.

10. See Madison's speeches in the constitutional convention in Farrand, *Records of the Federal Convention*, vol. 1, 551, 554 (July 7, against equal votes in the Senate), 568–69 (July 10, on size of the House of Representatives).

11. The formula for apportioning representation in the House of Representatives and direct taxes was changed by the Fourteenth Amendment in 1868 to eliminate the provision on "other persons."

12. Compare the amendments proposed by the Massachusetts, South Carolina, New Hampshire, Virginia, and New York state ratifying conventions in Helen E. Veit et. al., *Creating the Bill of Rights: The Documentary Record from the First Federal Congress* (Baltimore, 1991), 14–28.

A Rhode Island Reflection

Antifederalism was stronger in Rhode Island than in any other state. This tiny political entity offered more amendments to the Constitution (eighteen, plus eighteen more "certain and natural rights"), took longer to approve it (until May 29, 1790), and ratified it by the narrowest margin (34 to 32). The principal objections posed by the Rhode Island ratifying convention (which met first in early March 1790 and adjourned over Federalist protest until late May) were the absence of a bill of rights, the Constitution's three accommodations with slavery, and the failure to adequately check the growth in power of the central government, especially that government's direct taxing power.

In the contest over ratification Rhode Island defied the instructions of the Constitution's Framers by holding a popular referendum on their handiwork. This "mobocratic" tactic so outraged local Federalists that they refused to participate. That episode is worthy of notice here.

When the federal convention completed its labors on September 17, 1787 (with Rhode Island absent), it transmitted the Constitution to Congress with the recommendation that the document be submitted to the states for ratification by popularly elected conventions. Congress complied with this suggestion and gave the states official notice of its action.

The Rhode Island legislature, with agrarians in control, took the new Constitution under advisement at its October 1787 session. It thereupon voted for the distribution of one thousand copies of the proposed document to allow the freemen "an opportunity of forming their sentiments" upon it. This approach was consistent with the dominant Country Party's practice of governing by referendum.

With most of the freemen thus apprised of the federal charter's contents, the February 1788 session assembled. Then, to the consternation of Federalists within the state and without, the General Assembly authorized a popular vote on the Constitution and scheduled it for the fourth Monday in March. This ratification procedure was irregular and contrary to the recommendations of the Philadelphia delegates, but the legislature was not deterred by this unique departure from the norm. In fact, the February session specifically rejected a motion to call a ratifying convention. Over the course of the next twenty-three months, a total of eleven such efforts by Federalists would be spurned.

The popular referendum on the Constitution was held according to schedule. Although the result was predictable—239 for and 2,711 against—the margin of defeat is deceptive. The federal port towns of Providence and Newport boycotted the referendum; just one vote was cast in the former community and only eleven were registered in Newport. These ballots, with one exception (in Newport), were cast by so-called "Antifederalists." The only towns in the Federalist column were the bay settlements of Bristol (26–23) and Little Compton (63–57). The critics of the Constitution, however, registered lopsided victories in many rural communities, among them Glocester (228–9), Coventry (180–0), Foster (177–0), and Scituate (156–0).

The total vote in this referendum was 2,950 (tabulations vary slightly), as compared with the 4,287 who had voted in the well-contested gubernatorial election of 1787. Newport and Providence accounted for most of the abstainers, for these towns, according to fairly reliable estimates, together had between 825 and 900 freemen in 1788. Yet it is obvious that even if these communities had turned out en masse for the Constitution, it would have been rejected by an impressive margin.

Though as much an act of defiance by the rural-based, pro-paper-money Country Party as an act of grass-roots democracy, this unique referendum was a harbinger of future constitutional practice at the state level, where popular referenda on constitutions and amendments thereto have become the almost universal procedure throughout America.

Rhode Island's Distinctive Contribution to American Constitutional Development
William M. Wiecek

HE MOST APPROPRIATE WAY to celebrate Constitution Day 2006 here in Rhode Island might be to identify the ways in which Rhode Island has made a distinctive contribution to the larger American constitutional tradition. I do not refer to those occasional United States Supreme Court cases that merely happened to originate in Rhode Island, like *Lynch* v. *Donnelly*, the 1984 Christmas creche case that came out of Pawtucket, or *Lee* v. *Weisman*, the 1992 school prayer case from Providence. Rather, let us consider how Rhode Island contributed something distinctive to the evolution of the American constitutional system.

Pat Conley's book *Democracy in Decline*, published in 1977, provides a background thesis for our subject. The book contends that Rhode Island constitutional experience in the nineteenth century witnessed a declension from the democratic potential present in Rhode Island's origins. Conley concluded his study on an optimistic note, suggesting that despite the constitutional settlements of 1843, Rhode Island eventually overcame the carefully crafted restrictions in the 1843 constitution and has enjoyed a subsequent expansion of democracy. I will return to this thesis in conclusion.

Rhode Island's most significant contributions to American constitutionalism occurred early in her history. First, the Ocean State originated the social compact as a working instrument of government, not just a speculative theory, and used it to establish local government and then the governments of the colony and the state. This provided the foundation of the truly democratic potential in American governments. Second, Roger Williams's ideas about liberty of conscience provided a basis for the American understanding of religious freedom, expressed in the federal Constitution as the linked concepts of free exercise and nonestablishment of religion. And finally, Rhode Island's unique constitutional event, the Dorr Rebellion, affected the ways in which we think about popular sovereignty and the nature of republican government. Our public law today is different from what it might otherwise have been had it not been for these three distinctive contributions of the nation's smallest state.

First, let us examine the social contract as a basis for American democracy. When English people began to settle Rhode Island in the early seventeenth century, they adopted the social compact as an agreement among people about how they are to be governed. That was a product of the Protestant Reformation. The many congregations that had been formed under compacts had perfected the technique of agreeing to form a social unit, such as a church. These church compacts had vertical and horizontal dimensions. The vertical dimension was the relationship between God and people; the horizontal was the agreement among the members of the congregation themselves, agreeing to form their ecclesiastical society. Such churchly compacts translated readily into secular and civil counterparts that would serve as the basis for organizing civil government.

Rhode Islanders were not the first American settlers to use the compact idea to form civil polities. Two better-known social compacts have overshadowed the Rhode Island compacts: the Mayflower compact of 1620, signed by the Pilgrims who would settle Plymouth, and then the Fundamental Orders of Connecticut in 1639, which was the first written constitution that created a structure of government in America. The Rhode Island compacts differed from the Massachusetts model in a crucial way. The latter was based on the assumption that the majority of people in the community had to impose order on the minority—a minority differentiated on religious or social terms. The Rhode Island compact, in contrast, was entirely democratic and rejected the majority-controls-minority version of the Mayflower Compact.

The earliest Rhode Island compact, the Providence "town fellowship" of 1637, was formed and signed by the male settlers of Providence. In creating a basis of town government, it specified that the town's powers would be limited to secular matters, thereby anticipating the separation of church and state (which I will address in my second topic). The Providence settlers deliberately rejected the ideal of a theocracy that combined, or at least intimately linked, church and state, the structure favored in Plymouth and Massachusetts Bay.

Another compact, the Providence Plantation Agreement of 1640, guaranteed liberty of conscience and, significantly, included a number of women among its signatories. When Portsmouth established its town government by compact in 1638, the settlers declared that its form of government was to be "democratical," which they defined as being based on "the free and voluntary consent of all or the greater part of these inhabitants." The Portsmouth compact and the compact uniting the two towns of Portsmouth and Newport in March 1640/41 were authentic town constitutions, and as such they formed the basis for the law of that little island society. In this understanding, both government and laws emanated directly from the exercise of popular sovereignty, as it was represented by the social compact. In March 1643/44 Parliament recognized Rhode Island as a colony, thereby guaranteeing the stability and permanence of these formative compacts.

When John Locke theorized about the social compact in his *Two Treatises of Government* (1690), a work that is usually cited as the source of compact theory in the United States, he was merely confirming Rhode Island's experience and providing a theoretical justification for it. What, then, did American society as a whole derive from the democratic model of the Rhode Island compact? First, the Rhode Island compacts affirmed popular sovereignty and the related theory of limited government. As Roger Williams wrote, "all true civil magistrates have not the least inch of civil power but what is measured out to them from the whole — the whole people." Elsewhere he insisted that "governments have no more power nor for no longer time than the people consenting shall entrust them with." The democratic impulse of the Rhode Island social compacts provided a basis for the theory of popular sovereignty (which constitutes my third theme) and for the idea of limited government, namely, that governments are responsible and accountable to the people who put them in place.

Second, the compacts are a basis of fundamental law: the idea that there is a law superior to ordinary legislation. This fundamental law is derived from the sovereignty of the people. This gets us ahead of our story by a little over a hundred years, but Rhode Island's experience with compacts nevertheless anticipates the idea of the constitution as fundamental law.

Third, implicit in the compact is the idea that all individuals have fundamental rights of which they cannot be deprived by governmental action. Because all individuals have these same fundamental rights, to that extent individuals are all equal among themselves. Thus the notion of fundamental rights and equality is implicit in the Rhode Island constitutional experience. Finally, the Rhode Island compacts, like the Massachusetts and Connecticut compacts, were the precursors of written constitutions, an innovation that distinguishes us from the mother country.

Rhode Island's second major contribution to American constitutionalism is Roger Williams's ideal of what he called "liberty of conscience" or "soul liberty." In 1647, over a decade after Williams had been exiled from Massachusetts, he carried on a debate with John Cotton, the most prominent theologian of the Bay Colony at the time, over the problem of church-state relationships. Williams's first contribution was a tract entitled *The Bloudy Tenent of Persecution, for Cause of Conscience* (1644). In this book-length argument Williams laid out his thoughts about liberty of co nscience. The ideas that Williams expressed there were not the only paradigm for the ways that Americans as a whole think about religious freedom or religious establishment. Their place in our constitutional tradition may be better likened to the role of an instrument in an orchestra, where no single instrument or section dominates a symphonic performance, but each is often so uniquely expressive that we cannot imagine a piece being played without it, or with some substitute. (Think of the English horn in the slow movements of Berlioz's *Symphonie Fantastique*, Dvořák's *New World Symphony*, or Sibelius's *Swan of Tuonela*.) Williams's ideas on religious liberty are like that: however much Williams may have been an outcast or ignored in his own time, we cannot imagine our constitutional tradition today without him.

In the *Bloudy Tenent*, Williams insisted that the state is "merely civil." It is a purely secular instrumentality, having no religious component to it at all, and no authority over religious matters. Under his doctrine of popular sovereignty, government is derived from the people for secular ends, and it has no power to rule the churches. In the sort of model that Williams had in mind, the churches are self-constituting and self-governing bodies, over which the civil magistrate can claim no legitimate authority. From thence Williams went to the core of his argument—the problem of what he called "soul oppression" or the "rape of conscience." Williams played out that rape metaphor at vivid length, arguing that any attempt to force people to adopt or forswear a religious position that is contrary to their conscience is offensive to God and to the individual. In addition, such an attempt is practically useless, because forced conversions are seldom effective and "stink in God's nostrils."

It follows that the state must protect the religious autonomy of all, including the liberties of the Papist, the Jew, the Turk, and the infidel. The state cannot enforce religious uniformity and should not suppress dissent. In Massachusetts Bay, John Cotton insisted that the state needed the power over conscience that the Bay Colony theocracy claimed for itself as necessary for preserving civil peace, the unity of the community, and a common morality. Williams rejected that argument, claiming that Cotton had got it altogether backwards. All attempts at forced observance of religious practice or profession of belief disrupt the possibility of civil peace, disturb the community, and are in themselves a moral violation.

Implicit in Roger Williams's concept of religious liberty is the principle of separation of church and state. He warned the settlers who were establishing religious commonwealths in New England that "when they have opened a gap in the hedge or wall of separation between the garden of the church and the wilderness of the world, God hath ever broke down the wall itself, removed the candlestick and made His garden a wilderness as at this day." That metaphor of the candlestick requires explanation, because it was a powerful image for Williams's audience. The candlestick he referred to was the menorah of the temple in Jerusalem when the future Roman emperor Titus suppressed the Jewish rebellion in 70 A.D. In keeping with Roman military custom, the victorious soldiers carried off the temple furnishings as trophies of war to be displayed at Rome in a triumphal parade. The loss of the temple menorah not only represented the beginning of the Jewish Diaspora and the destruction of Judaea as a semiautonomous state; it also marked the end of Jewish temple religion. After the destruction of the temple, Judaism assumed an entirely different form of religious identity and observance. Williams was using a historical event, the destruction of the temple, to suggest the violence and disruption that awaits a community that violates its covenant with God.

Williams's primary concern was to preserve the purity of the church against the corruptions of the state. Thomas Jefferson, who also employed the metaphor of a wall a century and a half later to describe church-state relations, was concerned with the opposite problem, namely, the corruption of the secular realm by involvement of clergy in state government. Williams's thought on church-state relations represents an enduring tradition in American constitutional development that is today more relevant than ever to the way that we think about our constitutional order.

My third topic is popular sovereignty and republican government as exemplified in the Dorr Rebellion. Speaking to an audience of Rhode Islanders, I may not need to identify that rebellion, but the coterie of Dorr scholars here today—Pat Conley, Marvin Gettleman, and I—who did scholarly work in the 1960s and 1970s on that popular uprising of the early 1840s learned that the subject is not as well known to Americans as it ought to be. So let me recap it briefly.

After American independence the royal charter of 1663 continued to serve as Rhode Island's constitution. Together with Connecticut, Rhode Island was one of only two states that did not adopt a new republican state constitution during the Revolutionary era. As Rhode Island found itself in the forefront of industrialization in the 1820s and 1830s, a wave of European immigrants, many of them Roman Catholics from Ireland, began to flow into the state to work in the mills of the Blackstone and Pawtuxet valleys. Problems of both malapportionment and disenfranchisement were severe. Scholars estimate that in 1840 the overwhelming majority of adult males in Providence could not vote. The power of the rural towns in the southern and northwestern parts of the state far outweighed the representation of Providence and the industrializing towns in the state legislature. Suffrage reformers tried throughout the 1820s and 1830s to correct these problems without success, coming up against the immovable complacency of those who benefited from the status quo. Finally, in 1841, the reformers became more organized and restive, and they decided to abandon mere political protest and try a much more radical approach toward resolving the difficulties of constitutional government in their state. The result was the Dorr Rebellion of 1842, an effort to exercise popular sovereignty based on the constitutional theory of America's Revolutionary era.

Three distinctive constitutional theories emerged from the struggles of the so-called Dorr War. These positions sort themselves out in a Hegelian dialectic of thesis, antithesis, and synthesis. In 1841 the Rhode Island Suffrage Association, a group of reformers who abandoned their futile demands for suffrage reform, decided to take matters into their own hands. They drew up a new constitution for the state and submitted it for ratification to the entire white adult male populace, thereby hoping to create a new government on an authentically republican basis. They believed that if the people of Rhode Island were literally and truly sovereign, they must be able to act in that sovereign capacity, to function as the people without the mediation of the reactionary state legislature. (The reverberations of the Protestant Reformation three centuries earlier are unmistakable.) That was how they framed the question of popular sovereignty. Thomas Wilson Dorr, a prominent Providence attorney, emerged as the leader of the Suffragist forces and was the principal draftsman of the People's Constitution, which was overwhelmingly ratified by popular vote in December 1841. In May 1842 Dorr became the People's governor under the provisions of this purported basic law.

This action raised a cluster of constitutional issues of profound importance for all Americans: popular sovereignty, democracy, the legitimacy of government, the right of revolution, the nature of republican forms of government, and the appropriate place of conservative constitutional thought. Consider each of the three contrasting opinions that emerged from this political melee. First was the People's Constitution, drafted by a "People's Convention" called into existence through the efforts of the Rhode Island Suffrage Association. The delegates to this convention took Thomas Jefferson's grand rhetoric in the Declaration of Independence literally. The People's Constitution proclaimed that "the people have an unalienable and indefeasible right in their original, sovereign, and unlimited capacity to ordain and institute government and in the same capacity to alter, reform, or totally change it." Acting on those ideas, the suffrage reformers-turned-militants ignored the restricted franchise that had evolved under the royal charter, which had limited political power to males who paid taxes on real estate assessed for at least $134 and to their eldest sons, and threw the franchise open to all adult males (excluding African Americans). They also provided for a moderate reapportionment of the Rhode Island legislature. Their core idea in the passage just quoted was that the people have the ability to act in their original sovereign capacity.

The antithesis came in the response of the existing government, known variously as the Freeholders' government, the Charter government, or the Law and Order party. In March 1842 it proposed its own alternative, the Freeholders' Constitution, which advanced a distinctly different theory of governance. Unfortunately the freeholders did not encapsulate their theory in a brief, neat quotation as did the Suffrage Association, so we must be content with a paraphrase. The freeholders believed in a distinction between what they called the "natural people" and what they called the "corporate people." The natural people comprised all human beings located within the jurisdiction, including women, infants, lunatics, foreigners, and persons otherwise excluded from political power for reasons of race, religion, or other disabilities. The corporate people were those endowed with full political rights who exercised sovereignty, a power that existed not in the natural people but only in the corporate people. In Rhode Island as of 1841, this meant only the "freeholders," those legally empowered to vote, namely, the men owning $134 worth of real property and the eldest sons of these men, an arrangement that traced back to statutes that were enacted to implement the royal charter of 1663.

The second vital characteristic of the freeholders constitutional theory was that it was essential to follow established and legitimate procedures for modifying government. In addition, there was a strong streak of nativism and anti-Catholicism in the freeholders' position: they were willing to enfranchise all native males but retained the $134 real estate qualification for naturalized male citizens. They also reapportioned the legislature somewhat less extensively than did the People's Constitution. When the freeholders government submitted its constitution for ratification, even the restricted electorate rejected it, although by a small margin.

The synthesis of these conflicting positions occurred after the freeholders suppressed the Dorr Rebellion and produced the so-called Law and Order Constitution in November 1842. This document (which became the state constitution in May 1843) contained a two-sentence summary of the synthesis position: "the basis of our political systems is the right of the people to make and alter their constitutions of government." Up to that point these conservatives sound like Jefferson, Washington, and the suffragists. But there followed a semicolon, and then a "but." In that kind of syntactical construction, the real import of the sentence follows the exception: "but that the Constitution which at any time exists until changed by an explicit act of the whole people is sacredly obligatory upon all." The existing constitution must be respected because it provided the only legitimate structure within which to work for change. The Law and Order Constitution finally provided Rhode Island with a republican constitution, drawn up and ratified by the "people" of the state (however defined) sixty-six years after American independence had been declared. It provided for moderately improved apportionment and contained a complex system of franchise reform, but one that discriminated against naturalized citizens. So the question presented by the Dorr Rebellion is this: did popular sovereignty ultimately prevail as a result of the rebellion, or was the reform effort a great and lasting failure in the exercise of popular sovereignty? The question lingers into our own times, as the studies of Conley, Gettleman, and others suggest.

In concluding, let us return to Pat Conley's thesis in *Democracy in Decline*. In each of these three areas discussed above—democracy, religious liberty, and popular sovereignty—are we better off today than we were when the people of Rhode Island confronted these issues in the past? I am more pessimistic than Pat's 1977 cautiously optimistic conclusions. Take democracy, for example: due in part to developments like marketing software that can analyze consumption patterns with such great accuracy that you can predict how people are going to vote down to the neighborhood level, followed by the use of that software to apportion state legislatures in ways that lock in the political extremes in many legislative districts, American democracy is seriously threatened today in terms of its ability to respond to the will of the people. The two-party system stifles third-party challenges, and as it operates today, it has an unhealthy tendency to encourage parties to appeal to the extremes of their bases.

Second, consider Roger Williams's ideal of liberty of conscience: church and state should have no ability to interfere in each other's operations, producing an absolute separation of church and state. Williams's metaphor of the wall separating the garden from the wilderness is under worrisome attack today, particularly by evangelicals. Williams, who was their ancestor in evangelical religion, would be appalled to see his descendants attacking the vision he so passionately promoted.

And finally, in the matter of popular sovereignty: many Americans think that the ability of the American people to control their representatives in any effective way has eroded to the point where governments are beyond accountability, at least at the national level. In presidential elections, for example, voters in all but the ten or so battleground states are effectively disfranchised. To the extent that the Dorr Rebellion is able to provide lessons for us today, it lies in the example of courageous people risking "our Lives, our Fortunes, and our sacred Honor" to reform a government that had grown unjust in its very structure, and consequently in its operations. But is it imaginable that American citizens today could emulate the courage of Thomas Wilson Dorr and his fellow suffragists in taking direct action to assert the people's effective control over their government?

Unfortunately the gradual implementation of structural reforms in the Constitution of 1843 in the century and a third following its adoption, as described by Conley in his epilogue to *Democracy in Decline*, has not fulfilled in practice these three distinctive Rhode Island contributions to the American constitutional tradition.

A Rhode Island Reflection

Thomas Wilson Dorr is the pivotal figure in Rhode Island history. He drew his heritage, training, and moral values from the old order and applied them towards the betterment of the new. He exemplified the best traits attributed to old-stock Rhode Islanders—individualism, daring, defiance of unjust authority, and a passion for democracy and self-determination. Simultaneously he inaugurated the role of patrician reformer, typified in the modern era by such Rhode Island statesmen as Theodore Francis Green (who admittedly drew inspiration from Dorr), Claiborne Pell, and John Hubbard Chafee.

Dorr thus serves as the bridge between early and modern Rhode Island, between old stock and new, and between the Charter government that served Rhode Island for 180 years and the present constitutional order.

More than any other person, Thomas Dorr influenced the governmental transition from the old royal-charter regime to a new political system based upon a written constitution. And although his preferred basic law—the People's Constitution—was denied implementation, its provisions and principles were gradually incorporated into the Rhode Island constitution throughout the more than sixteen decades since Dorr's defeat.

But Dorr was not merely a force for constitutional change; he was the quintessential reformer of America's first great age of reformist activity. In the economic realm, he drafted and secured the enactment of the first statute in any state providing for governmental regulation of state-chartered banks, and he worked diligently for the abolition of imprisonment for debt. He might well be described as Rhode Island's first consumer advocate. Dorr also attacked neomercantilism, whereby the state granted special privileges and monopolies to private business corporations; such a practice, he declared, was a violation of equal rights. Dorr was a pioneer in his advocacy of an economic system regulated in the public interest—the modern regulated economy.

Dorr's reformist zeal also extended to the social order. He was an early member of the American Anti-Slavery Society, led by William

Lloyd Garrison and Rhode Islander Arnold Buffum, and he fought, albeit unsuccessfully, to enfranchise blacks via the People's Constitution. His efforts were extolled, in the aftermath of his defeat, by the abolitionist poet John Greenleaf Whittier.

Governor Dorr also encouraged the involvement of women in the public sphere. His leadership of the People's party in 1842 inspired the first large-scale involvement of Rhode Island women in the political process. Support of Dorr's cause and sympathy for him because of the harsh treatment accorded the deposed People's governor led women to undertake such unprecedented political activities as forming free-suffrage associations, raising funds for the relief of those imprisoned for supporting the People's government, staging rallies and clambakes in support of reform, organizing a campaign for Dorr's liberation, and writing political and legal defenses of the People's movement, most notably *Might and Right* (1844), by Frances Harriet Whipple.

In addition, Dorr made a major contribution towards the development of free public education in Rhode Island, both as a state legislator, when he earmarked the famous federal deposit of 1836 for the permanent school fund, and as a member and then president of the Providence School Committee, when he played the leading role in implementing such modern improvements as the appointment of Providence's first superintendent of schools, the establishment of teacher certification and training programs, the creation of Rhode Island's first public high school, and the construction of modern school facilities.

On the burning issue of foreign immigration, Dorr attacked the nativism of his day. As early as 1833, when nativist violence first erupted, he made a public appeal for toleration toward Roman Catholics. Dorr's exhortation to his fellow Rhode Islanders revealed his humanity:

> It is quite time that a better state of feeling should prevail, and that narrow illiberal prejudices should be discarded. Whatever good the division into sects may have done, it is time that they should overlook the party lines behind which they have entrenched themselves, and extend to each other the hand of fellowship. If men cannot agree in religious opinions—and, from the constitution of the human mind,

such an agreement can never exist—they certainly can agree to differ peaceably. There is a common ground of good will and charity on which they can and ought to meet as brethren.

Consistent with his principles and pronouncements, Dorr befriended and defended the Irish Catholic immigrants of the 1840s, structuring the People's Constitution to give naturalized Irishmen equal rights with native-born citizens. He helped to organize the defense for John Gordon in the famous Amasa Sprague murder trail, and he then spoke against the death penalty meted out to this hapless Irish Catholic merchant of Spragueville.

Optimistic, articulate, concerned—these were among the qualities of Thomas Dorr. Belief in fundamental human goodness, the brotherhood of men, and majoritarian rule were basic articles in his political creed. Liberty and equality were to him, as much as to any reformer of this remarkable age, the indispensable conditions of human activity.

Dorr's 1843 lament—"All is lost save honor"—may well have been the story of his rebellion and his life, but it is not his legacy nor the ultimate verdict of history. At the conclusion of his trial for treason, Dorr made an impassioned plea: "From the sentence of the court I appeal to the People of our State and of our Country. They shall decide between us. I commit myself without distrust to their final award." To his credit—and to ours—the confidence of this optimistic, if somewhat naive, democrat continues to experience an inexorable, though painfully gradual, vindication. In the many decades since his defeat and death, the judgment against him from a biased court has been properly overruled by time and experience.

To my foregoing profile, which some may say is in the nature of a eulogy, I append a true eulogy that appeared in the *Providence Journal* shortly after Dorr's death at the age of forty-nine in December 1854. It was written by Dorr's most bitter rival, *Journal* editor Henry Bowen Anthony, former governor (1849–1851), later U. S. senator (1859–1884), and the principal founder of Rhode Island's Republican Party. According to Anthony (who will be the villain in this book's final essay), Dorr's misguided idealism cost him dearly:

He was a man endowed with intellectual powers, which had they been rightly directed, would have secured him commanding influence. Those powers, too, were disciplined by an education more accomplished perhaps than any other man of his age in Rhode Island had been privileged to obtain. As a man of science and letters, he might have attained honorable distinction, had he chosen to dedicate his time to science or to letters. As a statesman he might have rendered his native State substantial service. He might have been a truehearted, private gentleman, honored by the respect and confidence of the community in which he resided.

As Dorr's friend John Greenleaf Whitter wrote in his wistful poem "Maud Muller": "For of all sad words of tongue or pen, / The saddest are these: 'It might have been!'"

Incorporation or Amendment?
The Standardization of the Rules
of Criminal Procedure
Joseph R. Weisberger

FTER THE GENEROUS, even lavish, introduction by Dr. Conley, let me now talk about my contribution—my inadequate contribution—to this series of Constitution Day addresses.* I think I have been present at all of them and have enjoyed them greatly.

My assignment today is to talk about the selective incorporation of the Bill of Rights into the Due Process Clause of the Fourteenth Amendment. As you know, Article V of the Constitution of the United States provides for amendments, and the amendment process is neither easy nor short. By vote of two-thirds of the members present in both houses (assuming the existence of a quorum), Congress may propose an amendment to the Constitution, and that amendment will become part of the Constitution if ratified by three-quarters of the states, either by vote of the legislatures or by conventions called specifically for that purpose. Also, two-thirds of the states may apply to Congress to call a convention to recommend amendments that will become part of the Constitution, again if ratified by three-quarters of the states. This method has never been used.

Today, however, I am going to talk about another very significant manner of amendment that has taken place in the United

---

*Editor's note: My lengthy introduction was based on a biographical profile of Justice Weisberger, entitled "Joseph R. Weisberger: A Life in Law," that I wrote on the occasion of his retirement as chief justice in February 2001. It was prepared at the request of the Rhode Island Bar Association and was published in the *Rhode Island Bar Journal* 49 (February 2001): 5–9, 32–42.

States over an extended period of time. This amendment procedure probably began in 1925 and reached its zenith by 1969, with several periods of inactivity in between. I speak of amendment by judicial fiat.

If we harken back to that 1787 summer in Philadelphia when the Constitution was framed, we can note that many of those who were active in the drafting of the Constitution were somewhat disappointed because it did not contain a bill of rights. Indeed, George Mason of Virginia, the author of the Virginia Bill of Rights, refused to sign the proposed Constitution, and he was not the only holdout. The dissenters were worried about what might happen with a central government that might become so strong as to threaten the liberties of individuals in the several states.

John Kaminski, your second Constitution Day speaker, has reminded me that the citizens of the various colonies—the soon-to-be-free citizens of the United States—distrusted each other deeply. In all likelihood they may have distrusted each other more than they distrusted the British. After all, most were loyal subjects of the king until Parliament decided to tax them. This action enhanced their distrust of a remote central government. These Americans had what they thought was a bad experience with Parliament.

Conversely, there were many in the country who thought Parliament was right. The Revolution was not supported by all the colonists; about a third remained loyal to the king. They realized that Britain had spent twelve million pounds to defend the colonies from the French in the recent war. These loyalists thought, as did Parliament and Lord North, that England had a right to recoup some of these expenses by taxing the colonists—a fiscal remedy seldom exercised by the mother country in the 150 years since the establishment of the earliest settlements.

When the Constitution was completed and the new government was about to be formed, many revolutionaries, as well as many former Loyalists, were worried. When they thought of this remote central government, whether it would be located in New York or Philadelphia, they felt that it was a long way from their area of the country, and that its newly granted power was too far removed from most of the people. They felt that this potentially powerful entity should be restrained by a bill of individual rights. This concern created a groundswell of opinion during the ratification process that rights-related amendments should be added to the Constitution to protect individual liberties. Consequently, in 1789 the First Congress, with James Madison in the lead, recommended a bill of rights that included twelve proposed amendments, ten of which were ratified by December 1791. The individual rights are set forth in the First through the Eighth Amendments. These are really our Bill of Rights in the full sense of the term.

It is clear that these amendments were designed as limitations upon federal power. No one at the time had any notion that they were designed to limit or in any way inhibit state action. The citizens of the various states felt quite capable of handling their own General Assembly, General Court, House of Burgesses, or whatever else they might have called their legislature. They were worried mainly about their new national government and sought protection from it.

Chief Justice John Marshall, in the 1833 case of *Barron* v. *Baltimore* (7 Peters 243), solemnly determined that the Bill of Rights was designed to limit the federal government, and that was all. At issue in this case was a Fifth Amendment right to just compensation, something that the people of Baltimore, or at least the governing council of Baltimore, did not want to give for taking the property of a private person. John Marshall and his court decided that the Fifth Amendment and its requirement of just compensation had no bearing on the state of Maryland or the municipal rulers of the city of Baltimore. It was very clear in 1833 that the Bill of Rights was applicable only as a limitation on federal power.

That ruling by Marshall went unchallenged, and things stayed pretty much the same until 1868, when the Fourteenth Amendment was added to our Constitution. It contained a clause stating that no state could "deprive its citizens of life, liberty or property without due process of law," thereby reiterating and embracing the Due Process Clause of the Fifth Amendment. It also contained an Equal Protection Clause and a Privileges and Immunities Clause; but the Due Process Clause was destined to have the greatest influence in regard to the applicability of the Bill of Rights to state action in my particular field of law.

The Fourteenth Amendment's primary purpose and effect was to define national citizenship with blacks included within that definition, so as to enable the federal government to protect the rights of its citizens. Therefore, the amendments's early focus was more on race than on the expansion of rights to the general populace. Illustrative of this fact was the court's 1873 decision in the *Slaughter-House Cases* (16 Wallace 36), emanating from the state of Louisiana.

This early ruling defined the rights of U.S. citizens (their "privileges and immunities") narrowly and left most rights under state jurisdiction and regulation. This limitation of the scope of the amendment was reinforced by the Court's 1877 ruling in *Munn* v. *Illinois* (94 U. S. 113), when it refused to apply the amendment to protect substantive economic rights from state interference, and its 1883 opinion in the *Civil Rights Cases* (109 U.S. 3), when the Court distinguished illegal state actions, prohibited by the Fourteenth Amendment, from private acts of discrimination, which were not prohibited. Then, in *Hurtado* v. *California* (1884),[1] the Court ruled that the Due Process Clause of the Fourteenth Amendment did not require the states to indict by grand jury in capital crimes or, by implication, to follow other Fifth Amendment rules governing criminal procedure under federal jurisdiction.

A full forty years after the Fourteenth Amendment was ratified, the Supreme Court held that there was no limitation placed upon state power by the Fifth Amendment. The ruling in *Twining* v. *New Jersey* (211 U.S. 78) involved the privilege against self-incrimination. As a result of the *Twining* doctrine, a state could regard refusal to testify as tantamount to an admission of guilt. However, the Court also declared in *Twining* that some rights protected by the Due Process Clause were similar to rights enumerated in the first eight amendments to the Constitution. Though denying an express textual identity, the justices suggested that there existed some correlation between the Fourteenth Amendment and the Bill of Rights.

The first chink in the armor of state procedural primacy came in 1925 in a case called *Gitlow* v. *New York* (268 U.S. 652). Fred Gitlow precipitated this controversy when he issued what was called a left-wing manifesto that advocated the overthrow of all capitalistic governments. Obviously a disciple of Marx, Lenin, and other socialists, Gitlow suggested that our government should be overthrown and that people ought not to enlist in the army or register for the draft. He was therefore charged in New York with violation of the state's criminal syndicalism statute, and he was convicted. In Gitlow's appeal to the Supreme Court of the United States, Justice Edward Sanford, who wrote the majority opinion, promulgated in just a few sentences an "assumption" that the free speech and free press clauses of the First Amendment were limitations on state power, because the First Amendment to the Constitution of the United States applies to the states. Despite having made that assumption, Sanford affirmed the conviction because a certain category of speech — that advocating the overthrow of the government — was constitutionally unprotected and "inherently unlawful."

Justices Oliver Wendell Holmes Jr. and Louis A. Brandeis dissented from the affirmation of the conviction, but not from the assumption that the First Amendment constituted a limitation upon state power. The *Gitlow* decision was the first step towards incorporation, and it was the result not of what one might call a detailed analysis but rather of a simple assumption.

Things really did not change markedly from 1925 until 1937, when an unfortunate person named Palko appeared before the high court (302 U.S. 319). He was tried by the State of Connecticut for murder in the first degree, but he was found guilty only of second degree murder and was therefore sentenced to life imprisonment. The State of Connecticut was not satisfied with that result. It took a statutory appeal to its Supreme Court of Errors, which found that there had been substantive and procedural mistakes in the trial, such as the admission and exclusion of certain evidence and faulty instructions to the jury. The Supreme Court of Errors sent the case back for retrial, at the conclusion of which the unfortunate Palko was found guilty of murder in the first degree and sentenced to death.

When the *Palko* case reached the Supreme Court of the United States, the issue was double jeopardy. In a federal court the Fifth Amendment ban on double jeopardy would have made Palko's second trial an impossibility. Justice Benjamin Nathan Cardozo, one of the great judges of his time or any time, crafted an opinion which analyzed the whole history of the Bill of Rights and its application to the states and made the determination that only those elements of the Bill of Rights which were "implicit in the concept of ordered liberty" (a key phrase) would be a limitation upon state power. He used as his example the First Amendment, "without which a free state could hardly exist." Having so stated, Cardozo then examined the Fifth Amendment's ban on double jeopardy, declaring that it is not of the same fundamental character as the First Amendment. Why shouldn't the State of Connecticut get a trial free of error, he queried, just as the defendant had the right to expect one? So poor Palko was left to a difficult fate.

May I digress to tell you a side story? Pat Conley referred to my teaching at the National Judicial College, where I lectured for thirty-three years. At one point, about the middle of that period, I was talking about *Palko* v. *Connecticut* to a group of judges, one of whom had been Palko's lawyer. This unsuccessful defense counsel had afterward become a member of the Superior Court of the State of Connecticut. Though Palko met a bad end, I was pleased to learn that his lawyer was alive and well

As we move along this cobbled road towards the application or incorporation of the federal Bill of Rights to state actions and procedures, the mileposts of *Gitlow* and *Palko* will give way to a rapid series of cases analogous to ten-yard lines, especially during the heyday of the Warren Court in the turbulent decade of the 1960s.

Proceeding along our path, we come upon the 1947 case of *Adamson* v. *California* (332 U.S. 46). Its appellant had allegedly killed a person who in those days was romantically called his "paramour." Because he had a prior record, Adamson decided not to take the stand, and under California law he had that right. However, the California prosecutor and the judge also had a corresponding right to comment to the jury about his failure to deny matters within his personal knowledge, and therefore to suggest to the jurors that they might draw an adverse inference from Adamson's reticence. They did. Adamson was convicted and then sentenced to death. When the case came to the Supreme Court, the question again arose of whether or not the Fifth Amendment privilege against self-incrimination, or the right to comment upon its exercise, is applicable to the states. Justice Stanley Reed wrote a somewhat routine opinion citing *Palko* v. *Connecticut* and *Twining* v. *New Jersey*. His conclusion was "no," the Fifth Amendment's privilege against self-incrimination is not applicable to the states.

The interesting aspect of *Adamson*, however, is what one might call its debate between a concurring opinion by Justice Felix Frankfurter and a dissenting opinion by Justice Hugo Black. The latter took the position that there should be a total incorporation of all of the elements of the Bill of Rights into the Due Process Clause of the Fourteenth Amendment, because our federal practice is America's standard for due process. To the contrary, Frankfurter observed that in the eight decades since the ratification of the Fourteenth Amendment, Black's argument had been presented to forty-three justices, and of those forty-three, only one — who might respectfully be called an eccentric exception — had suggested that wholesale incorporation should be adopted. Such a broad-brush doctrine is unacceptable to the Court, said Frankfurter, and has been all along. (By the way, Justice Frankfurter was not referring to his colleague, Justice Black, but to the elder Justice Harlan as the eccentric exception.)

In any event, Frankfurter had a further argument. He pointed out that the Fifth Amendment also has a Due Process Clause and asked whether his colleague was suggesting that Madison and his contemporaries would have put a Due Process Clause in the Fifth Amendment if due process embraced all of the rights in the other provisions of the first eight amendments. Could the Framers have crafted so much useless language? Could those masters of the English tongue be so redundant? Frankfurter believed that the Due Process Clause rested solidly on its own bottom and forbade only those procedures that would violate the canons of decency which all English-speaking peoples would respect. What are these "canons of decency?" For Justice Black (or so I believe), the canons of decency are set forth in the first eight amendments to the Constitution of the United States.

Although Frankfurter won the debate in *Adamson* in the sense that he was concurring and Black was dissenting, the latter lived to see the "ordered liberty" doctrine, first stated by Justice Cardozo in *Palko*, expanded so that almost all of the elements of the Bill of Rights have been incorporated into the Due Process Clause.

A selective list of selective incorporation would include the following Supreme Court decisions: In *Wolf* v. *Colorado* (338 U.S.

25, 1949), Frankfurter himself, writing for the Court, said that the Fourth Amendment, or more precisely the right to privacy at the core of the Fourth Amendment, was implicit in the concept of ordered liberty and consequently a limitation upon state power in the sense that a state could not affirmatively condone violations of the Fourth Amendment. In *Wolf,* Frankfurter declined to include the exclusionary rule of *Weeks* v. *United States* (232 u.s. 383), a 1914 ruling that had prevented federal courts from allowing evidence to be admitted if obtained in violation of the Fourth Amendment.

However, the exclusionary rule eventually prevailed twelve years later in *Mapp* v. *Ohio* (367 u.s. 643, 1961). Justice Tom Clark (he was never called Thomas), writing for the Court, said that without the exclusionary rule, the *Wolf* v. *Colorado* decision was an empty promise. Then, in somewhat rapid succession (at least by Supreme Court standards), *Robinson* v. *California* (370 u.s. 660) incorporated the ban on cruel and unusual punishment into the Due Process Clause of the Fourteenth Amendment in 1962. *Robinson* involved a California statute making it a crime to be an addict — specifically, a drug addict. Such a status crime, said the Court, was cruel and unusual punishment.

Then, in the 1963 case of *Gideon* v. *Wainwright* (372 u.s. 335), the Court decided that the right to counsel in a felony case was implicit in the concept of ordered liberty and was therefore applicable to the states via the Due Process Clause. In 1964 *Malloy* v. *Hogan* (378 u.s. 1, 1964) incorporated the Fifth Amendment privilege against self-incrimination, overruling *Twining* and building upon what you might call our evolving national rules of criminal procedure. The year after that, in *Griffin* v. *California* (380 u.s. 609, 1965), another case involving comment on the failure of a defendant to take the stand, such a reference was found to be a violation of the Fifth Amendment and was incorporated to inhibit state power. Thus *Adamson* v. *California* was specifically overruled.

Next in this inexorable year-by-year march of the incorporation doctrine was *Pointer* v. *Texas* (380 U.S. 400, 1965), a decision declaring that the right to confront prosecution witnesses was incorporated into the Due Process Clause and became an inhibition on state power. The year 1966 produced the most cited incorporation ruling, *Miranda* v. *Arizona* (377 U.S. 201), and three related cases, proclaiming a person's fundamental right to be informed of his or her right to remain silent or to consult with an attorney from the outset of a custodial interrogation.

In 1968 *Duncan* v. *Louisiana* (391 U.S. 145) established one's right to a jury trial in a criminal felony case, a right that also was incorporated into the Due Process Clause and became a limitation on state power. And finally, in *Benton* v. *Maryland* (395 U.S. 784, 1969) the Court came around full circle from its 1937 ruling in *Palko* and determined that the ban on double jeopardy was applicable to the states by incorporation. At that point Justice Black, in effect, had nearly achieved a full victory, with the notable exception of *Hurtado* v. *California* (see footnote 1) relating to grand jury indictment.

However, I do not want to overlook another decision that was written by Justice William Douglas, which I wish to consider a bit out of chronological order. The name of this 1965 case is *Griswold* v. *Connecticut* (381 U.S. 479), and it involves a Connecticut statute that forbade the use of contraceptives, even among married couples. The law was challenged, and when the appeal reached the United States Supreme Court, Justice Douglas, who wrote the opinion, promulgated some very interesting theories. According to Douglas, the first eight amendments to the Constitution have "penumbrae and emanations," and those penumbrae and emanations, when read together with the Ninth Amendment (which says simply that the specific guarantees in the first eight amendments do not preclude the existence of other liberties and rights to which the people are entitled) create a zone of privacy into which state power may not intrude. That "zone of privacy," of course, was the precursor of *Roe* v. *Wade* (410 U.S. 113, 1973), and it constitutes the beginning of the second generation of substantive due process in the area of criminal procedure.

Appropriately, the final case upon which I have chosen to comment relates to the death penalty. One can get no more final than that! The Court's 1972 decision in *Furman* v. *Georgia* (408 U.S. 238) and several related cases involved the issue of whether or not the death penalty violated the Eighth Amendment's ban on cruel and unusual punishment. That said, let me briefly digress:

When the new building of the National Judicial College was being dedicated, I had the privilege of being on the dais. Sitting next to me was Erwin Griswold, who was then solicitor general of the United States but who had been dean of the Harvard Law School when I was a student there. We struck up a conversation, during which he mentioned that *Furman* v. *Georgia* was pending. He asked, "Do you think the Supreme Court can overturn the death penalty?" I replied, "Well, it seems a little hard for me to believe that it would." "Well, to me, it seems impossible," he replied. He then went on to observe that the death penalty is specifically mentioned in the Constitution, so that it would not be possible to declare it a violation of the Constitution. Well, the dean was not often wrong, but his ability to prophesy was not working at its best on that occasion. In eight separate opinions the Supreme Court, in a *per curiam* judgment, overturned the death penalty because it constituted cruel and unusual punishment.

Two of the justices in *Furman*, William Brennan and his colleague Justice Thurgood Marshall, stated that under evolving standards of decency the Due Process Clause made the death penalty, per se, unconstitutional. The three other justices simply said that it was applied so capriciously and so irrationally in this instance that it was unconstitutional. Marshall and Brennan never changed their opinion that the death penalty was per se unconstitutional. They consistently took the same position even after the death penalty regained validity in the 1976 case of *Gregg* v. *Georgia* (428 U.S. 153), where the Court upheld it because the state statute was not applied in an arbitrary or capricious manner, as it was in *Furman*.

The death penalty decisions are a fitting end to my saga. There are other cases, of course, in which the court has, in effect, nationalized criminal procedure by incorporating the Bill of Rights into the Due Process Clause of the Fourteenth Amendment. One may ask, however, whether in doing so the court has improved criminal procedure. In all likelihood, it has. Certainly the rights of the defendants have been enormously increased by cases such as *Miranda* v. *Arizona* and the like, but I ask you to draw your own conclusions. Does our process of selective incorporation actually amend the Constitution by mere interpretation? Interestingly, we have seen the Rehnquist Court, and to some lesser extent the present court, move in the other direction.

To preserve the Constitution as an eternal document that is the symbol of our national unity, do we want to subscribe, at least theoretically, to the Frankfurter doctrine of abstention from a judicial interpretation that constitutes an amendment of our basic law, or do we accept the Black-Brennan-Douglas doctrine of expansive interpretation, in which sometimes, for good and noble reasons, the Constitution may be amended by interpretation or judicial fiat? The answer to that question would have to be made by each of us. I can only say that the Constitution is this year, 2007, is quite different from what it was perceived to be at the outset of 1937—ironically the year in which FDR launched his unsuccessful Court-packing scheme to counteract conservative judicial obstruction of New Deal policies.

Thank you very much for your attention; I hope these observations are food for thought, and being a reasonable judge, I do not wish to deny any of you an appearance at the bar.

NOTE

1. 110 U.S. 516 (1884). The *Hurtado* decision has survived the tidal wave of incorporation. The delegates at the 1973 Rhode Island Constitutional Convention, by a vote of 90 to 4, proposed an amendment to the state constitution (subsequently ratified by a popular vote of 60,400 to 35,808 as Article of Amendment XL) that allowed an alternative to grand jury indictment for felonies, namely, "one information in writing signed by the Attorney General or one of his designated assistants." This substitute method had been recommended by a legislative committee chaired by Senator Joseph Walsh to expedite criminal processing and procedure. Attorney Martin Malinou, one of the four delegates to dissent, cited *Hurtado* as allowing such a method of indictment, but he expressed the belief that the numerous recent incorporations indicated that "the United States Supreme Court will hold that the requirement of indictment by a grand jury is required under the XIV Amendment . . . due process" clause and will be "made binding on the states." Malinou's imperfectly stated fears have yet to be realized, although it should be noted that the *Hurtado* ruling involved murder, a capital crime, whereas Rhode Island's amendment does not allow criminal informations in certain instances, including any offense "which is punishable by death or imprisonment for life." That amendment is now Article 1, Section 7, of the recently revised Rhode Island Constitution. For these debates, see Patrick T. Conley, ed., *The Proceedings of the Rhode Island Constitutional Convention of 1973* (Providence, 1973), 129–32, 155, 158.

A Rhode Island Reflection

To ascertain where Justice Weisberger stands on the questions he posed at the conclusion of his address, one might refer to the biographical sketch I wrote on the occasion of his retirement as chief justice. In preparing that profile, Joe confided to me that those who attempted to impose federal models upon him in their arguments before his court were perhaps unaware that his "hero" was Justice John Marshall Harlan (1955–1971), whom Weisberger described as "a magnificent judicial craftsman and also an advocate of judicial restraint." Harlan often allied with Felix Frankfurter to resist the activism of the Warren Court. According to his biographer, "Harlan frequently voted to sustain the objections to the Supreme Court's power to decide" because of "his concern lest the Congress, the legal profession, and the general public lose confidence in the judiciousness and self-restraint of members of the Court." Harlan's caveat in his *Reynolds* v. *Sims* dissent in 1964 has been echoed by Weisberger's rulings in the local controversy over the separation of powers: "the vitality of our political system . . . is weakened by reliance on the judiciary for political reform."

Coupled with his restraint was Harlan's federalism, so evident in several of Weisberger's rulings. Harlan's philosophy of federalism, as stated in his *Reynolds* dissent, relied upon "the people, that is, upon political solutions devised and implemented by the people's representatives, rather than federal judicial formulas that have the effect of placing basic aspects of state political systems under the pervasive overlordship of the federal judiciary."

When he was a member of the Rhode Island Superior Court, Joe Weisberger was a fine trial judge, and he is a specialist in the constitutional aspects of criminal law. For nearly four decades, beginning in 1966, he taught courses to new trial judges on the Fourth Amendment (search and seizure) and the Fifth Amendment (custodial interrogation, double jeopardy, and the privilege against self-incrimination) at the National Judicial College in Reno, Nevada. Hence his foregoing analysis of incorporation theory relates primarily to the rights of the accused in criminal cases. Rhode Island has produced no landmark U.S. Supreme

Court decisions in this realm, not that we lack criminals, but three key rulings have emanated from Rhode Island involving the religion clauses of the First Amendment.

There is a tinge of irony in the fact that the state which pioneered religious liberty and church-state separation in America has recently become a leading source of major U.S. Supreme Court decisions using the incorporation doctrine to implement the Establishment Clause of the First Amendment. A fundamental reason for this seeming anomaly is that the state's predominantly Catholic population has fostered an interpretation of establishment at variance with the prevailing Supreme Court view. The high court has generally supported a wall of strict separation between church and state, prohibiting any direct governmental assistance to any religion. The Catholic view accepts government aid if it is evenhanded and does not support or advance any religious sect at the expense of another. Curiously, one of the most persuasive and succinct historical defenses of that position has been written by a Rhode Islander about a Rhode Islander.

Professor Mark DeWolfe Howe — late professor of law at Harvard, secretary to Justice Oliver Wendell Holmes, and author of *Cases on Church and State in the United States* — wrote a book entitled *The Garden and the Wilderness: Religion and Government in American Constitutional History* (1965), a title derived from a metaphor by Roger Williams. Here Howe demonstrates that the "wall of separation" phrase employed by the modern Supreme Court originated not with Jefferson but with Williams. However, says Howe, "when the imagination of Roger Williams built the wall of separation, it was not because he was fearful that without such a barrier the arm of the church would extend its reach. It was, rather, the dread of worldly corruptions which might consume the churches if sturdy fences against the wilderness were not maintained." Howe contends that "there is a theological theory of disestablishment traceable to Roger Williams," and that "the Court, in its role as historian, has erred in disregarding the theological roots of the American principle of separation" in favor of Jefferson's secular view.

Howe further states that the First Amendment's prohibitions at the time of their promulgation "were generally understood to be more the expression of Roger Williams's philosophy than that of Jefferson's." The conclusion Howe eventually reaches is that the First Amendment was designed to prevent government interference with religion and not to prevent "government advancement" of religion generally. If Howe is correct, then the posture assumed by Rhode Island in the three major establishment cases that it has sent to the Supreme Court since 1971 does no violence to Williams's position on the relation of church and state.

During the tumultuous and ideologically divisive 1960s, the liberal Warren Court rendered several decisions on the relationship between religion and education that ran counter to the "government advancement" view described by Howe. In Rhode Island, most legislative efforts to aid the state's financially troubled Catholic schools were thwarted by this Court's new and expansive view of the First Amendment's Establishment Clause. In 1969 the state legislature passed an act to supplement the salaries of teachers in parochial elementary schools. After an ACLU challenge, the U.S. Supreme Court in the landmark case of *DiCenso* v. *Robinson* 403 U.S. 602 (1971) struck down the measure because it provided "substantial support for a religious enterprise" and caused "an excessive governmental entanglement with religion."

DiCenso has been obscured because it was joined for decision with the Pennsylvania case of *Lemon* v. *Kurtzman*, which involved a law authorizing that state's superintendent of public instruction to reimburse nonpublic schools for teachers' salaries, textbooks, and instructional materials in secular subjects. Both cases, however, are significant as a statement of the Supreme Court's view of impermissible "entanglement." In fact, the three-prong test and other rulings associated with *Lemon* actually were part of the *DiCenso* decision! Shortly after *DiCenso* the federal district court for Rhode Island invalidated a state school-bus law requiring towns to bus private-school pupils beyond town boundaries if necessary. This decision prompted the resourceful legislature to create regional bus districts to circumvent the court's ruling.

In 1973 the high court made its controversial decision on abortion in *Roe* v. *Wade,* using incorporation to impose upon the states a right of privacy concocted from the Fourth Amendment's alleged "penumbras." Since that time the Rhode Island state legislature has displayed much more opposition to abortion than the general population, as evidenced by the decisive defeat of a pro-life amendment proposed by the 1986 state constitutional convention. Although abortion is basically a moral rather than a religious issue, in Rhode Island the battle has assumed sectarian overtones and church-state implications. Numerous laws to blunt the effect of *Roe* have passed the General Assembly, including one declaring that life begins at conception, another requiring spousal or parental permission for abortions, and another requiring the informed consent of the prospective patient, followed by a forty-eight-hour waiting period. Most of these laws have failed to pass constitutional muster in our federal district court.

The next church-state issue to pierce the thin veil of local ecumenism involved the use of public funds for religious displays. Here Rhode Island produced another nationally significant case in *Lynch* v. *Donnelly*, 465 U. S. 668 (1984). In this confrontation the ACLU challenged the city of Pawtucket's inclusion of a Nativity scene in its Christmas display. In a 5-to-4 decision, Chief Justice Burger, speaking for the majority, dismissed the complaint in part because "it has never been thought either possible or desirable to enforce a regime of total separation" of church and state. The Court majority felt that in the predominantly secular context of Pawtucket's display, the primary purpose and effect of the Nativity scene were not to promote religion but only to acknowledge the spirit of the holiday season. The decision continues to generate interest and has prompted a book-length analysis entitled *The Christ Child Goes to Court* (Temple University Press, 1990), by Wayne R. Swanson, professor and chairman of the Government Department at Connecticut College.

The final major establishment case, *Lee* v. *Weisman*, 505 U. S. 577 (1992), developed from a graduation ceremony at Nathan Bishop Middle School in Providence at which a student, Weisman, objected to school principal Lee's invitation to clergymen to give the invocation and benediction. The Supreme Court ruled in a 5-to-4 decision that a school requirement that a student stand and remain silent during a "nonsectarian" prayer at the graduation exercise in a public school violated the Establishment Clause, even though attendance at the ceremony was completely voluntary. The student, said the Court, should not be required to give up her attendance at the graduation, "an important event in her life, in order to avoid unwanted exposure to religion."

The bitterness with which these three Supreme Court cases were contested reveals that even in the land of Roger Williams, where religious liberty has always existed and where no established church ever reigned, history seems to support Montesquieu's cynical observation that "there has never been a kingdom given to so many civil wars as that of Christ."

Article III, Section 2, and the Bloody Background of *Van Horne's Lessee* v. *Dorrance*

Christopher Collier

RTICLE III OF THE U.S. CONSTITUTION establishes the judicial department of the U.S. government; Section 2 of that article lays out federal jurisdiction. As of late August at the Constitutional Convention of 1787, that jurisdiction included "controversies between two or more States, (except such as shall regard Territory or Jurisdiction) between a State and Citizens of another State, between Citizens of different States, and between a State or the Citizens thereof and foreign States, citizens or subjects."[1] Note the significant exception for controversies regarding territory or jurisdiction. The delegates further defined federal jurisdiction on August 27. A number of amendments were proposed; some were accepted and some not as the day wore on, when at last Roger Sherman of Connecticut "moved to insert after the words 'between Citizens of different States' the words, 'between Citizens of the same State claiming lands under grants of different states,'" noting the clause's precedent in the Articles of Confederation. Sherman's motion was agreed to "nem con," and the hot and tired debaters adjourned for the day.[2]

Behind this most obscure clause of our hallowed but much anatomized national constitution lies a saga more tragic and bloody, perhaps, than any in the annals of the nation's Revolutionary history.[3] Our story begins in 1662, 125 years before the convention.

In 1662 Charles II granted Connecticut a charter which, for the first time since its founding in 1634, gave the colony legal legitimacy and, more significant for our story, defined Connecticut's geographical bounds. Those bounds included what in 1776 became the state of Connecticut, as well as a long strip extending to the Pacific Ocean with the same south-to-north bounds as are Connecticut's today.[4] Until the mid-eighteenth century, Connecticutters never pressed these western claims while the Hudson River Valley was filling up with patroons, settlers, and speculators, and while Pennsylvania speculators bought up Indian rights to the territory constituting the northern third of modern Pennsylvania. But then, when population pressures pressed on the rocky soil of Connecticut proper, local speculators spied an opportunity to relieve population pressure and get rich quick.[5]

In 1753 a group of Connecticut entrepreneurs, who soon co-opted some of the highest and most influential leaders in the colony's government, formed the Susquehannah Company to take speculative advantage of the century-old charter bounds. They arranged in the usual manner — which involved liquor, deceit, and bribery — to buy the land from the Senecca and other Iroquois Indians of the Six Nations who lived there. One Pennsylvanian characterized these proceedings as "a scene of the vilest fraud and grossest forgery."[6] Nevertheless, Pennsylvania's governor James Hamilton proposed a land swap that would give the Susquehannah Company compensatory lands west of Pennsylvania's bounds — lands which were also claimed by Virginia. Hamilton's proposal went nowhere at the time, but it was prophetic of the ultimate resolution of the affair forty years later. Too bad; a Susquehannah acceptance in 1754 would have saved hundreds of lives and indescribable misery for thousands of Connecticut and Pennsylvania pioneers.[7]

The French and Indian War, which began in 1754, intervened to slow down land speculation and settlement, but in 1768 the Treaty of Fort Stanwix with the Indians opened the way for Connecticut pioneers. By the beginning of the War for Independence against the king and Parliament, thousands of farm families from Connecticut had bought land from the Susquehannah Company and were settled in the area. Pennsylvania speculators objected, of course, and "there followed a tedious and trying succession of strategic movements, skirmishes, sieges, countersieges, sorties, sallies, captures, capitulations, and evictions of one party or the other, all without permanent result."[8] Indeed, a number of skirmishes between the Pennsylvanians and the redoubtable Yankees, some west of the King's Proclamation Line of 1763, cost each side a dozen lives or more. During the Revolution, organized military forces of Loyalists and Indians engaged the Connecticut settlers in large-scale bloody battles, some of them no less than massacres.[9]

The bloodiest of these was the great Wyoming Massacre of July 3, 1778, a "crowning calamity . . . a sweeping butchery that was soon to appall the whole world." A "heterogeneous herd of [about 1,200] murderous soldiers and savages"—Tories, Pennsylvania land jobbers, disciplined British provincial troops, and undisciplined Senecca, Mohawk and other Indians— descended on the Wyoming settlement of about 450 Yankee men and their families. The Loyalist/Pennamite forces, Alfred Mathews tells us in his overwrought and one-sided account, included "soldiers, Indians, renegade whites, all brutalized by three years of fierce frontier warfare; a majority by lifelong savagery; many incited by bitter personal animosity, and some by simple thirst for blood; energized by cupidity and cruelty; goaded by race hatred and by human hatred."[10]

The British commander pleaded later that he could not control the Indians, who slaughtered women and children and clubbed, scalped, and burned to death about half of the Yankees who died that day. A few days later one investigator in Pennsylvania lands—no friend of the Yankees—wrote this description: "I never in my Life saw such Scenes of distress; The River and the roads leading down it, were covered with Men women and children flying for their lives, many without any Property, at all, and none who had not left the greatest part behind."[11]

The Yankees, who had pleaded in vain for Congress to send

reinforcements, had several days' notice and could have sent their families away—indeed could have discretely disappeared themselves. But they never stood a chance. One hundred and fifty of them died in battle, and an equal number were captured and tortured to death. Three hundred widows and six hundred orphans were made in a few hours.[12] The tragic decision to stay and face the attack shows the Yankee families' powerful attachment to their hard-pioneered farms. In their desperate commitment and sacrifice lies the substance of the legal battle that ran for yet another seventeen years before, during, and after the writing and ratification of the U.S. Constitution.

Jurisdictional control of Wyoming and its environs was an early and ardent objective of the Susquehannah Company founders. Settlers wanted to legitimize their claims to their farmsteads through local registration by official clerks and courts if necessary; and as one modern historian has suggested, "legitimate political authority could . . . go a long way toward validating . . . inhabitants' extralegal pursuit of property for with [jurisdiction], mobs could become militias and illegal dispossessions [could become] legal ejectments."[13] Thus the speculators who established the Susquehannah Company—there were 850 founders—carried on a decades-long campaign in Connecticut for endorsement by the General Assembly, and in 1754 the Assembly approved the project.[14] But at this point, hostilities with the French, always rumbling, burst the surface and threatened English colonial interests throughout the entire valley of the Mississippi. French and, especially, Indian claimants to Wyoming made settlement on Susquehannah Company lands impossible, with the "war-whoop within hearing of nearly every frontier cabin." Indeed, the Delaware tribe was so put off by the machinations of the Susquehannah Company's agents that the "Connecticut purchase had been one of the chief causes" of the French and Indian War.[15] At the conclusion of the war in 1763, Connecticut pioneers rushed in.

By this time the conflict between Pennsylvania proprietors and the Susquehannah Company, each with supporters in their colony's government, had come to the attention of the king's Board of Trade. The board issued an order-in-council calling for a joint commission to resolve the matter. Nothing came of this at the time, but efforts by the government in England to bring the two colonies together continued until the outbreak of the Revolution in 1775.[16]

Meanwhile, back on the frontier, the first settlers sponsored by the company had arrived on the frontier in 1760, surveyed three townships and some home lots, and built log cabins, a sawmill, and a gristmill. They told agents of the Pennsylvania speculators, who were traveling incognito, that they expected many more settlers to come in their train. Indeed, one Pennsylvanian reported that "Early in the spring [of 1761] these deluded people will come over like blackbirds and settle all before them." The company implemented settlement by offering huge land grants to individuals and families who would venture into such Indian-infested wild lands. As the company's most authoritative scholar puts it, "it was a determined effort at forcible possession; ... the settlers that were attracted in were of a hardened, rough, and even desperate type. They constituted, of course, an armed force."[17]

Back in Connecticut the company continued to exert political pressure both on grassroots voters, many of whom faced dismal prospects in Connecticut's overworked and overpopulated agricultural lands, and on the delegates to the General Assembly, the lower house of which faced elections every six months. During the early 1770s the issue of state sponsorship of the company's claims dominated Connecticut politics. In 1771 the Assembly declared that the lands in question "are well contained within the boundaries and descriptions of the Charter granted by King Charles 2d" and authorized the colony's agents in England to prosecute the case against Pennsylvania. Rushing ahead of events in England, in

1774 the General Assembly, now dominated by supporters of the company, authorized a survey of the disputed territory, described its bounds, and organized the settlers there into a town — Westmoreland — which, with expanded bounds, was made a county in 1776 by one of the very first acts of the now independent state.[18]

Meanwhile, attempting to carry on the war against England, the Continental Congress found intercolonial conflict counterproductive. Ameliorative efforts in the Continental Congress focused on the creation and implementation of articles of confederation. Delegates from both Pennsylvania and Connecticut — including Roger Sherman — sat on the committee assigned to write the document. Nothing endangering to either state's claims would find a place. Several states without western land claims (most notably Maryland) refused to ratify the document until all states had ceded their claims to the United States. All but one of them did; the lone holdout was Connecticut. Though Connecticut and Pennsylvania ratified the Articles in 1778, some landless states continued to refuse, and the required unanimous ratification was not achieved until in 1781.[19] Pennsylvania immediately moved to bring Connecticut to court under Article IX of the Articles of Confederation, and Connecticut responded affirmatively to this motion in January 1782.[20]

Article IX of the Articles of Confederation provided that Congress shall be "the last resort on appeal in all disputes and differences that hereafter may arise between two or more states concerning boundary, jurisdiction or any other cause whatever." It then established an elaborate process involving the quarreling states in the selection of five judges to hear the case. A trial was set for November 1782 in Trenton, New Jersey.[21] The case was argued by each state's most distinguished attorneys, with support and assistance from their governments. Connecticut sent William Samuel Johnson, who had been trained at the Inns of Court in England; Eliphalet Dyer, the leading figure among the

Susquehannah Company's founders; and Jesse Root, a most eminent, but largely provincial, lawyer. The Pennsylvania delegation consisted of four of the state's most successful lawyers, including James Wilson, thought by many to be the best lawyer anywhere in the colonies. Wilson was an infamously heavy plunger in real estate, and he held a large interest in the disputed lands.[22] The case was argued from November 12 to December 24.[23]

The question, remember, was not who actually owned the real estate but which state had jurisdiction over it, and therefore had the right to grant out the lands. The conflicting royal charters were the central and essential elements in the dispute. Connecticut's sea-to-sea charter of 1662 antedated the king's grant to William Penn by nineteen years, but it lacked the customary "saving clause" that protected the lives and property of any Christian people living in the granted territory. But at bottom Connecticut's charter bounds, reaching as they did to the Pacific Ocean, were absurd and defied common sense. The lawyers, of course, found scores of points, historical and legal, to dispute. But finally—almost inevitably—the five-judge panel decided unanimously and unqualifiedly for Pennsylvania.[24]

To the thousands of settlers who had come to the Wyoming territory from Connecticut, the decision at Trenton was not an unmitigated disaster. Their most pressing concern—the rights to the soil—was still unresolved, at least from their perspective. And indeed, the many farmers there from overpopulated Connecticut could hardly be expected to give up without a fight. They were desperate young men with no prospects at home, men who had fought off Tories and Indians, men who had spilled blood and lost relatives. Some had dug deep local roots after a decade or more of building and rebuilding their communities, and some, in fact, were no longer young.[25]

The Pennsylvania proprietors—their land titles confirmed by the highest court in the land, now that independence had been achieved—had the law and the full authority of government on their side and they meant to take possession. They offered the settlers one-year leases and compensatory lands elsewhere, but they had few takers, and they sent troops to the area to harass the embattled settlers. Both sides agreed at this point to petition Congress for a new trial to test the soil rights of the Connecticut claimants. That trial never took place.[26] Instead, Connecticut's delegates to the old congress used their political skills to draw Pennsylvania's delegates into a cabal that would help Connecticut get congressional approval of a qualified cession of what Connecticut still construed as her territory. Connecticut would withdraw support from the settlers and cede all its claims to western lands except for a large area just west of Pennsylvania's bounds—the famous Western Reserve—if Pennsylvania's delegates would support the western reservation. It was, as one congressman told James Madison, "nothing but a State juggle contrived by old Roger Sherman to get a side wind confirmation to a thing they had no right to." The deal cemented majority support in Congress for acceptance of the Connecticut cession, with its reserve of nearly 4,688 square miles.[27]

The Pennsylvania speculators now sought to drive the pioneer farmers out of the territory. But though they had supporters in the Pennsylvania Assembly, most Pennsylvanians, in and out of the Assembly, had trouble justifying claims of speculators to lands whose ownership was gained by juggling paper, while actual settlers who had fought and bled attempting to keep Indians at bay would be run off farms where some had lived for twenty years. The settlers pleaded their case before the Pennsylvania Assembly, in which some representatives were their elected delegates and many others were sympathizers.[28]

The result was a political settlement called the Confirming Act. The act was passed by the Pennsylvania General Assembly on March 28, 1787, a month after Congress issued its call for states to send delegates to a constitutional convention, and about six weeks before delegates began drifting into Philadelphia. As we shall see, events on Pennsylvania's frontier were very much on the minds of the statesmen gathered in Pennsylvania's metropolis.[29]

The Confirming Act stipulated that settlers who had "acquired" and "occupied" lots in the Susquehannah Company's vast tract before the Trenton decree of 1782 could get legal title to the lands by submitting their claims, within eight months, to a commission established by the Pennsylvania Assembly, and then gaining the commission's approval. Left out were the hundreds of new pioneers who had come onto company lands after December 1782, as well as the absentee speculators who sat warmly at home stoking fires in the Connecticut General Assembly. Pennsylvania speculators whose lands were taken up by Connecticut pioneers were given compensatory lands elsewhere in their state.[30]

The Confirming Act became the subject of the U.S. Circuit Court case central to this essay. The statute appeared to violate one of the most fundamental common-law rights of Anglo-American jurisprudence: Legislators lacked the authority, as did kings and governors, to take property from A and give it to B without adequate compensation and a public necessity. The statute enacted by the Pennsylvania Assembly deserves to be quoted at length:

> That all the said rights, or lots, now lying within the County of Luzerne, which were occupied or acquired by Connecticut claimants, who were actually settlers there at or before the termination of the claim of the State of Connecticut, by the decree aforesaid, and which rights, or lots, were particularly assigned to the said settlers prior to the said decree, agreeably to the regulations then in force among them, be and they are hereby confirmed to them and their heirs and assigns; *Provided*, that all the claimants whose lots are hereby confirmed, shall, by themselves, guardians, or other lawful agents, within eight months next after the passing of this act, prefer to the Commissioners hereinafter mentioned their respective claims to the

lots aforesaid, therein stating the grounds of their claims and sufficiently describing the lots claimed, so that the same may be made known and ascertained, and support the same by reasonable proofs.

The Confirming Act actually produced almost no effects on the ground; no lots were confirmed in the year after it was passed. The act was repealed by the Pennsylvania Assembly in 1790.[31]

The repeal was a thunderclap on the frontier, giving the Pennsylvania speculators everything they could have hoped for. It read, in part:

[T]he act, entitled "An act for ascertaining and confirming to certain persons called Connecticut claimants, &c," . . . be and the same is hereby repealed, and all proceedings had under said act are hereby render ed void, and declared to be null and of no effect; and all titles and claims which might be supposed to be affected by said act are hereby re-vested in the former owners, in as full and ample a manner as if the said act had never been enacted, anything in the same to the contrary notwithstanding.[32]

The settlers' partisans in the Pennsylvania Assembly protested strenuously. One of them declared the repeal legislation a "mockery of justice, and a satire on the House." The locally elected sheriff would eject no one, regardless of the strength or weakness of the claims or when they had been first asserted.[33] The Repealing Act of 1790 — which had been preceded by a suspension of the Confirming Act in March 1788 — explicitly noted the private property implications inherent in the situation. "The reasons set forth in the preamble" of the Confirming Act, the Assembly declared, "do not appear sufficient to warrant any legislative interference or departure from the established rules of justice, in respect to private property, nor hath [the act] had the effect proposed."[34]

Meanwhile, in Philadelphia, fifty-five delegates from twelve states had drafted a constitution with very immediate implications for the Wyoming settlers. Representing Connecticut at the convention were the potent political operative Roger Sherman and the attorney who had pleaded the pioneers' cause at Trenton, William Samuel Johnson. Local politics influenced the behavior of every one of the delegates, of course, and in no case was the relationship more evident than in the Wyoming imbroglio.

Though the Connecticut cession with its attached Western Reserve had been resolved in the old congress politically, as we have seen, the plight of the Connecticut settlers who chose to stay in the Connecticut townships was still dire; titles to their claims had not been legitimated, and indeed the settlers faced a challenge in the Pennsylvania courts, or perhaps in another Article IX suit. Their fate at the hands of Pennsylvania courts was clear; they could not get a fair trial. Everyone knew this; and Sherman and Johnson had protection of the Western Reserve and amelioration of their pioneer constituents high on their list of priorities at the convention. Legal challenges to their real estate had to be kept out of Pennsylvania courts. The convention offered an opportunity to do just that — but through a back-door opening that was quickly noted by the crafty politician and the astute lawyer.[35]

The back door was the clauses in Article III of the draft constitution. The version put forward by Edmund Randolph on May 29 provided that there should be inferior courts and a supreme court appointed by the legislature, with jurisdiction over cases involving piracies, foreign citizens, collection of the national revenue, impeachments of national officers, "and questions which may involve the national peace and harmony."[36] After weeks of discussion and refinement, the convention's Committee of Detail produced a draft:

> The Jurisdiction of the Supreme Court shall extend to all cases arising under laws passed by the Legislature of the United States; to all cases affecting Ambassadors, other Public Ministers and Consuls; to the trial of impeachments of Officers of the United States; to all cases of Admiralty and maritime jurisdiction; to

controversies between two or more States, (except such as shall regard Territory or Jurisdiction) between a State and Citizens of another State or the Citizens thereof and foreign States, citizens or subjects. In cases of impeachment, cases affecting Ambassadors, other Public Ministers and consuls, and those in which a State shall be party, this jurisdiction shall be original. In all the other cases before mentioned, it shall be appellate, with such exceptions and under such regulations as the Legislature shall make.[37]

In particular, we should note the parenthetical exclusion of cases "such as shall regard Territory or Jurisdiction." The parentheses imply the intention to revisit such cases. When the delegates arrived at this point in the committee draft, a number of verbal and substantive changes were proposed, some of which were rejected, some accepted. Then, at the end of the day (a Monday), "Mr. Sherman moved to insert after the words 'between citizens of different states' the words 'between Citizens of the same State claiming lands under grants of different states'—according to the provision of the 9th art: of the Confederation—which was agreed to nem: con:"[38]

That Sherman's motion brought unanimous approval was not because of the lateness on a hot day; there was a wide consensus that the cases covered by his motion should be assigned to the federal courts. Alexander Hamilton summed up that consensus in *Federalist 80*:

> The reasonableness of the agency of the national courts in cases in which the state tribunals cannot be supposed to be impartial, speaks for itself. No man ought certainly to be a judge in his own cause, or in any cause in respect to which he has the least interest or bias. This principle has no inconsiderable weight in designating the federal courts as the proper tribunals for the determination of controversies between different states and their citizens. And it ought to have the same operation in regard

to some cases between the citizens of the same state. Claims to land under grants of different states, founded upon adverse pretensions of boundary, are of this description. The courts of neither of the granting states could be expected to be unbiased. The laws may have even prejudged the question, and tied the courts down to decisions in favour of the grants of the state to which they belonged. And even where this had not been done, it would be natural that the judges, as men, should feel a strong predilection to the claims of their own government.[39]

Hamilton pointed out the unique but necessary inclusion of the cases covered by Sherman's motion: Federal jurisdiction must extend "to cases between the citizens of the same state, *claiming lands under grants of different states. These fall within the last class, and are the only instance in which the proposed constitution directly contemplates the cognizance of disputes between the citizens of the same state.*"[40] In another place, Hamilton wrote that

> The most discerning cannot foresee how far the prevalency of a local spirit may be found to disqualify the local tribunals for the jurisdiction of national cause; whilst everyman may discover that courts constituted like those of some of the states, would be improper channels of the judicial authority of the union. State judges, holding their offices during pleasure, or from year to year, will be too little independent to be relied upon for an inflexible execution of the national laws.[41]

Many years later Justice Joseph Story reiterated the conventional wisdom: "The constitution has presumed . . . that state attachments, state prejudices, state jealousies, and state interests might sometimes obstruct or control the regular administration of justice." Alluding to *Federalist 80*, in almost identical language, Story reiterated Hamilton's view in his still-revered *Commentaries* of the 1830s.[42]

The consensus on state partiality no doubt brought easy acceptance of Sherman's motion, but the motion would never have been made had it not been for conditions on the ground in the Wyoming Valley. As one commentator — a partisan in the legal battles of the 1790s — noted in 1801, "It is probable this controversy was the moving reason for the insertion of this clause in the constitution."[43] Thus the final draft of the Constitution linked federal jurisdiction to the special circumstances of Sherman's Wyoming constituents.

Pennsylvania speculators holding grants from that state had been entering suits for ejectment in Pennsylvania courts throughout the 1780s, especially after the Trenton decree of 1782. The injury and palpable unfairness to the pioneers of the legal results of these cases had led to the Confirming Act of 1787. The repeal of that act in 1790 did not abort these suits, but a new action to test them all was initiated in 1791. It became the defining case, *Van Horne's Lessee* v. *Dorrance*.[44]

The case of *Van Horne's Lessee* v. *Dorrance* is known to constitutional scholars principally for William Paterson's long disquisition, in his charge to the circuit court jury, on the common-law principle of vested rights. This principle, the plaintiffs' attorney argued, held that there were some personal rights so fundamental as to be beyond the range of government action, and perhaps the most important of these was the right to possess and employ private property. "The right of acquiring and possessing property and having it protected," Paterson declared, "is one of the natural, inherent, and unalienable rights of man." Did the Confirming Act violate the vested rights of Pennsylvania-based grantees? Did the Pennsylvania General Assembly take from A and give to B without adequate cause and compensation? If it did, that legislation "ought to be viewed with jealous eyes, examined with critical exactness, and scrutinized with all the severity of legal exposition."[45]

The facts underlying the suit are complicated, and their interpretation depends largely on which colony's royal charter took precedence, the status of purchases from Indians, and the material situation on the ground—who first came onto the lots, constructed buildings, and cultivated the soil. The specific facts of these last considerations are these:

John Dorrance bought a lot or lots in 1772 from one Ezek Peirce. Dorrance claimed that he was the first to build on the lots; the Van Hornes said that they themselves were. Significantly, Dorrance had fulfilled all the steps necessary to gain legal title under the Confirming Act except the final one—the issuance and receipt of a patent.[46]

Thomas Van Horne had bought 190 acres for £40 for himself and 177 acres for his son, Cornelius, for the same price at the same time, April 1771. Van Horne made the purchase from Richard Penn's agents; Penn had bought—under a Pennsylvania grant—from the Indian Six Nations. Van Horne soon sent out "planters" furnished with tools and other necessary accouterment, and these men were immediately run out by "the Connecticut Party." This seems to have happened in 1773.

Apparently the Dorrances lived unmolested on the land for nine years until the Trenton decree inspired the sons of Thomas Van Horne to recapture the lots. In 1791 the Van Hornes leased 900 acres to Richard Fenn, who moved onto the lots; but "with Force and Arms &c" John Dorrance "ejected" Fenn "from his farm and [did] other Wrongs" to him "to the great Damage to the said Richard Fenn and against the Peace and Dignity of the United States of America."[47]

Under these charges Dorrance was summoned to appear before the federal circuit court in Philadelphia at the spring term of 1792, in accordance with Article III, Section 2, of the new U.S. Constitution, the obscure clause inserted by Roger Sherman in expectation of exactly this contingency: Federal jurisdiction shall extend to cases "between Citizens of the same state claiming Lands under Grants of different states." And since the question of jurisdiction had in a legal sense been resolved at Trenton, this suit was contesting rights to the soil: which individual actually owned the lots?[48] After much legal maneuvering the suit was finally heard in 1795. Alexander Dallas, the court reporter, remarked that "This was a cause of great expectation, involving several important questions of constitutional law."[49]

Paterson first gave short shrift to Connecticut's long-held premise that its charter of 1662 preempted Pennsylvania's 1681 royal grant, merely asserting, that it "does not cover or spread over the lands in question." Perhaps with more justice, Paterson declared the purchase from Indians "radically defective and faulty; . . . fraud is apparent on the face of it."[50] If the Susquehannah Company's purchase from the Indians was invalid and the state of Connecticut had no jurisdiction over the tract—as the Trenton decree had already declared—the rest of the Paterson's job was easy, or could made so by applying the new principles of judicial review.

Addressing the jury, Paterson explicitly previewed John Marshall eight years before *Marbury* v. *Madison*.[51] Paterson told the jury that he would help them to a verdict by first instructing them on "the *constitutionality* of the confirming act." The American system, he declared, was fundamentally different from the English practice where Parliament was supreme and (quoting Coke) "transcendent and absolute . . . the authority of Parliament runs without limits, and rises above control . . . absolute and transcendent . . . omnipotent."[52] But, he said, "[i]n America the case is widely different." "Every State in the union," Paterson lectured the jury,

> has its constitution reduced to written exactitude and precision. What is a Constitution? It is the form of government, delineated by the mighty hand of the people, in which certain first principles of fundamental laws are established. The Constitution is certain and fixed; it contains the permanent will of the people, and is the supreme law of the land; it is paramount to

the power of the Legislature, and can be revoked or altered only by the authority that made it. The life-giving principle and the death-doing stroke must proceed from the same hand. In short, gentlemen, the Constitution is the sun of the political system, around which all Legislative, Executive and Judicial bodies must revolve. Whatever may be the case in other countries, yet in this there can be no doubt, that every act of the Legislature, repugnant to the Constitution, is absolutely void.[53]

Having thus laid out the principle upon which he would reason, Paterson turned to the matter at hand—the legitimacy of the Confirming Act in taking land from the Pennsylvania grantees and giving it to the Connecticut claimants, speculators as well as settlers.

The attorney for the defense, William Rawle, of course argued that the Cofirming Act should be upheld and the repealing act undone. That act, said Rawle for Dorrance, "in the extent & weight of its injustice becomes equivalent to the long catalogues of recorded oppression which load the leaves of despotic history." The repealing act was "a bill of perfidy . . . a patent of iniquity." The Confirming Act was consistent with common law that permitted governments to take property when a common convenience and public necessity required it and when adequate monetary compensation was supplied. Furthermore, Rawle insisted, the repealing act was ex post facto legislation forbidden the states under Article I, Section 9, of the new U.S. Constitution.[54] Plaintiffs asserted that the Confirming Act was both an impairment of contracts and an ex post facto law, both denied to the states under Article I, Section 10. Thus the defendants employed common-law eminent domain principles, while the plaintiffs counterposed the new Constitution's clause prohibiting state impairment of contracts.[55]

Pointing out that the Confirming Act had been passed before the new Constitution was written or went into effect, and that the act was subsequently repealed, Paterson declared the ex post facto claim irrelevant. The act was, however, an impairment of the obligation of contracts. "[I]t is clearly void, because it tends, in its operation and consequences, to defraud the Pennsylvania claimants, who are third persons, of their just rights; rights ascertained, protected, and secured by the constitution and known laws of the land.... As a contract, it could convey no right, without the owner's consent; without that, [the Confirming Act] was fraudulent and void." Indeed, said Paterson, an act of a legislature taking property from A and giving it to B "would be a monster in legislation, and shock all mankind." Further, "It is inconsistent with the principles of reason, justice, and moral rectitude; it is incompatible with the comfort, peace, and happiness of mankind; it is contrary to the principles of social alliance in every free government; and lastly, it is contrary both to letter and spirit of the constitution."[56]

The settlers, the Susquehannah Company, and the state of Connecticut had no valid claim separately or collectively to the land, and the Pennsylvania legislature "had no authority to make an act divesting one citizen of his freehold, and vesting it in another." Paterson wished to be unambiguous. In notes taken during argument he wrote, "the *Connecticut* settlers were, in legal estimation, trespassers and intruders. They purchased the land without leave, and entered it without right." Paterson instructed the jury that "The confirming act is unconstitutional and void. It was invalid from the beginning, had no life or operation, and is precisely in the same state, as if it had not been made.[57]

In a last desperate move for a new trial, Rawle entered an exception to Paterson's charge to the jury, but this got his cause nowhere. The jury followed Paterson's course of legal reasoning and found for the Van Horne plaintiffs. But seeing little justice in ejecting pioneers who had lost limbs, lives, and relatives protecting the Pennsylvania frontier, and who had cultivated the soil, built homes, and put down roots over a generation or more, the jury awarded Van Horne's lessee seven cents in damages and seven cents in costs.[58]

A significant number of representatives in the Pennsylvania General Assembly still thought justice had been ill-served and continued to make grants to displaced Connecticut settlers. Dorrance family members were well served: two of them in 1795 and 1796 were given at least 64,000 acres — 100 square miles — in several frontier townships.[59]

NOTES

1. Max Farrand, *The Records of the Federal Convention of 1787*, 4 vols. (New Haven, Conn.: Yale University Press, 1937, reprinted 1987), 2:186. The Committee of Detail had written, "Controversies between (States,—except those wh. Regard Jurisdn or Territory,—betwn) a State and a Citizen or Citizens of another State, the) Citizens (of any of the States) (thereof) and foreign States, Citizens or Subjects." Ibid., 173, 432.
2. Article IX of the Articles of Confederation reads, in part:

   > The United States, in Congress assembled, shall also be the last resort on appeal in all disputes and differences now subsisting, or that hereafter may arise between two or more states concerning boundary, jurisdiction or any other cause whatever. . . . All controversies concerning the private right of soil, claimed under different grants of two or more states, whose jurisdictions, as they may respect such lands and the states which passed such grants, are adjusted, the said grants, or either of them, being at the same time claimed to have originated antecedent to such settlement of jurisdiction, shall, on the petition of either party to the Congress of the United States, be finally determined, as near as may be, in the same manner as is before prescribed for deciding disputes respecting territorial jurisdiction between different states.

   Merrill Jensen, *The Articles of Confederation: An Interpretation of the Social-Constitutional History, of the American Revolution, 1774–1781* (Madison, Wis.: the University of Wisconsin Press, 1959, 266–67. "nem con": *nemine contradicente*, without opposition.

   The clause has figured in adjudication by the U.S. Supreme Court only six times, from 1789 to 2009, according to a very sophisticated and thorough search done by John Nann at the Yale Law School library. Jurisdiction was rejected in at least four cases, those heard in 1799, 1817, 1895, and 1951. In addition to the circuit court case discussed in this article, the Supreme Court decided cases involving this clause in 1809 and 1970.

   Max Farrand found among George Mason's papers a document of August 27, 1787, not in Mason's handwriting, that includes a nearly verbatim replication of Sherman's motion.

3. The story of Connecticut's charter is most succinctly told in Robert J. Taylor, *Colonial Connecticut: A History* (Millwood, N.Y.: KTO Press, 1979), chap. 2. See also Robert C. Black, *The Younger John Winthrop* (New York: Columbia University Press, 1966), chap. 15, and Charles M. Andrews, *The Colonial Period of American History: The Settlements, vol. 2* (New Haven, Conn: Yale University Press, 1936), chap. 4.

4. The demographics and politics of eighteenth-century land settlement are described in Richard L. Bushman, *From Puritan to Yankee: Character and the Social Order in Connecticut, 1690–1765,* (Cambridge, Mass.: Harvard University Press, 1967).

5. Quoted in Robert J. Taylor, "Trial at Trenton," *William and Mary Quarterly*, 3rd ser., 26 (October 1969): 532. The whole area claimed constituted more than 15,000 square miles, 9.6 million acres, only a small fraction of which was being actively contested.

6. Julian P. Boyd and Robert J. Taylor, eds., *The Susquehannah Company Papers*, 11 vols. (Wilkes-Barre, Pa., and other places: Wyoming Historical and Genealogical Society and other publishers, 1931–71), 1:lxxiv (hereafter SCP). The story of the Susquehannah Company is most fully told in the Introduction section of each of the eleven volumes of the *Papers*. A short account is Julian P. Boyd, "The Susquehannah Company: Connecticut's Experiment in Expansion," *Journal of Economic and Business History* 4 (1931): 36–69. A recent account is Paul B. Moyer, *Wild Yankees: The Struggle for Independence along Pennsylvania's Revolutionary Frontier* (Ithica, N.Y.: Cornell University Press, 2007).

7. Alfred Mathews, *Ohio and Her Western Reserve: A Story of Three States* (New York: D. Appleton and Company, 1902), 72.

8. The Indian policy of George III attempted to protect tribes from encroaching pioneers. To implement the Proclamation of 1763, the Board of Trade ordered the Connecticut settlers of the Susquehannah lands to withdraw, as they had settled west of the line set in the proclamation. This order, however, was "never executed." SCP 10:xxxv–xxxvi.

9. Mathews, *Ohio.* 82, 83, 90, 88–89. Near present-day Wilkes-Barre, Pennsylvania, the term Wyoming was then, as now, applied to a stretch of the Susquehanna bottoms about 21 miles long and averaging 3 miles in width, shut in by actual mountain walls 1,000

feet in height. "Fertile and fair as heart could wish, abounding in the richest growth of all that was natural to the clime, watered by the broad river and by innumerable cascades that leaped down the verdure-clad hills, it must, in its primeval condition, have seemed to those pioneers a veritable garden of the gods." Mathews, *Ohio*, 90.

10. Ibid. SCP, 7:xxii, xvi; Mathews, *Ohio*. 92–96; SCP, 7:46, quoting William Maclay. Homesteads burned, livestock stolen, and personal effects looted were valued by the Connecticut General Assembly at over £38,300 — a bit more than $22 million in year 2000 dollars. SCP, 7:xvi–xvii; John J. McCusker, *How Much Is That in Real Money? An Historical Commodity Price Index . . .* (Worcester, Mass.: American Antiquarian Society, 2001), 52, 59.

11. Mathews, *Ohio*, 90, says 300 Yankees died. A better source says 450 went out of the fort; 60 returned. SCP, 10:298.

12. Moyer, *Wild Yankees*, 39.

13. Charles J. Hoadly, ed., *The Public Records of the Colony of Connecticut*, 15 vols. (Hartford: various publishers, 1850–90), 10:378. The company's petition is fraught with legal obscurities. The request was for permission to petition the king to grant the tract, while at the same time describing Connecticut's bounds as already encompassing the area. The objective, the petitioners claimed, was "to cement and fix the Indians of the Six Nations . . . in friendship with his Majesty's subjects." Ibid, 10:378.

14. SCP, 3:v, II:xv.

15. Ibid., 2:xvi.

16. Ibid. xvii, xix, xxv.

17. Hoadly, *Records of the Colony*, 13:27, 14:218, 15:13, 197; Charles J. Hoadly, et al., eds., *The Public Records of the State of Connecticut*, 19 vols. to date (Hartford: various publishers, 1894—), 1:7, 229.

18. The relationship between western land claims and debate over the Articles of Confederation is thoroughly described in Jensen, *Articles*.

19. SCP, 7:50–51, xvii, xx. I have described the Connecticut political context of western lands in Christopher Collier, *All Politics Is Local: Family, Friends, and Provincial Interests in the Creation of the Constitution* (Hanover, N.H.: University Press of New England, 2003).

20. Jensen, *Articles*, 266; SCP, 7:xvii, xx.

21. Sherman, Johnson, and Wilson are the subjects of full-scale biographies. All five are included in the *Dictionary of American Biography*.

22. Taylor, "Trial"; SCP, vol. 7 generally.

23. SCP, 7:245. Taylor points out that the resolution of the controversy was seen at the time as a pathbreaking peaceful settlement of an international dispute. "Trial," 546.

24. The Connecticut perspective can be traced through letters of Eliphalet Dwyer in vol. 7 of SCP, keeping in mind that Dwyer was heavily invested in Susquehannah lands.

25. SCP, 8:xv, 7:xxxiv.

26. Christopher Collier, *Roger Sherman's Connecticut: Yankee Politics and the American Revolution* (Middletown, Conn.: Wesleyan University Press, 1971), 147, 144–48, 219–21.

27. The best account of the machinations of the various settlers, speculators, and Connecticut and Pennsylvania legislators is in the Introductions to vols. 8 and 9 of SCP. Something of the context of this legislation was an effort by Ethan Allen and others to carve out a new state in the area. The Confirming Act would undercut those rather fanciful efforts. Mathews, *Ohio*, 121; SCP 8:xxxvii; Moyer, *Wild Yankees*, 78–79.

28. SCP, 9:xix, 83.

29. Ibid., 10:112–13.

30. Ibid.,112.

31. Ibid.,115; James E. Brady, "Wyoming: A Study of John Franklin and the Connecticut Settlement into Pennsylvania" (unpublished dissertation, Syracuse University, 1973), 263–64, 278–79.

32. SCP, 10:342, 112.

33. Ibid.

34. I have described the play of local politics and its effects on the language of the Constitution in *All Politics Is Local*. See especially 25–28, 73–75, 170 n. 73.

35. Farrand, *Records*, 1:21–22.

36. Ibid., 186.

37. Ibid., 2:431–32. Despite Sherman's religious aversion to doing business on Sundays, the frequency of consummated compromises on Mondays clearly hints at his Sabbath Day work.

38. Jacob E. Cooke, ed., *The Federalist* (Middletown, Conn.: Wesleyan University Press, 1961), 538.

39. Ibid. 540. Emphasis in original. During the ratification debate in Virginia, James Monroe also pointed to this unique characteristic of cases included by Sherman's motion: the clause provided "the one possible case . . . where a controversy between citizens of the

same state can be carried into the Federal court." Monroe's *Writings*, 1:384–87, quoted in Philip B. Kurland and Ralph Lerner, eds., *The Founders' Constitution*, 5 vols. (Chicago: University of Chicago Press, 1987), 4:251. A perusal of documents collected in SCP, especially in the later volumes, leads conclusively to the conviction that Connecticut settlers could not get a fair trial in Pennsylvania courts. Further evidence lies in descriptive narratives of the pioneers' hardships. See, for instance, Moyer, *Wild Yankees*, passim, or Brady, "Wyoming," 298–99.

40. Cooke, *The Federalist*, "Federalist No. 81," 547.

41. *Martin* v. *Hunter's Lessee*, 1 Wheaton 304 (1816), quoted in Kurland and Learner, *Founders' Constitution*, 4:310. Other cases of a similar nature dealt with claims by citizens of New Hampshire who claimed lands in what became Vermont; e.g., *Town of Pawlet* v. *Clark*, 9 Cranch 292 (1815).

42. SCP, 11:39. The SCP editor thinks it more likely that the clause drifted in the course of the convention debate into the Constitution from the Articles of Confederation. 10:39n2. I do not agree.

43. 2 Dallas, 304 (1795); SCP, 10:292, 488, 416. Sometimes spelled Vanhorne, Van Horne is the preferred form. A company member, George Eddy, bankrolled Dorrance; the state sponsored and financed Van Horne. As one contemporary wrote, the men whose names entitle the case "were only nominal parties": "Van Horne knew nothing about it. Dorrance . . . had as little to do with it."

44. *Van Horne*, 310, 318.

45. SCP, 10:252n, 254, 310; 9:325; 10:326–27. Dorrance was a well established settler, elected a justice of the peace in 1787 and to other minor omit offices. A relative—perhaps his father—was a lieutenant colonel who died in the Wyoming Massacre of 1778. Cornelius Van Horne was of dubious character, having been charged with stealing horses on more than one occasion, and at the time of the trial was hiding out in New Jersey. Ibid., 9:19, 116 n. 3, 512; Mathews, *Ohio*, 93; SCP, 10:328.

46. SCP, 4:207–08, 207 n.i; 10:309; 9:325; 10:152–53, xxi.

47. Ibid., 10:152–53. By the terms of the Confirming Act, the Connecticut settlers had been given the option of Pennsylvania citizenship.

48. *Van Horne*, 304.

49. Ibid. 306.

50. *Marbury* v. *Madison*, 1 Cranch 137 (1803). Paterson was not the first jurist to elucidate judicial review. There is a long line of state and

national commentaries advancing this doctrine; for a recent discussion of them, see Philip Hamburger, *Law and Judicial Duty* (Cambridge, Mass.: Harvard University Press, 2008). Note also Patrick Conley's "reflection" on Gordon Wood's essay, *supra.*

51. *Van Horne*, 307. Emphasis added.

52. Ibid., 308.

53. SCP, 10:573, 567, 569.

54. In Article I, Section 10, the U.S. Constitution prohibits any state from passing any bill "or Law impairing the Obligation of Contracts."

55. *Van Horne*, 320, 310. Paterson also held that compensation to the Pennsylvania grantees under the confirming Act—had it been upheld—should have been in gold or silver specie, not in unlocated land elsewhere in the state. *Van Horne*. 315.

56. SCP, 10:311; *Van Horne*, 310.

57. SCP, 10:327, 327 n. 19.

58. Ibid., 573, 567, 569.

59. Ibid.

A Rhode Island Reflection

Connecticut's corporate charter of 1662, a contributing factor in the Pennsylvania land disputes described in fascinating detail by Kit Collier, almost awarded Connecticut an east-west domain from sea to shining sea. In fact, such a grandiose grant was contained in the Connecticut constitution until it was modified by Rhode Island's royal charter of 1663.

Connecticut's first boundary dispute was not to the west but to the east. Connecticut governor John Winthrop Jr. not only got a royal decree that swallowed up New Haven colony; he secured one that gulped down southern Rhode Island to the westerly shore of Narragansett Bay. This area, popularly known as the Narragansett Country and now called South County, was inhabited by the Narragansett tribe of Indians and a smaller, subject group called the Niantics. In the late 1630s Roger Williams and John Smith Sr. had each established a trading post near Narragansett Bay around present-day Wickford in the northeast corner of the Narragansett Country. By the late 1650s, however, a group of Connecticut speculators formed the Atherton Company and laid claim to a large swath of these South County lands by virtue of its 1659 purchase of a tract called Quidnesset (the area from the Potowomut River to the port village of Wickford) and another called Namkook (now the Boston Neck area of the town of Narragansett).

The younger Winthrop, who was not only governor but a member of this acquisitive land company headed by Humphrey Atherton, secured the following boundary language for his colony from King Charles II:

> All that Part of Our Dominions in New England in America, bounded on the East by Narragansett River, commonly called Narragansett Bay, where the said River falleth into the Sea . . . From the said Narragansett Bay on the East to the South Sea [i.e. Pacific Ocean] on the West Part . . .

Rhode Island's colonial agent Dr. John Clarke, a resident of Newport and a colleague of Williams, vigorously sought to redefine this boundary in the process of obtaining Rhode Island's famed royal corporate charter of 1663, asserting that Winthrop "hath injuriously swallowed up half of our colonie."

According to Winthrop's biographer Robert C. Black III, the Connecticut agent eventually gave valuable assistance to Clarke. Beset by problems back in his colony, Winthrop compromised on the thorny question of Connecticut's eastern boundary, much to the eventual consternation of both the Atherton men and his own legislature. Thanks to Winthrop's just but reluctant decision, Rhode Island (now a whopping 1,214 square miles) is about 400 square miles larger than it might have been!

The tenacious Clarke was aided in reversing the 1662 boundary grant by a panel of five arbitrators. After their deliberations in April 1663, the harried and homesick Winthrop conceded the Pawcatuck River as the boundary between the two colonies. Thus Rhode Island's basic law, dated July 8, 1663, set a boundary

> on the west or westerly, to the middle of a channel or a river there, commonly called and known by the name of Pawcatuck, alias Pawcatuck River; and so along the said river, as the greater or middle stream thereof reacheth or lies up into the north country, northward into the head thereof, and from thence by a straight line drawn due north, until it meets with the south line of the Massachusetts Colony.

When Connecticut refused to accept Winthrop's compromise, tensions mounted in the disputed area. Each colony arrested and jailed alleged trespassers, and armed clashes seemed imminent. To avert more serious confrontations, a board of royal commissioners investigated the rival claims in 1665. Their decision pleased neither colony. The commissioners declared the disputed Narragansett Country to be the King's Province, an independent enclave open to settlement by both colonies, but under Rhode Island judicial supervision. This situation endured for over sixty years. Wilkins Updike, an early historian of South County, describes the confusion: "Claimants occupied under both governments. Proclamations fulminated from both colonies. . . . Arrests and captures were made by officers, aided by troops of horse, and laws were enacted by each government, threatening forfeiture of estate to all who claimed under or acknowledged the jurisdiction of the other."

Through it all, Rhode Island persisted. It had a geographical advantage, a claim based on its original parliamentary patent of 1644, a long-standing association with the area's native tribes, even after King Philip's War, and a charter grant that apparently superseded an earlier provision in Connecticut's basic law. It had even established four towns in the Narragansett Country—Westerly (1669), North Kingstown (1674), East Greenwich (1677), and South Kingstown (1723).

Finally, after several failed intercolonial conferences and attempted settlements, Rhode Island appealed to the King-in-Council in 1720 and later sent its deputy governor, Joseph Jencks, to join its agent, Richard Partridge, in London to conduct the hearing. Despite a long delay, during which the Board of Trade suggested that the two warring colonies "might be annexed to New Hampshire," this effort was crowned with success for Rhode Island. In February 1726/27 the council promulgated its decision, establishing the Pawcatuck River as the boundary, thus allocating all of the King's Province to Rhode Island, except for a narrow strip along its western border.

By the following year Rhode Islanders had begun the process of marking the line of demarcation with stone heaps at precise intervals, a project performed with Connecticut's concurrence. In June 1729 Rhode Island's General Assembly created King's County, comprising most of the Narragansett lands except for East and West Greenwich, which in 1750 joined Warwick and Coventry in the newly formed county of Kent.* Thus ended this incredibly convoluted and protracted dispute, but one without the mayhem attendant upon Connecticut's western boundary—except for the annual summer invasions of South County beaches by thousands of fun-seeking Connecticutters.

In an attempt to reconcile the conflicting boundary provisions of the two charters, some ingenious draftsman, commissioner, or arbitrator named the waters at the outflow of the Pawcatuck "Little Narragansett Bay." Even today that amorphous stretch of salt water bears this repetitive name, one born of compromise.

If only some clairvoyant court commissioner had inserted "a/k/a Hudson River" after "South Sea" in the 1662 Connecticut charter, then the bloody and bitter Pennsylvania land controversies Kit describes would have been averted with a stroke of the pen, and Mark Twain's classic novel may have been entitled "A Connecticut Patroon in King Arthur's Court."

*The final decision, complete with the council's rationale and its history of the dispute, is reproduced in Elisha R. Potter Jr., *The Early History of Narragansett* (Providence, 1835), 206–211. An excellent summation is Roland Mather Hooker, *Boundaries of Connecticut* (New Haven, 1933). For technical information, consult John Hutchins Cady, *Rhode Island Boundaries, 1636–1936* (Providence, 1936), and Henry Wolcott Buck, "Connecticut Boundary Line Surveys," a paper presented at the 54th annual meeting of the Connecticut Society of Civil Engineers (1938). In the many years since the 1727 settlement, this boundary has been tweaked, most notably in 1840. However, as late as 2004 border commissions appointed by each state made small adjustments necessitated by the movement of markers and by the use of new surveying technology, including the Global Positioning System. I was a member of this most recent Rhode Island Boundary Commission.

Rhode Island and the People's Sovereignty, 1776–1843

Ronald P. Formisano

E LIVE IN A POLITICAL WORLD we call a democracy. But when we think more than superficially about our form of government, we know it is not a democracy. We look around the globe at authoritarian governments in countries where the people enjoy few freedoms, and we boast that "here the people rule." But in contemplating more carefully what is, in theory, the people's sovereignty, we realize that the people do not rule. Rather, representatives that the people elect periodically do the ruling, not to mention unelected officials such as judges and bureaucrats in positions of power. We can claim, however, to live in a representative democracy.

We hold our constitutions sacred, especially the Constitution of the United States. But at the same time controversy attends the interpretations of constitutions. The federal Constitution provokes debate, particularly between those jurists and legal scholars who claim to know the *original meaning* of the Founders in 1787 and others who contend that the Constitution, as originally written, embodied compromises among *multiple meanings* that were debated by Madison, Wilson, Washington, Hamilton, and their colleagues.[1]

In the era of the Founding, however, many Americans looked at constitutions with a perspective shaped by their Revolution, an outlook that, while it lasted for several decades, no longer exists today. Indeed, well before the Civil War this view of constitutions declined, and one of the signature episodes marking its eclipse occurred in Rhode Island.

The idea of popular constitutionalism, as historians have labeled it, grew out of the American Revolution, because the leaders of the movement for independence from Britain necessarily appealed to natural rights and the *people's sovereignty* for legitimacy. As historian Edmund S. Morgan explained, the concept of the people's sovereignty originated during the preceding century and a half in England and in the colonies as a "fiction" created to justify government—not by the people but, in actuality, by the few. The people's sovereignty is a fiction, because while the people may be the source of legitimacy, they themselves cannot rule; rather, elites rule in the name of the people.[2]

In the early United States, as now, this disconnect between theory and reality helped to create a populist political culture that over time has given rise to many protest movements and political parties, and that routinely leads to unrealistic expectations among many citizens. In the late eighteenth and early nineteenth centuries, the populist ideal of the people's sovereignty, in promising more than it could deliver, led to instability and challenges to authority. These popular insurgencies, however, modeled themselves on the same kinds of actions that had brought about the American Revolution. And they also expressed a determined vigilance to maintain the people's liberties.[3]

In the 1760s and 1770s Americans drew repeatedly on the notion of the people's sovereignty to justify crowd actions, riots, and then armed resistance to British rule. After 1765 the conflict with British officials called into play an extraordinary outburst of crowd violence and popular protests. This had long-running consequences: the patriots' uprisings established a template for later movements that would attempt, in the name of "the people," to end social injustice, or what those movements saw as the corrupt sway or oppression of powerful officials (a perception that was sometimes correct).

But who were "the people"? Opinions differed in the early republic, especially among the upper classes. The lawyers, merchants, and officials who led the Revolutionary cause defined "the people" according to different degrees of inclusiveness. Most would not admit women to the status of citizens, for example, or persons of color, or even the lowest class of white men. Over time, however, the boundaries encompassing the people broadened, in part because the notion of the people's sovereignty was like a genie out of a bottle, and it kept expanding and growing more inclusive.

When new state and federal governments were established after the Revolution, many Americans continued to engage in crowd and mob actions, riots, and even armed insurgencies to protest injustice, hard times, bad laws, and arrogant out-of-touch authorities. But an important point must be made here regarding the character of these popular "armed insurgencies." During the 1780s, 1790s, and early 1800s, from New Hampshire and Maine to the Carolinas, backcountry farmers and rural folk frequently gathered in a military manner, armed with muskets, clubs, and axe handles, and they engaged in vigilante and illegal actions such as closing courts to stop foreclosures, or preventing absentee landlords from collecting rents on lands improved by settlers, or marching to free prisoners who had not paid taxes that the protesters believed unfair or oppressive. In Virginia, mobs even burned courthouses. But in most of these protests, which saw armed demonstrators taking the law into their own hands, these self-proclaimed "people" did not intend to start shooting. Rather, they usually aimed to avoid bloodshed by mobilizing large numbers to overawe the authorities.[4]

During the 1760s in North Carolina, the corruption of colonial officials, sheriffs, and large speculators provoked riots, court closings, and finally an unwanted battle in 1768. The protesters — mostly backcountry settlers who included many members of pious religious sects — called themselves Regulators. So, too, did the often armed insurgents of the 1780s in New Hampshire, Vermont, Maine, Massachusetts, Pennsylvania, and elsewhere. The best known of these popular mobilizations in Massachusetts became misnamed Shays's Rebellion after a Revolutionary war captain from a hill town in western Massachusetts. But insurgents had been seeking redress from the legislature, and then closing courts in several counties, well before one Daniel Shays joined the protests, and they too called themselves Regulators. One historian recently labeled the Massachusetts Regulation "the mother of all populist insurgencies against government run in the interest of financial elites."[5]

Subsequently, many of New England's Regulators tended to become opponents of the 1787 U.S. Constitution, calling themselves Antifederalists after the Constitution's proponents cleverly appropriated the name Federalist for their cause. Most Antifederalists held a view of the Constitution very different from its nationalist or Federalist supporters.

The Constitution's opponents feared a strong central government—they called it "consolidation"—and wanted the balance of power to reside in the states. Above all, though, the Antifederalists "repeatedly drew distinctions between 'the people' and 'the government.'. . . they argued that an enumeration of rights would affirm the right of citizens to act *independently* of government." Let me repeat that phrase: *independently of government.* In addition, the Antifederalists saw correctly that the Federalists wanted to ensure rule by gentlemen, by "the better sort," and to limit the chances of ordinary men—or "the middling sorts," in the language of the day—to hold office.[6]

A generation ago many historians criticized the Constitution's opponents as shortsighted and narrow-minded. Recently, however, historians have credited the Antifederalists with contributing positively to shaping the Constitution and gaining a bill of rights. More to the point here, to quote Edmund Morgan again, "Antifederalists were right. Government and people could not be the same."[7] But as localists, they wanted the government to be as close to the people as possible.

Though the Antifederalists lost the larger struggle over the Constitution, their perspective persisted within the nation's public life well into the nineteenth century. In the 1790s and 1800s backcountry insurgencies similar to the earlier "Regulations" erupted in several states from Maine to the Carolinas. The Indian disguises worn at the Boston Tea Party would reappear in Maine from 1800 to 1810 as settlers harassed and scared off deputies, surveyors, and land agents acting for large land speculators. In the 1840s, although often ignored in textbooks and traditional histories, three decades after the heyday of Maine's "White Indians" tens of thousands of tenant farmers in eastern New York disguised themselves as Indians to engage in similar actions. Roving bands on horseback, mostly young men, waged vigilante resistance against law officers and agents sent to collect back rents by the great semifeudal landlords, or patroons, of the upper Hudson and Mohawk Valleys.

The Anti-Rent wars of New York crested in the mid-1840s, but episodic disturbances continued up to the Civil War. The Anti-Renters, driven by economic hardship, justified their outlaw vigilantism with the central idea of the American Revolution: the people's sovereignty. Although never redressing Anti-Rent grievances satisfactorily, many New York political leaders of both major parties gave lip service to the same democratic rhetoric invoked by many Anti-Renters who turned from insurgency to electoral politics.[8]

In the years in between the White Indians of Maine and the Anti-Rent riders of New York, various reform and protest movements put themselves forward as champions of the people, especially after the economic hard times that followed the Panic of 1819. By the late 1820s, however, most populist movements appealing to the people's sovereignty turned to the ballot box and organized themselves to work through politics, either as pressure groups or outright political parties.

The preeminent example of this transition of social movements to political organizations was the Anti-Masonic Party of the years 1828 to 1834. Anti-Masonry too has been given short shrift in the American story, but it delivered a lasting impact on our politics. The Anti-Masonic Party in 1832 held the first national presidential nominating convention, modeled on the church organizations in which many Anti-Masons had cut their teeth.

More importantly, the Anti-Masonic Party contributed significantly to the process by which the world's first mass political parties came to dominate politics. Simultaneously, the ideal of the people's sovereignty became more widely broadcast and established as political gospel. As universal white male suffrage took hold in the 1820s and 1830s, popular movements asserted "the people's right actually to rule."[9] By the 1840s the new Democratic and Whig Parties competed vociferously for the mantle of the true people's champion. It was in this changed environment that the doctrine of the people's sovereignty made a dramatic appearance in Rhode Island during the 1840s.

What is known as Rhode Island's Dorr War or Dorr Rebellion can be seen on one level as simply a struggle between political reformers and an entrenched political establishment unwilling to give up any of its influence or power. But it was also a sharp conflict between two competing views of constitutionalism that brought the state to the edge of civil war.[10]

In 1840 the state's fundamental law still derived from its 1663 colonial charter, which included no amending mechanism. Under that archaic document the General Assembly was omnipotent, and it had always imposed a statuatory real estate requirement for voting that it refused to remove. That statute limited the franchise to "freeholders" owning land (originally £40 worth, revised in 1798 to $134). As population grew, so did the number of landless adult males, such as artisans and factory workers, who were unable to vote, and so did inequity in legislative representation, which skyrocketed. Every small agricultural town, ranging in size from 182 to 461 freeholders, sent two representatives to the General Assembly, while Providence and Smithfield sent one delegate for every 5,793 and 4,767 freeholders. Nonfreeholders also lacked civil rights in matters of jury service, debt collection, and assault, making them second-class citizens.[11] Perhaps only one other state in the Union, South Carolina, came close to enjoying less democracy than Rhode Island.

The 1663 charter, ironically, has been described as "munificent" for its day, making Rhode Island "more democratic and self-governing" than any other colony. But the charter's "liberality" subsequently became a "cruel irony" of Rhode Island's constitutional history. Another irony: the state's heritage of religious liberalism also contributed to the persistence of an undemocratic polity. In Massachusetts and Connecticut, conflict over established churches, and dismantling of them, had already led to constitutional reform.[12]

From its founding, Rhode Island had been insular, other-minded, and suspicious of outsiders, and when the United States began to exist as a government in 1789, the state had not yet joined the Union: it stood "perfectly alone, unconnected with any state or sovereignty on earth." At the same time, nowhere else were the rights of local communities and individuals more jealously guarded. "The popular assembly, the popular initiative and referendum, frequent election of officials, as well as the preponderating influence of the legislature, all bear witness of their [Rhode Islanders'] solicitude."[13]

By the 1830s and 1840s, however, Rhode Island had fallen far out of step with the democratic, egalitarian climate of those decades, and the power and rigidity of the legislature constituted a formidable obstacle for reformers. A relatively cohesive elite of wealthy landowners, merchants, and manufacturers dominated state politics and wielded a controlling influence over elections. In 1840 "influence" meant that with the absence of the secret ballot and with virtually open voting, employers and creditors could know how debtors, tenant farmers, employees, and any dependents voted, since ballots (or "proxes," as they were called in Rhode Island) were of distinctive colors. The freehold qualification also induced landlords to sway elections by creating "freemen-for-a-day" by temporary conveyances of small tracts of land.[14]

Reformers appealed to the principle of the people's sovereignty inherited from the Revolution, and they, like many other Americans, believed that the people possessed an inherent right to revise their constitutions whenever they chose, and not necessarily through established procedures. The right "to alter or to abolish," originally asserted in the Declaration of Independence, found its way into many state constitutions. This meant that if sovereignty resided in the people, it was not transferred to written constitutions or to elected representatives, and so the people could act whenever they decided.[15]

But other Americans embraced a contrary view. They believed, rather, that "once the people created a government, it became the conduit and the enforcer of the people's will." Conservatives insisted that constitutional change could be effected only through already established procedures. This procedural constitutionalism held that the people were bound by the constitution they had imposed upon themselves. It was in the interest of Rhode Island's rulers, of course, to embrace this interpretation.[16]

A reform movement gained momentum during the 1820s and 1830s, but the legislature ignored or scornfully dismissed a series of petitions and conventions. By the 1830s a loose reform coalition had formed, composed of mechanics, artisans, and small businessmen as well as young lawyers and professionals.[17]

One such youthful lawyer was Thomas Wilson Dorr, a scion of the Providence gentry. Born in 1805, Dorr attended Harvard College, studied law in New York City, and entered the state legislature in the mid-1830s. He was affiliated with the Whig Party, and his reform enthusiasms extended beyond the suffrage to embrace many causes, including the rights of antislavery petitioners and religious radicals, abolition of imprisonment for debt, softening of the state's harsh penal code, better prisons, educational uplift, a more independent judiciary, and regulation of banking institutions.[18]

A note here about political parties: While many historians have associated the Democratic Party of Andrew Jackson with democratization during this period, the reverse held true in Rhode Island. The Democrats dominated the state, reactionary landowners and merchants controlled the party, and most top Democrats stood foursquare against change. (The events of the early 1840s, however, would bring about a realignment of the two major parties, the Democrats and the Whigs.)[19]

The exciting 1840 presidential election, won by the Whigs with their "Log Cabin and Hard Cider" campaign, mobilized the voters with such electioneering techniques as parades and huge camp meetings. These unprecedented tactics produced the highest voter turnout (of adult white males) of the period—80 percent. Rhode Island's citizens, even those who could not vote, caught the political fever, and the 1840 campaign prompted a new militant suffrage reform movement to emerge and attract many new supporters, including younger Democrats. Men who could not vote because they owned no land were especially resentful that they were nevertheless required to perform militia duty—and were the majority of those called upon for such duty. But the legislature continued to ignore the reformers' petitions and fed the sense of injustice by levying criminal penalties on anyone refusing militia service. The legislature further inflamed suffragists by absolving the state's small African American population—which was also seeking the vote—from town and state taxes. Many of Providence's blacks worked as servants for, or depended for their livelihood on, the antireform upper class, and for the most part they shared their employers' conservative outlook. Consequently, white reformers and blacks tended to be hostile to one another.[20]

Because the General Assembly refused to act, in 1841 the suffrage association asserted the right of citizens, inherent in the people's sovereignty, to call a constitutional convention on their own — to bypass the legislature, elect delegates, draft a constitution, and submit it to the electorate. During the spring and summer reformers held massive parades, rallies, and barbecues, and they even picked up significant support from freeholders, who were already voters.[21] This was nonprocedural constitutionalism borne along on a wave of popular enthusiasm.

After an August election to select delegates, the "People's Convention" met in October and drafted a "People's Constitution," extending the vote to adult white male Americans who had lived in the state for one year. The constitution increased representation ratios for Providence and the larger towns, though not on an equal basis. It also provided for a secret ballot, voter registration before elections, and an independent judiciary. The convention allotted three days, December 27 through 29, 1841, for a popular vote on the proposed document.[22]

In a well-run and closely supervised election, almost 14,000 approved the People's Constitution, including nearly 5,000 freeholders. Voters cast written or printed ballots that identified each one as an American citizen, a state resident, and a freeholder or nonfreeholder. Supporters of the Charter government boycotted the election, and only 59 negative ballots were cast.[23]

Unfortunately for reform, however, the People's Constitution generously provided that the Charter government keep office until May, giving the establishment four months to launch a counteroffensive. As historian Patrick Conley commented, "[S]eldom have revolutionaries been so obliging."[24]

Besides attacking the legitimacy of the proposed constitution, the state establishment, or Charterites, held a Landholders'

Convention in February 1842 that drafted its own constitution, one offering mild concessions, notably giving the vote to native-born citizens but keeping the property qualification for naturalized citizens. Indeed, Charterite nativists then launched an inflammatory scare campaign against the foreign-born and Catholics as a way to defeat the People's Constitution and promote the Charterite document. Even with landholder vote buying, however, their proposed basic law lost in the ensuing referendum by a vote of 8,689 to 8,013.[25]

But the state government, undeterred, now moved to crush the reformers, notably with laws decreeing harsh penalties for any actions implementing the People's Constitution. President John Tyler allied with the Charterites by promising assistance in case of insurrection and by stating that he would recognize no constitutional change unless blessed by state authorities.

But the Suffragists pressed on, holding their own election for state offices and electing an unopposed Thomas Dorr as the People's governor. Two days later the landholders reelected the incumbent governor, Samuel Ward King. Despite more repressive legislation and military preparations by the Charterites, now styled the Law and Order party, on May 3 Dorr's government held a festive inauguration ceremony, complete with brass band, marching militia, and troops of artisans and tradesmen. At this point, however, the People's movement faltered. The People's legislators marched past the locked statehouse and assembled instead in an unfinished foundry. Under a leaky roof, perhaps symbolic of their sinking cause, the Foundry Legislature, as it came to be called, enacted laws, but it failed to take possession of the statehouse. A friend of Dorr's called this a "fatal mistake," and in a later history a Dorrite wondered that "[m]en who dared to face a life sentence in prison [for defying the state] dared not . . . force a lock or break a pane of window glass in the State House."[26]

Worse was to come. The Charterite legislature declared that an insurrection existed and began arresting members of the People's government. Meanwhile, Dorr reluctantly joined a delegation to Washington to plead the reformers' case to an unsympathetic President Tyler. Returning, Dorr stopped in New York, where cheering Tammany Hall Democrats urged him to persist and volunteered their military services if needed; but the New Yorkers' posturing would turn out to be "empty promises." Back in Providence on May 16, an obviously tired and (given his subsequent actions) a mentally fatigued Dorr was welcomed by 1,200 admirers, to whom he gave a passionate speech proclaiming his willingness to die in defending the People's government.[27]

A day later, over the objections of Dorr's moderate allies, the People's governor led sixty armed Dorrites in a raid on a Providence armory and seized two Revolutionary War-era cannon. After midnight on May 27 Dorr and dozens of Suffragists stood in an open field in fog and darkness and prepared to assault the state's arsenal. Inside waited a well-protected and well-armed contingent of 200 that included Dorr's father and younger brother. After Dorr's antiquated cannon failed to fire, most of his men vanished. Dorr then fled the city and the state; and calling his action "deplorable," the entire Providence delegation to the People's legislature resigned. The reform coalition had collapsed, with many moderate middle-class reformers proving to be, as Dorr called them, "no force constitutionalists."

Dorr returned in late June to Chepachet, the site of an earlier Suffragist celebration, to reconvene the People's legislature, but he failed to rally any legislators or a significant number of supporters. Only two hundred or so artisans and farmers joined Dorr at Chepachet, and perhaps as many onlookers. After the reformers disbanded and Dorr again left the state, a Charterite force of 3,500 militia arrived from Providence and "stormed" an empty, undefended hill where the Suffragists had met. Cheated of a confrontation, the militia terrorized surrounding farms and villages, indiscriminately rounding up and mistreating suspected Dorrites. The loyalist militia men were mainly from rural southern and western counties, reflecting the geopolitical fault lines in Rhode Island's quasi-civil war; the Chepachet area had the misfortune of being in the more industrial north, which leaned heavily toward the People's cause.[28] The martial law invoked by the state government on June 25 would continue in effect until August 8.

In November the state government put forward a new constitution, and Suffragists largely boycotted the ratification of what some called "this bastard constitution." The new document contained a one-year residency requirement for freeholders and a two-year residency requirement for the native-born without real estate but owning $134 worth of personal property; the latter stipulation would give the vote to many of the native-born artisans, mechanics, and shopkeepers who had supported reform. But naturalized citizens still needed to clear the hurdle of the real estate qualification of $134, "a restriction," wrote Conley, "which made Rhode Island's basic law the most nativistic in the nation from the moment of its inception."[29]

The new constitution apportioned more legislative seats in the House to growing towns, but it capped the upper limit at twelve, thereby immediately costing Providence two seats. But representation in the Senate was wholly retrograde, with each town, regardless of size, having one vote. The conservative oligarchy that had resisted the People's movement retained control. This "rotten-borough" system prevailed, amid frequent controversy and only moderate relief for over 120 years, propping up unrepresentative rule by sometimes shifting coalitions of economic elites, political leaders, and their supporters in the electorate. To call it undemocratic is an understatement. Not until the 1960s did U.S. Supreme Court decisions end Rhode Island's peculiar republic by mandating "one man, one vote."[30]

In the short run, the defeat of the People's Constitution and reform in the 1840s hobbled representative government in Rhode Island. Repression continued, notably in the sentencing of Thomas

Dorr to life imprisonment in separate confinement. Released in 1845 after a political backlash and rehabilitated by legislators in the 1850s, Dorr died soon after in 1854 at the age of forty-nine, his health broken by the twenty months he had spent in prison.

In the long run, entrenched influence, political inequality, bribery, and coercion in elections, present in the 1840s, continued into the twentieth century. For another forty-five years after 1843 the subordination of naturalized citizens—primarily Irish Catholics—continued, until Republican leaders in the 1880s recognized the political capital to be gained in new groups of naturalized citizens who were non-Irish, non-Catholic, and potential supporters. However, the enfranchising amendment of 1888 (Article of Amendment VII) also continued a property tax-paying requirement for city council elections, a significant limitation in the size of municipal electorates that lasted until removed by Article of Amendment XX in 1928.[31]

In the larger context of the nation, though, the Dorrite defeat signified that the Revolutionary-era view of popular constitutionalism based on the people's sovereignty was being eclipsed. The People's Constitution had fully embraced the sovereignty of the people and "their inalienable right . . . to ordain and institute government, and . . . to alter, reform or totally change the same, whenever their safety or happiness requires." The Charterite constitution spoke only of the citizens' right, "in a peaceable manner, to assemble for their common good, and to apply to those invested with the power of government for redress of grievances or other purposes, by petition, address, or remonstrance."[32]

The conservative Charterite view would dominate the future in Rhode Island and the nation. In 1849 the U.S. Supreme Court reinforced proceeduralism in *Luther* v. *Borden*, a case arising out of Rhode Island's troubles. The Court's majority found that throughout the conflict only the incumbent state legislature and executive had been legitimate representatives of the state, and that neither

Congress nor the president had ever recognized the People's government.[33] Although Chief Justice Taney claimed that the Court declined to pass judgment "upon political rights and political questions," in fact the majority opinion implicitly validated procedural constitutionalism.

In dissent, Justice Levi Woodbury, a New Hampshire Democrat sympathetic to Dorr, reached a rather startling conclusion. He reasoned that the Suffragists had not gone far enough to establish their authority. He observed that the patriot revolutionaries of 1776 had won independence because they resorted to the uninhibited use of force. He implied that the People's movement failed because it had not gone far enough: "the popular movement," he wrote, "will generally succeed, though it be only by a union of physical with moral strength."[34]

So what was the significance of Rhode Island's near civil war to our understanding of constitutions and democracy in the United States? Historians have disagreed. Some legal scholars and historians have tended to view the Suffragists' constitutional position as illegitimate. Even a historian sympathetic to the reformers called their theory "an archaic and potentially dangerous relic of our Revolutionary era."[35] Another historian of the Dorr War went further and assessed the reformers' understanding of popular sovereignty as dysfunctional, irrelevant, and impractical. By 1840 a new historical consciousness prevailed, he argued, that had "lost contact with the founding period," while the Suffragists remained mired in the past and numbered a minority. Most Americans, he claimed, had moved on.[36]

Unfortunately we have no poll data to test that claim, but we do know of similar efforts at constitutional reform in other states during the decades from the Revolution to the 1840s. In these movements the idea of the people's sovereignty and the right of majorities to change governments and constitutions at will persisted and remained in dispute. One such political battle occurred in Maryland in the 1830s, for example, and it resulted ultimately in reforms.[37]

The legal historian Christian Fritz, the most recent and thorough historian of this general subject, observes that Dorr and his supporters hardly saw the Revolutionary principle of "alter or abolish" as outmoded or irrelevant. During the Revolutionary era and continuing afterward, several states included alter-or-abolish provisions in their constitutions or bills of rights. The Rhode Island Suffragists saw their principle as imbedded in the American constitutional tradition; it was the foundation of American governments, the great principle of the American Revolution, and, in the words of one Dorrite, "the public law of America."[38]

While Fritz's contention that Americans' beliefs about changing constitutions and governments remained in conflict and contested up to the 1840s, the failure of the People's movement in Rhode Island marked the waning of the reformers' interpretation. As we turn from the 1840s to the present political landscape, perhaps it is instructive to reflect on the tension that existed then, and endures now, between democratic rhetoric about the people's rule and the realities of our governance.

Notes

1. For the latter view, see Jack N. Rakove, *Original Meanings: Politics and Ideas in the Making of the Constitution* (New York, 1996).

2. Edmund S. Morgan, *Inventing the People: The Rise of Popular Sovereignty in England and America* (New York, 1988), 49–50, 53.

3. Ronald P. Formisano, *For the People: American Populist Movements from the Revolution to the 1850s* (Chapel Hill, N.C., 2008).

4. Ibid., 25–51.

5. Robert A. Gross, review of *Shays's Rebellion: The American Revolution's Final Battle*, by Leonard L. Richards (Philadelphia, 2002), *New England Quarterly* 76 (March 2003), quotation, 126; Marjoline Kars, *Breaking Loose Together: The Regulator Rebellion in Pre-Revolutionary North Carolina* (Chapel Hill, N.C., 2002). The *Oxford English Dictionary*'s first definition of "regulator" is "one who regulates," with a 1655 usage: "Such judges as may be appointed Regulators of the great abuses done thereunto." The second and third definitions of the infinitive "to regulate" similarly suggest persons or officials with special authority to correct abuses, as do the usages given: "b. To bring about or reduce [a person or body of persons] to order. . . . 1687 . . . . There are 6 commissioners appointed, who are to inspect all of the corporations of England, and regulate them, by turning out such as are against taking away the penall laws and test," and "c. To correct by control").

6. Wayne D. Moore, *Constitutional Rights and Powers of the People* (Princeton, N.J., 1996), 67, 68; see also Morgan, *Inventing the People*, 282, and Gordon S. Wood, *The Creation of the American Republic, 1776–1787* (Chapel Hill, N.C., 1969), 506–15. Saul A. Cornell, *The Other Founders: Anti-Federalists and the Dissenting Tradition in America, 1788–1828* (Chapel Hill, N.C., 1999), locates three varieties of Antifederalism in their social context.

7. Saul A. Cornell, "The Changing Historical Fortunes of the Anti-Federalists," *Northwestern University Law Review* 84 (fall 1989): 64; Morgan, *Inventing the People*, 284.

8. Among much fine work on these insurgencies are Alan Taylor, *Liberty Men and Great Proprietors: The Revolutionary Settlement on the Maine Frontier, 1760–1820* (Chapel Hill, N.C., 1990); Reeve Huston,

Land and Freedom: Rural Society, Popular Protest, and Party Politics in Antebellum New York (New York, 2000); and Charles W. McCurdy, *The Anti-Rent Era in New York Law & Politics, 1839–1865* (Chapel Hill, N.C., 2001). See also Formisano, *For the People*, 57–62, 176–89.

9. Glenn C. Altschuler and Stuart M. Blumin, *Rude Republic: Americans and Their Politics in the Nineteenth Century* (Princeton, N.J., 2000); Robert Weibe, *The Opening of American Society: From the Adoption of the Constitution to the Eve of Disunion* (New York, 1984), 155; Formisano, *For the People*, 65–158. In the 1840s "the sovereign people seemed everywhere on the march" (Daniel T. Rodgers, *Contested Truths: Keywords in American Politics since Independence* [New York, 1987], 101). This description of the prevailing rhetoric does not necessarily mean that the reality fit the rhetoric. Historians have often been skeptical of the extent to which mass political parties brought about more democracy. See, e.g., Altschuler and Blumin, *Rude Republic*.

10. The principal studies of the episode are Marvin E. Gettleman, *The Dorr Rebellion: A Study in American Radicalism: 1833–1849* (New York, 1973), and George M Dennison, *The Dorr War: Republicanism on Trial, 1831–1861* (Lexington, Ky., 1976); but Patrick T. Conley, *Democracy in Decline: Rhode Island's Constitutional Development, 1776–1841* (Providence, 1977), is indispensable. Also useful are Chilton Williamson, "Rhode Island Suffrage since the Dorr War," *New England Quarterly* 28 (March 1955): 34–50, and *American Suffrage: From Property to Democracy, 1760–1860* (Princeton, N.J., 1960), and Arthur May Mowry, *The Dorr War: The Constitutional Struggle in Rhode Island* (Providence, 1901; reprint, New York, 1970).

11. U.S. Congress, House, *Interference of the Executive in Affairs of Rhode Island*, Report No. 546, 28th Cong., 1st sess., 1844 (a large compilation of primary documents, also known as *Burke's Report* after Edmund Burke, the reform Democratic congressman who headed the committee that investigated events in Rhode Island); Dan King, *The Life and Times of Thomas Wilson Dorr* (Boston, 1859), 26–27; Williamson, *American Suffrage*, 243–46; Peter J. Coleman, *The Transformation of Rhode Island, 1790–1860* (Providence, 1983), 255–57. *Burke's Report* presented its material from a Dorrite-Democratic point of view to help elect Polk in 1844, and while "still the most

valuable published source on the Dorr Rebellion, was also a political campaign document"(Conley, *Democracy in Decline*, 359).

12. Quotations from Conley, *Democracy in Decline*, 21, 54; John L. Brooke, "Exhibition Review: Right and Might: The Dorr Rebellion and the Struggle for Equal Rights," review of an exhibition and catalog by the Rhode Island Historical Society," *Journal of American History* 80 (June 1993): 197.

13. First quotation from Providence Town Records, 7:141, quoted in Frank Greene Bates, *Rhode Island and the Formation of the Union* (New York, 1898), 170; second quotation, ibid., 208; Irwin H. Polishook, *Rhode Island and the Union, 1774–1795* (Evanston, Ill., 1969), 8–13, 22–51; John P. Kaminski, "Democracy Run Rampant: Rhode Island in the Confederation," in *The Human Dimensions of Nation Making: Essays on Colonial and Revolutionary America*, ed. James Kirby Martin, (Madison: State Historical Society of Wisconsin, 1976), 243–69. Among others, Polishook (p. 5) noted a "tradition of isolation and distrust" of outsiders and innovation.

14. Coleman, *Transformation of Rhode Island*, 268. Evidence of the openness of voting can be found in the lists of South Kingstown voters in the papers of Democratic leader and landowner Elisha R. Potter, Potter Collection, Rhode Island Historical Society, Providence (RIHS); see, for example, "Vote for 1st Rep., Aug. 1837," and "Vote for 2nd Rep., Aug. 1837." Also, see the 1842 circular letter of the Providence Central Committee, Law and Order Party, March 1842, Broadsides Collection, John Hay Library, Brown University, Providence (JHL). Abuses are described in testimony of Aaron White Jr., in *Burke's Report*, 277. For security, the landholders retained the grantee's note for the actual worth of the land, while the bogus voter "would vote as the grantor desired." In 1841 a prominent Democrat and defender of the freehold suffrage conceded privately to a reform Democrat that "there is fraud enough in our present system" (Elisha R. Potter to Dutee J. Pearce, Dec. 20, 1841, Pearce Papers, RIHS).

15. Christian G. Fritz, "Recovering the Lost Worlds of America's Written Constitutions," *Albany Law Review* 68, no. 2 (2005): 261–93, quotation, 273, and *American Sovereigns: The People and America's Constitutional Tradition before the Civil War* (New York, 2008).

For the Rhode Island Charterites' procedural constitutionalism, see Conley, *Democracy in Decline*, 317–19, and for a contemporary statement, N. R. Knight, William Sprague, and twenty-one others, "Address to the People of the United States" (Providence, Oct. 21, 1844), RIHS.

16. Fritz, *American Sovereigns*, 4. Michael Kammen observed that no "strong constitutional consensus" existed at the outset of the republic. *A Machine That Would Go of Itself: The Constitution in American Culture* (New York, 1986; reprint, 1994), 13.

17. Coleman, *Transformation of Rhode Island*, 264–66; Conley, *Democracy in Decline*, 237–39, 263; Jacob Frieze, *Concise History of Efforts to Obtain an Extension of Suffrage in Rhode Island from the Years 1811 to 1842* (Providence, 1842), 42–43.

18. Freize, *Concise History*, 27; Conley, *Democracy in Decline*, 249–52, 258–80, 283–85. Regarding Dorr's causes, see Thomas W. Dorr to Alexander H. Everett, Jan. 27, 1840, and Dorr to Robert Rantoul, Feb. 1, 1840, Dorr Papers, JHL, and a clipping of a Sept. 25, 1830, communication by Dorr to the *Providence Journal* in the Dorr Papers, RIHS.

19. On party realignment, see Conley, *Democracy in Decline*, 352–53. It was well underway by December 1842: *Address Adopted by the Democratic Convention Holden at the State-House*, Providence, Dec. 20, 1842, RIHS.

20. Robert J. Cottrol, *The Afro-Yankees: Providence's Black Community in the Antebellum Era* (Westport, Conn., 1982), 72–77, 85; J Stanley Lemons and Michael A. McKenna, "Re-enfranchisement of Rhode Island Negroes," *Rhode Island History* (February 1971): 7–10; William Goodell, *The Rights and Wrongs of Rhode Island* (Whitesboro, N.Y, 1842), 5–6.

21. Conley, *Democracy in Decline*, 300–03; Gettleman, *The Dorr Rebellion*, 37–40. "Convention Quick Step," Composed and Respectfully Dedicated to the Rhode Island Suffrage Association by Henry S. Cartee, performed by the American Brass Band, April 17, 1841 (Boston, 1841); this sheet music at the Newberry Library displays a lithograph of a huge procession of some 3000 participants and festivities on a plain above the city with beer, roasted ox, calf and hog. See Conley, *Democracy in Decline*, 302.

22. Conley, *Democracy in Decline*, 309–13. Through Dorr's insistence, a clause provided for a timely referendum on striking the word "white" from the suffrage qualification, but prominent abolitionists nevertheless came into the state to campaign against the entire document. Some Suffragists returned the favor by labeling the state antislavery society "a 'nigger party,' 'checkerboard party,' and 'amalgamationist'. . . raising the spectre of race mixing." Deborah Bingham Van Broekhoven, *The Devotion of These Women: Rhode Island and the Anti-Slavery Network* (Amherst, Mass., 2002), 45.

23. Welcome Arnold Greene, *The Providence Plantations, for Two Hundred and Fifty-Years* (Providence, 1886), 81–82; Coleman, *Transformation of Rhode Island*, 274–75; Conley, *Democracy in Decline*, 151–56, 315. Not surprisingly, the People's opponents challenged the validity of the referendum: A Citizen of Massachusetts [George T. Curtis], *The Merits of Thomas W. Dorr and George Bancroft: As They are Politically Connected* (Boston, 1844).

24. Conley, *Democracy in Decline*, 316.

25. Ibid., 317–23; Joshua A. Rathbun (Tiverton) to Thomas W. Dorr, Mar. 25, 1842, Dorr Papers, JHL; William Emmons to Dutee J. Pearce, Mar.18, 1842, Pearce Papers. See also "Native American Citizens Read and Take Warning!" (March 1842) and "No Right to Make Any Difference Between Native and Naturalized Citizens!" (March 1842), Broadsides Collection, JHL; William Wiecek, "Popular Sovereignty in the Dorr War: Conservative Counterblast," *Rhode Island History* 32 (May 1973): 35–51.

26. Dan King, *Life and Times*, 26–27; Thomas Williams Bicknell, *The History of the State of Rhode Island and Providence Plantations*, 6 vols. (New York: American Historical Society, 1920), 2:796; Francis H. Whipple McDougall, *Might and Right* (Providence, 1844), 236–37; Conley, *Democracy in Decline*, 327–29. Because of the Suffragists' paralyzing scruples, "the cause was defeated," said Dorr in 1843, "if not lost" (*Burke's Report*, 738).

27. Conley, *Democracy in Decline*, 333–38; Gettleman, *The Dorr Rebellion*, 107–18; quotation, David Grimstead, *American Mobbing, 1828–1861: Toward Civil War* (New York, 1998), 214, 336 (n. 43 and 44). Regarding the New Yorkers misleading Dorr, Mowry, *Dorr War*, 166–79. Mowry recorded the conflicting recollections of several witnesses

who heard Dorr's speech and concluded that whatever the exact words, they were inflammatory. (*Dorr War*, 176–78). Conley notes that "Dorr spoke of military action mainly in defensive terms" (*Democracy in Decline*, 336).

28. Frieze, *Concise History*, 112–15; Conley, *Democracy in Decline*, 344–51. For optimistic advice to Dorr regarding potential military support before Chepachet, see letters to Dorr from John S. Harris, June 12, 1842; Charles E. Newell, June 13, 1842; William J. Miller, June 15, 1842; J. Sprague (Chepachet) June 15, 1842; Burrington Anthony, June 17, 1842; Dorr MSS, JHL. For contrary advice, see Aaron White (Woonsocket) to Dorr, June 12, 1842, but compare Aaron White to Dorr, June 18, 1842; Dorr MSS. JHL. Some of Dorr's closest friends opposed his return to Chepachet: Benjamin Albro, Walter S. Burges, et al., "Remonstrance against the Proceedings at Chepachet by Several Suffrage Men," June 25, 1842. Dorr replied to Burges angrily, asking if "the brave men who have acted in support of the constitution by all necessary means" were simply to be "given up" to the Algerines. Dorr (Glocester) to W. S. Burges, June 27, 1842, Dorr MSS, JHL. A letter of apology written by Burges several months later is revealing of the pressures on Dorr at Chepachet. Burges to Dorr, Oct. 30, 1842, Dorr MSS, JHL.

29. Conley, *Democracy in Decline*, 351, 372–73; Coleman, *Transformation of Rhode Island*, 284–85; first quotation, David Parmenter to Dorr, Sept. 30, 1842, Dorr Papers, JHL; second quotation, Conley, *Democracy in Decline*, 373.

30. Historians have given surprisingly little attention to this feature of Rhode Island's history, but see the relevant essays in Patrick T. Conley, *Rhode Island in Rhetoric and Reflection: Public Addresses and Essays* (Providence, 2002), especially chapter 21, "The Constitution of 1843: A Sesquicentennial Obituary," and chapter 48, "Tradition and Turmoil: Government and Politics in Rhode Island, 1636–1986."

31. Conley, "The Constitution of 1843," 76–79. In 1905 muckraker Lincoln Steffens included Rhode Island in his exposé of political corruption: "Rhode Island: A State for Sale," *McClure's Magazine* 24 (February 1905): 337–53; also, Irving Berdine Richman, *Rhode Island: A Study in Separatism* (Boston, 1905), 323–31.

32. The constitutions are reprinted in Mowry, *Dorr War*; quotations, 323, 349.

33. Peter C. McGrath, "Optimistic Democrat: Thomas W. Dorr and the Case of *Luther* v. *Borden*," *Rhode Island History* 29 (August/November 1970): 10–11.

34. Quotation, McGrath, "Optimistic Democrat," 111; also, Conley, *Democracy in Decline*, 365–66 n. 95.

35. Conley, *Democracy in Decline*, 375. For the debate over the People's movement in the 1840s, Patrick T. Conley, "Popular Sovereignty or Public Anarchy? America Debates the Dorr Rebellion," *Rhode Island History* 60 (summer 2002): 70–91.

36. Conley, *Democracy in Decline*, 375; Dennison, *The Dorr War*, xiii, 6, 198–99; quotation, 198. While critical of the People's movement, Dennison presents a thorough understanding of the constitutional issues involved.

37. Formisano, *For the People*, 192–94.

38. Fritz, *American Sovereigns*, 261.

A Rhode Island Reflection

With Professors Wiecek and Formisano giving ample treatment herein to Rhode Island's Dorr Rebellion (buttressed by my previous eulogy to Dorr with an assist from his archenemy, Henry Bowen Anthony), my reflection here will be pointed and mercifully brief. Independent scholar Russell DeSimone is a close student of the Dorr Rebellion and a collector of ephemera relating to that event. When I was vice chairman of the now defunct Rhode Island Supreme Court Historical Society, I induced that organization to publish a book entitled *Broadsides of the Dorr Rebellion* and wrote its introduction. This well-annotated volume was compiled by DeSimone and Daniel C. Schofield mainly from the collections of Brown University's John Hay Library and the Rhode Island Historical Society.

Recently DeSimone has teamed up with Erik Chaput, a most promising young scholar who is completing his doctoral dissertation on the Dorr Rebellion at Syracuse University under the tutelage of Bill Wiecek. They are currently publishing pamphlets on neglected aspects of that Rhode Island cause célèbre.

Members of our diverse coterie of latter-day Dorrites—which also includes Professors Marvin Gettleman, George Dennison, Ron Formisano, Christian Fritz, Al Klyberg, Bob Laffey, and Scott Molloy, attorney James Marusak, and independent scholar Joyce Bothelo—sometimes reexamine this fascinating and pivotal event in Rhode Island history and attempt to assess its long-range impact upon Rhode Island political and constitutional development, its national importance and implications, and its significance in the development of democratic theory. Two recent doctoral dissertations have added new Dorr devotees to the roster: Ray Lavertue, "The People's Governor: Thomas Wilson Dorr and the Politics of Sacrifice, 1834–1843 (Oxford University, 2010), and Susan H Graham, "Call Me a Female Politician, I Glory in the Name! Woman Dorrites and Rhode Island's 1842 Suffrage Crisis" (University of Minnesota, 2006).

At a recent auction Russ DeSimone bought a handwritten statement by Dorr dated August 10, 1853, less than seventeen months prior to his death at age forty-nine. The hapless reformer entitled this brief farewell "The Doctrine of Sovereignty." I had never seen it or cited it in my work, nor had any other contemporary Dorr scholar (to my knowledge). Amazingly, however, it had been published verbatim in 1920 on page 804 in volume 2 of Thomas Williams Bicknell's five-volume narrative and biographical *History of Rhode Island*. Its appearance there suggests that Dorr promulgated his view in print.

Bicknell called Dorr "above all, a Christian statesman," because Dorr recognized that "there exists a higher law, superior to human, to which men, institutions, and constitutions must ultimately yield obedience." Dorr's "doctrine of sovereignty," quoted here, confirms this assessment:

> There is One over all, blessed forever; and under him the People are sovereign. His Revealed Word is the higher law, to whose principles and rules of action recourse is had by the framers of Constitutions and by legislators, to impart justice and equity to political institutions. The application of these principles and rules to the Constitutions and legislative acts of States, and to men in their political relations, is what has been called the democracy of Christianity. Rights are the gift of God. The definition and protection of them are the objects of just government.

> Providence, R.I.   Thos W. Dorr
> Aug. 10th, 1853

Such idealism sustained Dorr in his crusade for equal rights. His selflessness is indicated by many of his actions and decisions. For example, he favored others to stand for People's governor in April 1842 and became the party's candidate by default when those timid reformers would not step forward. Sadly, Dorr's view of sovereignty exists only in utopia, not in the world of realpolitik where there are too few of Dorr's kind to sustain it.

No Landless Irish Need Apply: Rhode Island's Role in the Framing and Fate of the Fifteenth Amendment
Patrick T. Conley

IVEN RHODE ISLAND'S BOYCOTT of the 1787 Philadelphia Convention, discussion concerning the state's influence on the federal Constitution usually centers upon the religion clauses of the First Amendment. Much has been written regarding the influence of Roger Williams, Dr. John Clarke, Isaac Backus, and the Baptist tradition upon the Framers who drafted the Free Exercise and Establishment Clauses. My view is that the American church-state outlook has issued chiefly from two parallel positions: the Rhode Island dissenting tradition with its biblical base, initiated by Williams, and the eighteenth-century Virginia Enlightenment tradition rooted in natural law and natural rights, expounded by Thomas Jefferson and James Madison.[1]

Whereas Rhode Island's contribution to the First Amendment is widely discussed and salutary, the state's impact on the Fifteenth Amendment is little known and negative. For a state where the right to vote was widely dispersed during its formative era, Rhode Island's sharp reversal of form in the nineteenth century is cause for criticism and embarrassment, as Rhode Island became a democracy in decline. Reformers waged the Dorr Rebellion from 1841 to 1843 to gain the vote for landless white males, but the state constitution that emanated from that conflict denied the vote to landless naturalized citizens, most of whom were Irish Catholics. In the ensuing decades this discriminatory provision made the battle for voting rights more intense, divisive, and enduring in

An adaptation of this essay appeared in Rhode Island History *68 (summer/fall 2010): 79–90.*

Rhode Island than it was in any other state.[2] During the nineteenth century, local resistance to broadening the suffrage helped to shape and limit the United States Constitution, specifically the Fifteenth Amendment. That controversy is now worth recalling for those who take their right to vote for granted.

In the period immediately following the Civil War, the movement in Rhode Island for general suffrage reform intensified. It centered upon the real estate requirement for voting imposed on naturalized citizens by the Constitution of 1843. State statistician Dr. Edwin M. Snow noted in his 1865 state census that "only one in twelve or thirteen of the foreign-born of adult age was a voter."[3] Political leaders in the drive for liberalization of the franchise included Governor Ambrose Burnside, the former Civil War general, who supported the vote for naturalized veterans, many of whom had served under his command; former Democratic congressman Thomas Davis, a Dublin-born Protestant who had been ousted from the United States House of Representatives by the Know-Nothing landslide of 1854; Providence Republican mayor Thomas Doyle, a Protestant also of Irish descent; Democratic state senators Sidney Dean of Warren and Alexander Eddy of Gloucester; and Republican state senator Charles C. Van Zandt of Newport, a future governor from a heavily Irish-American community.[4]

The most fervent and outspoken advocate of suffrage reform in the postwar era, however, was young, energetic, and articulate Charles E. Gorman from the Wanskuck area of North Providence, a section that was annexed by the city of Providence in 1873–74. Gorman was born in Boston in 1844, the son of Charles and Sarah J. (Woodbury) Gorman. His father was a native of Ireland, but his mother was descended from one of the original settlers of the Massachusetts Bay Colony.

Admitted to the bar in 1865 at the age of twenty-one, elected as a Democrat to the Rhode Island General Assembly in 1870 and to the Providence Common Council in 1875, Charles Gorman is reputed to have been the first Irish Catholic to achieve each of these distinctions. During the last third of the nineteenth century he devoted most of his legal talent and his political energy to the cause of constitutional reform, or "equal rights," as the movement was then called.[5]

In 1870 freshman representative Gorman and Senator Dean each sponsored bills calling for an unlimited state constitutional convention to reform suffrage and representation, but the measures failed to pass. As a concession, however, the Assembly approved a resolution proposing three constitutional amendments, one of which called for the repeal of the real estate property qualification for naturalized citizens. This proposal met defeat in October 1871 by a wide margin — 3,236 votes were cast in its favor, but 6,960 of the electors rejected it. The vote came less than three months after New York City's infamous "Orange Riots" between Catholic and Protestant Irishmen, a bloody civil strife that prompted Henry B. Anthony's *Providence Journal* to equate suffrage extension with "mob government." The *Journal*'s editorial views prevailed over the exhortations of three small and short-lived newspapers (the pro-labor *Rhode Island Lantern,* the *Weekly Review,* and the *Weekly Democrat*) founded by Irish Catholics in 1870 to publicize the need for political and labor reforms.[6]

In November 1876 an effort was made to allow foreign-born soldiers and sailors to vote on the same terms as native citizens, but it too proved futile — 11,038 for to 10,956 against. This measure (which required a three-fifths vote) did not succeed until April 1886, when under Gorman's lead it became Article of Amendment VI to the Rhode Island Constitution.[7]

The most reasoned and elaborate defense of Rhode Island's voting provisions during these two decades of agitation was penned by Chief Justice Thomas Durfee (1875–1891), the son of Chief Justice Job Durfee (1835–1848), who presided with great partiality over the treason trial of Thomas Dorr and then sentenced him to life imprisonment. Among the younger Durfee's several justifications of the existing voting laws was the assertion that immigrants in a small manufacturing state were a "floating population" that does "not take root and grow. . . in the social and political soil and air of Rhode Island." Besides, said Durfee, "the main body of our foreign-born population . . . have only the crudest political ideas. They have but little time and no good opportunities to improve themselves. How can they discharge an electoral trust in a proper manner? They cannot. They are necessarily more or less at the mercy of men who are ready to mislead or corrupt them."[8] Perhaps the absence of a secret-ballot law and a work week consisting of six days and sixty-six to seventy-two hours gave some credibility to Durfee's assessment.

Finally, said the chief justice, "The peculiarity of our constitution is notorious. It has been bruited abroad to the four corners of the world. There is probably not a naturalized citizen in Rhode Island, who has any interest in politics, who did not know, when he came to the State, that he could not vote here without a freehold qualification. If he came knowing this, he came accepting it, and why should he quarrel with a condition which he voluntarily accepted?"[9] Thus the defense rested.

But our focus here is not upon the machinations to alter the state Constitution but on the ways in which the federal Constitution impacted Rhode Island and vice versa. Determined but not optimistic regarding support for reform from the Republican-controlled legislature, the state supreme court, or, for that matter, the conservative, old-line leadership of Rhode Island's Democratic party, Charles Gorman launched a decade-long effort to enlist the support of the federal courts and the U. S. Congress on behalf of Rhode Island's naturalized citizens. The bases for Gorman's federal crusade were the newly ratified Fourteenth (1868) and Fifteenth (1870) Amendments to the United States Constitution.[10]

While Gorman was pressing for suffrage reform, Rhode

Island's Republican United States senator Henry B. Anthony worked in an equally zealous manner for restriction on both the state and federal levels.[11] His effect on the framing of the Fifteenth Amendment is especially significant. During debate on this voting-rights amendment in February 1869, Republican senator Henry Wilson of Massachusetts submitted a plan to broaden the measure by banning all state qualifications for voting and office holding based on "race, color, nativity, property, education, or religious creed," but did not bar states from setting other qualifications for holding office. In effect, Wilson posed the controversial question of whether the amendment should confine itself to black suffrage or undertake sweeping reform of voting and office-holding qualifications. Ironically, Wilson had first been elected to the Senate in 1855 by the Massachusetts legislature as an anti-slavery candidate with essential support from the American party, a militantly anti-Irish-Catholic organization popularly referred to as the Know-Nothings.

Wilson's added language was accepted by the Senate on February 9 by a vote of 31 to 27, with Rhode Islanders Anthony and former governor William Sprague in opposition and eight men "absent." Then the Senate voted final passage of the expanded amendment by a margin of 39 to 16, thereby meeting the constitutionally required two-thirds vote. Again Anthony and Sprague resisted.

When the proposed Fifteenth Amendment went to the House for concurrence and debate on February 15, it was eloquently supported by John Bingham of Ohio, one of the principal architects of the Fourteenth Amendment. Unfortunately the momentum was lost when House leader, amendment manager, and black-suffrage advocate George S. Boutwell of Massachusetts objected on the somewhat baseless ground that the Senate version omitted the words "previous condition of servitude." His motion not to concur passed by a vote of 133 to 37. Five days elapsed before Bingham got things back on track.

After much political maneuvering, the matter again came to the floor of the House on February 20, when Bingham's motion to adopt the broad Senate language—except for adding "previous condition of servitude" and deleting "education"—passed by a margin of 92 to 70, with another sixty representatives listed as "not voting." Since the House and Senate versions of the proposed amendment did not precisely agree, Congress created a six-man conference committee with William Stewart (Nevada), Roscoe Conkling (New York), and George Edmunds (Vermont) representing the Senate. All three had voted against the Wilson amendment on February 9. They would be guided by the fact that while the House was debating, the Senate had voted on February 17 to recede from Wilson's proposal by a margin of 33 to 24, with nine absences. Henry Anthony, who would become the Senate's president pro tem in a month and hold that post in the next three Congresses, worked diligently behind the scenes to effect this reversal.

But this is not to suggest that Anthony was a one-man wrecking crew; far from it. William Gillette, who has written the most authoritative and detailed account of the Fifteenth Amendment's enigmatic course through Congress and the states, describes that measure's incredibly complex twists, turns, changes, and reversals during its labyrinthian journey through the House and Senate in February 1869.

Republican divisions over the amendment's scope, Democratic maneuvering to create delay, the imminent expiration of the Congress's "lame duck" session, political expediency, rivalry between the two chambers, personal pressures, the triumph of realism over principle, and other influences, both rational and irrational, all contributed to the amendment's final racially restricted language. And as moderate and radical Republicans exchanged views and vituperation, some political pragmatists in Congress and in the media made the preposterous insinuation that Wilson (who would become vice president in March 1873) and Bingham had crafted their changes for the purpose of ensuring the amendment's eventual defeat by the state legislatures that would decide its fate.

After days of seemingly endless, confusing, and repetitious debate, with the Fortieth Congress set to expire in less than a week, its members voted to send the Fifteenth Amendment to the states in its present limited form, thereby ending its exercise in futility. A practical and weary Wilson was compelled to concede that "my own amendment . . . I am sorry to find, is too broad, comprehensive, and just to be sustained by the country. . . . it is too broad, too comprehensive, too generous, too liberal for the American people of today. Rhode Island, Connecticut, New Hampshire, Massachusetts, and some other states desire to preserve their own notions, even if their notions are contrary to the rights of citizens of the United States."

The conference committee's report not only recommended the blacks-only version; it inexplicably deleted the office-holding provision as well, despite its approval by both houses. On February 26, as the Senate prepared to concur with the report (as the House had done the day before), a final bitter exchange took place between Wilson and Anthony that revealed a potent argument used by Anthony in urging his colleagues to retreat from sweeping reform.[12] To understand his remarks, one must understand the main political passion of the xenophobic Anthony.

Unlike Wilson, Henry Bowen Anthony never wavered in his virulent nativism during a forty-six-year public career that began in 1838 when, as editor of the *Providence Journal*, he railed against the enfranchisement of the "foreign vagabond" (read "Irish Catholic"). Anthony frequently compared the "purity" of Rhode Island's elections to those of the "immigrant infested" city of New York, where Irish Catholics had gained a foothold in the Democratic Party. His hostile and unyielding attitude towards these new arrivals was illustrated by his expressed belief that "they have come here un-invited, and upon their departure there is no restraint."

During the Dorr Rebellion the People's Constitution, drafted mainly by Thomas Wilson Dorr, eliminated the real estate voting requirement for all white male citizens. The existing government countered with a document known as the Freemen's (or Land-holders') Constitution, which retained the real estate require-ment for naturalized citizens. In urging ratification of the latter, Anthony alarmed the native-born electors when he exclaimed in the pages of his *Providence Journal* that under the People's Con-stitution "foreign elements . . . would neutralize your power and effectiveness." He admonished that "the great difference between the two constitutions lies in the provision respecting foreigners. Everything else is nothing to this!"[13]

Constant and true to form despite the passage of time, Anthony took sharp issue with Wilson on the floor of the Senate during the final debate on the Fifteenth Amendment. After Wilson made derogatory remarks about Rhode Island's restrictive voting system, the eloquent and strident Anthony chided him for inter-ference in Rhode Island's affairs. His state's voting laws, warned Anthony, "were not made for the people of Massachusetts; they were made for us, and whether right or wrong, they suit us, and we intend to hold them; and we shall not ratify any amendment to the Constitution of the United States that contravenes them, and we have the satisfaction of knowing that, without our State, the necessary number of twenty-eight states cannot be obtained for the ratification of any amendment whatever."

The anti-Irish Anthony, a publisher and the founder of the Government Printing Office, knew Rhode Island's support for the Fifteenth Amendment was critical because several southern states would likely reject it. Anthony was referring to the fact that the four border slave states and the seven states of the former Confederacy already readmitted to the Union were doubtful ratifiers, and California and Oregon, where anti-Chinese senti-ment ran high, were almost certain to reject any mention of "race." Four other Confederate states still awaited readmission. Congress would make ratification a condition of their restoration, a decision that would finally save the amendment.

It was evident to the Senate that Rhode Island's rejection could be fatal to the cause of ratification and that Anthony was the most powerful political voice in his home state. This situation undoubt-edly inspired Anthony's threatening remark and convinced his lis-teners that his was no idle threat. The influential and media-savvy Rhode Island senator and a majority of his colleagues, who were animated by varied motives, eventually prevailed. In its final form the Fifteenth Amendment was limited to the black vote ("race, color, or previous condition of servitude"), leaving such oppressed immigrant minorities as the naturalized Irish of Rhode Island unprotected.[14]

When the Fifteenth Amendment came to Rhode Island for ratification in 1869, the controversy centered on the Irish rather than the black vote. Rhode Island blacks had enjoyed the suffrage since 1843, so the amendment would not affect their status, but some overly cautious Republican conservatives among the group led by Anthony, U.S. Senator William Sprague, and Congress-man Nathan F. Dixon clouded the issue by expressing fears that the word "race" in the amendment could be interpreted to mean "ethnicity" and thereby invalidate Rhode Island's real estate voting requirement for the foreign-born. In fact, several histories of Ire-land have referred to "the Irish race."

Nativism blinded some Republicans to the great advantage their party would gain nationally by the black vote. Their atti-tude was reminiscent of the sentiments expressed against Thomas Dorr's People's Constitution in 1842, when that document granted suffrage to natives and naturalized on equal terms, while the Freemen's Constitution, offered by conservatives as an alternative, proposed a real estate requirement for the foreign born. As one of Dorr's followers in Tiverton confided to him, "this right to exclude naturalized citizens is strongly insisted upon here, and has perhaps operated against us more than anything else. Men were called upon not to vote for a constitution but to vote against Irishmen." When blacks were given the ballot by the Law and Order Convention of November 1842, Congressman Elisha Potter, a moderate, perceptively observed that although some opposed this concession, "there is not so much scolding about letting the blacks vote as was expected"; the delegates "would rather have the Negroes vote than the damned Irish."[15]

Although a generation had passed, prejudice persisted. As one journalist for the Providence *Morning Herald* observed on May 28, 1869, during the protracted ratification debate, "many Republicans were afraid of the amendment not because they liked the Negroes less but because they feared the Irish more." Some Rhode Island Republicans opposed it because they feared it might give the naturalized Irish the vote; most Democrats opposed it because they believed that it would not.

Supporters of ratification included Republican governor Seth Padelford and G.O.P. congressman Thomas A. Jenckes, the father of civil service reform. This left the dominant Republican Party divided on the issue. Lucius G. Ashley, a resourceful Republican advocate of ratification, assured his more cautious legislative colleagues that if the amendment were interpreted to allow naturalized citizens equal voting rights, a literacy test could then be imposed to disfranchise many of them.

The state senate voted its approval in May 1869 by a margin of 23 to 12, but the House deferred action until January 1870, when at the urging of Governor Padelford it gave its assent by a margin of 57 to 9. Thus Rhode Island grudgingly became the last New England state, and the twenty-fourth overall, to ratify the Fifteenth Amendment. It did so despite factional feuding, intraparty disputes, mixed motives, constitutional confusion, and ethnic tension, but the amendment had been so emasculated by Anthony and his congressional colleagues that neither it nor the Fourteenth Amendment seemed to afford Charles Gorman and his Irish Catholic followers any comfort or relief.[16]

Undaunted, in May 1870, four months after the ratification debate ended, the resourceful Gorman personally carried a petition signed by nearly three thousand Rhode Island citizens to Washington and presented it to the U.S. Senate and to the House of Representatives. The petition asked Congress to determine whether Rhode Island's real estate voting requirement for naturalized citizens conflicted with the Fourteenth and Fifteenth Amendments. Simultaneously, P. O'Neil Larkin, editor of the *Rhode Island Lantern* and a supporter of the radical Fenian movement, submitted a three-hundred-signature petition urging Congress to enact legislation, based upon the new amendments, that would give naturalized citizens equal rights with those who were native-born.

Anthony, now president pro tem of the Senate, immediately attacked these petitions, exclaiming that there was nothing in the constitution of Rhode Island that contravened the Constitution of the United States. Several days later the Senate Judiciary Committee issued a report dismissing the reformers' claims. It further stated that the Privileges and Immunities Clause of the Fourteenth Amendment did not include the right of suffrage. As to the Fifteenth Amendment, the committee observed that Rhode Island's constitution did not preclude any citizen from voting because of race, color, or previous condition of servitude. In fact, the state had specifically banned slavery and enfranchised blacks by its Constitution of 1843.[17]

When Congress disclaimed jurisdiction and was eliminated as a source of support, at least temporarily, Gorman turned to the federal courts in his quest for equal rights. In 1872 he took preliminary steps to bring Rhode Island's real estate qualification before the United States Circuit Court, citing the guarantees of the Fourteenth Amendment, including the Privileges and Immunities Clause, a remedy first suggested by state senator Charles Van Zandt. Before the case was argued, however, the Supreme Court undercut that position in three related decisions, emanating from Louisiana, that curtailed the reach of this amendment. The high court's ruling in the *Slaughter-House Cases* (since repudiated) limited the number of civil rights and liberties under federal jurisdiction and protection, thus leaving most "privileges and immunities" (such as the economic rights of white butchers in Louisiana and, presumably, the voting rights of foreign-born citizens of Rhode Island) to the discretion of state government for their scope and protection. Surprisingly, at that time little thought was given to the Equal Protection Clause, which has since become a bulwark of voting rights in our modern era.[18]

Next the persistent Gorman sought relief under the Fifteenth Amendment, but he was undercut by the Supreme Court decisions in *U.S.* v. *Reese* (1875) and *U.S.* v. *Cruikshank* (1876), in which the Court asserted that the Fifteenth Amendment did not confer the right of suffrage on anyone; it merely prohibited the states from excluding a person from the franchise because of race, color, or previous condition of servitude. The primary control of suffrage remained with the states. With respect to state elections, said the Court, Congress could only legislate against discrimination based on race.[19]

Eventually, in response to the demands of Rhode Island's equal rights advocates, as expressed by Gorman in a long essay entitled *An Historical Statement of the Elective Franchise in Rhode Island* (1879), an investigation of Rhode Island's governmental system was conducted by a committee of the United States Senate, chaired by Pennsylvania Democrat William A. Wallace. The committee's majority report in 1880 concluded that "the rights of suffrage to *foreign-born* citizens of the United States is [*sic*] abridged by the constitution and laws of Rhode Island to a greater extent than anywhere in the nation," and observed that "Rhode Island is the only State in the Union in which native and foreign born citizens stand on different grounds as to State qualifications for the right of suffrage." The committee's findings also disclosed a widespread practice of political intimidation by mill owners of their employees who were eligible to vote. Because of the absence of a secret ballot, the senators observed, "at almost every election for years these men voted under the eye of their employers' agents who were Republicans, and in very many cases under circumstances showing intimidation and fear of loss of work." The committee concluded that there were good grounds for the complaints made that the government of Rhode Island "is nearer an oligarchy than a democracy."[20]

In his 1879 statement to the Wallace committee, Gorman also alleged that the Rhode Island's two-standard system of voting was "unrepublican" and urged Congress to invoke the Guarantee Clause of Article IV, Section 4, to assure that Rhode Island had a republican form of government "and thus to redress any wrong inflicted upon the disfranchised citizens." In addition, citing federal naturalization laws, he asserted that a state's imposition of "additional qualifications upon naturalized citizens" would be recognizing the existence of a right whereby a state could abrogate and set aside federal naturalization laws, thereby "controlling a power which is exclusively vested in Congress" by Article I, Section 8, Clause 4, a federal constitutional provision that gives it the duty to establish a "uniform rule of naturalization."[21]

The Wallace committee's investigation was also a response to an 1878 petition from the relentless Gorman, signed by 1,100 citizens and backed by the state convention of the Democratic Party, demanding a federal constitutional amendment guaranteeing naturalized citizens the right to vote by prohibiting any state from denying such right based upon one's "place of nativity." Although Wallace favored such an amendment in theory, he realized the impracticality of submitting to all the states an amendment that affected only one.[22]

Finally, Wallace and Gorman explored the notion that Congress could invoke Section 2 of the Fourteenth Amendment to deprive Rhode Island of a congressman because its real property requirement deprived one-third of its adult male population of the vote. The clause they considered reads as follows:

> But when the right to vote at any election for the choice of electors for President and Vice President of the United States, Representatives in Congress, the Executive and Judicial officers of a State, or the members of the Legislature thereof, is denied to any of the male inhabitants of such State, being twenty-one years of age, and citizens of the United States, or in any way abridged, except for participation in rebellion, or other crime, the basis of representation therein shall be reduced in the proportion which the number of such male citizens shall bear to the whole number of male citizens twenty-one years of age in such State.[23]

At this suggestion the ailing Henry Anthony sprang into action, blasting the report of Democratic partisan William Wallace and denouncing the suggestion that Rhode Island be constitutionally penalized. His vigorous remarks were reprinted as a *Defense of Rhode Island, Her Institutions, and Her Right to Representatives in Congress*. Needless to say, the threat proved hollow, and the state kept its congressional delegation undiminished.[24]

Anthony penned a final defensive essay in December 1883 for the popular *North American Review*, upholding "Limited Suffrage in Rhode Island" and repeating his oft-stated argument that the real estate requirement for naturalized citizens had an "excellent effect" in elevating the character of the foreign-born by providing them with an incentive to acquire property. If this incentive were taken away, said Anthony sarcastically, a main element in the foreign population's "good order, stability, and thrift" would be removed.[25]

On September 2, 1884, shortly after this last salvo, Anthony died in office of a kidney ailment, with his lifetime legacy intact and no federal or state constitutional remedy to disturb it as yet.

Eventually, in 1887—when Gorman himself was Speaker of the Rhode Island House of Representatives (the first House session controlled by Democrats since 1854)—the Bourn Amendment was passed by the General Assembly, and a year later it was ratified by a narrow margin to become Article of Amendment VII to the state constitution. It removed the real estate requirement for voting that had discriminated against the foreign-born, but it did so at a time when native-born citizens of Irish descent greatly outnumbered naturalized Irish.

Sponsored by former Republican governor Augustus O. Bourn, the amendment in effect allowed newly arrived British, Swedish, German, Franco-American, and Italian immigrants to vote in state elections immediately upon naturalization. Republican leaders hoped these disparate groups would align themselves with the G.O.P. and consequently check the rising political power of the native-born Democratic Irish, from whom these newer ethnics were culturally estranged. Their hopes were realized. This political effect may explain how powerful Republican boss Charles R. Brayton, Anthony's protégé and successor, could give his indispensable support to this pseudo-reform. "Be careful what you wish for; you may get it!" Gorman himself may have mused. But the Bourn Amendment is another complex story—one which shows that the political rivalry of Yankee and Celt, spawned during the Dorr Rebellion of the 1840s, was still alive and virulent at the end of the nineteenth century and well beyond.[26]

Sadly, because of the emasculation of the Fifteenth Amendment, America waited ninety years and more for the federal government to provide by judicial interpretation and congressional legislation what Henry Wilson, John Bingham, and their fleeting majority of House and Senate members attempted in February 1869. But Wilson was undoubtedly correct, as was Anthony, when they concluded that the nation was not ready for such idealism and that a broad-based amendment could not have been ratified.[27]

Ironically, the removal of the ban on property and education as suffrage qualifiers left southern blacks vulnerable to disfranchisement. In the decades following Reconstruction, southern Democrats could (and eventually did) impose literacy tests and poll taxes to prevent blacks from voting. Perhaps a creative court could even have interpreted "nativity" as applying to condition of birth as well as place, thereby invalidating the South's notorious grandfather clauses.[28] In 1869, however, some northern Republican moderates seemed heedless of these possibilities. In effect, the Republicans abandoned their long-term hopes for the party in the South when they settled for a Fifteenth Amendment that left the states in practical control of the franchise.[29]

The U.S. Supreme Court has expanded voting rights dramatically in modern times under the aegis of the Fourteenth Amendment and its Equal Protection Clause. The broad interpretation of this amendment has vindicated the scattergun appeal of Charles E. Gorman, who, like his role model Thomas Dorr, eventually prevailed. Henry Anthony, who triumphed over both in life, now suffers the fate of many demagogues and bigots—remembered for his flaws rather than for his achievements.

Notes

1. "Rhode Island: Laboratory for the 'Lively Experiment'," in Patrick T. Conley and John P. Kaminski, eds., *The Bill of Rights and States: The Colonial and Revolutionary Origins of American Liberties* (Madison, Wis., 1992), chap. 6, 123–61.

2. Patrick T. Conley, *Democracy in Decline: Rhode Island's Constitutional Development, 1636–1841* (Providence, 1977), contains a detailed analysis of these events with ample documentation.

3. It is my considered opinion that the Republican Party instituted this mid-decade state census to keep a close track of the rapidly increasing foreign-born population of Rhode Island and to gather therefrom data that could be used for partisan political advantage. To buttress the validity of this opinion, consider the statement of statistician Edwin M. Snow at the outset of his 1865 state census, the first in the nation to record the demographic factor of parentage: "It seems to me," said Dr. Snow, "to be of the utmost importance that in our censuses, and in all our statistical investigations, that we should be able to classify the population, not only by nativity but also by parentage, that we should be able to show not only the facts related to those of foreign birth, but also those relating to their children, as distinguished from the children of American parents." *Report upon the Census of Rhode Island*, 1865 (Providence, 1867), lvi–lvii. See also Mary Cobb Nelson, "The Influence of Immigration on Rhode Island Politics, 1865–1910" (doctoral dissertation, Radcliffe College, 1954).

4. The most detailed analysis of this post-rebellion suffrage agitation is Robert M. Laffey, "The Movement to Achieve Suffrage Reform in Rhode Island, 1829–1888" (master's seminar paper, Providence College, 1978), a 156-page study written by Professor Laffey in my seminar. A regular attendee of Constitution Day, Bob completed his doctoral studies at the University of Notre Dame. Also helpful are Patrick T. Conley and Matthew J. Smith, *Catholicism in Rhode Island: The Formative Era* (Providence, 1976), 39–55, 76–83, 96–103; Conley, *Democracy in Decline*, 309–79, which emphasize the ethnoreligious aspects of the suffrage controversy; and Chilton

Williamson, "Rhode Island Suffrage since the Dorr War," *New England Quarterly* 28 (March 1955): 34–50.

5. Conley and Smith, *Catholicism*, 96–103, and Patrick T. Conley, *Liberty and Justice: A History of Law and Lawyers in Rhode Island, 1636–1998* (Providence, 1998), 353, 358, 365, 367, 370. There are several contemporary accounts of the 1870s reform effort by its advocates: Charles C. Van Zandt, *A Constitutional Convention* (Providence, 1870), a speech delivered in the state senate, March 1, 1870; Sidney Dean, *A Constitutional Convention* (Providence, 1871), a speech delivered in the state senate on February 1 and 9, 1871; Charles E. Gorman, *An Historical Statement of the Elective Franchise in Rhode Island* (Providence, 1879); Abraham Payne, *The Elective Franchise; An Argument . . . for a Constitutional Convention* (Providence, 1882); and Charles S. Bradley, *The Methods of Changing the Constitutions of the States, Especially That of Rhode Island* (Providence, 1885).

6. Conley and Smith, *Catholicism*, 97–98; Laffey, 68–76.

7. For the votes on these constitutional referenda and on general elections, consult the appropriate volume of the *Rhode Island Manual*, a detailed biennial handbook from the secretary of state that began publication in 1867 and continued until 1994.

8. Thomas Durfee, *Some Thoughts on the Constitution of Rhode Island* (Providence, 1884), 7–17. In a similar vein is William P. Sheffield, *The Mode of Altering the Constitution of Rhode Island, and a Reply to Papers by Hon. Charles S. Bradley and Honorable Abraham Payne* (Newport, 1887). Durfee makes frequent reference to the working class in his justificatory treatise. Professor Scott Molloy, our Constitution Day announcer, has written two in-depth studies of the Rhode Island labor movement during this era, emphasizing the Irish workforce and the relationship between labor and constitutional reform efforts: *Trolley Wars: Streetcar Workers on the Line* (Washington and London, 1996) and *Irish Titan, Irish Toilers: Joseph Banigan and Nineteenth-Century New England Labor* (Durham, N.H., 2008). Not until 1902 did Rhode Island workers get the ten-hour day (for a six-day workweek). The reform gave a big break to women and children by cutting their workweek to only fifty-eight hours. Molloy, *Trolley Wars*, 112–13, and Banigan, 90.

9. Durfee, *Some Thoughts*, 11–12.. 10

10. Gorman, *Historical Statement*, 15–20.

11. On Anthony, his career, and his nativist views, see Patrick T. Conley, "Henry Bowen Anthony," in *The Encyclopedia of American Political Parties and Elections*, ed. Louis Maisel (New York, 1990); William M. Ferraro, "Henry Bowen Anthony," in *American National Biography* (1990); William Barrie Thornton, "Henry Bowen Anthony: Journalist, Governor, and Senator," (master's thesis, University of Rhode Island, 1960); Robert C. Power, "Rhode Island Republican Politics in the Gilded Age" (unpublished honors thesis, Brown University, 1972); and Mary N. Tanner, "The Middle Years of the Anthony-Brayton Alliance, or Politics in the Post Office, 1874–1880," *Rhode Island History* 22 (July 1963): 65–76. Anthony speaks for himself with unwavering fervor from his opening remarks in the *Providence Journal*, August 16 and 29, 1838, as a twenty-three-year-old to his swan song at age sixty-eight: Henry Bowen Anthony, "Limited Suffrage in Rhode Island," *North American Review* 137 (1883): 413–21. At the start of the state constitutional reform effort in 1870, Anthony wrote a lengthy account of the Dorr Rebellion, defending his victorious Law and Order faction as "the men who vindicated Constitutional government and the union of liberty with law," with the clear implication that Gorman, Dean, Larkin, and company were on the same rabble-rousing course as Dorr: *Manufacturers' and Farmers' Journal* (Providence), November 28, 1870.

12. *Congressional Globe*, 40th Cong. 3rd sess. (1869), passim. These debates are conveniently compiled, arranged, and reproduced in a single volume: Alfred Avins, ed., *The Reconstriction Amendments' Debates* (Richmond, Va., 1967), 335–417. For a good general survey of the battle over this constitutional issue, consult William Gillette, *Politics and the Passage of the Fifteenth Amendment* (Baltimore, 1965). Gillette's very detailed and analytical description of the January and February debates in both houses (46–78) is impressive, except for the fact that it makes only one fleeting reference to Henry Anthony. The final House vote on the Fifteenth Amendment was 145 in favor, 44 against, with 35 congressmen "not voting," while the Senate approved with 39 yeas, 13 nays, with 14 "absent." See also Alexander Keyssar, *The Right to Vote: The Contested History of Democracy in the United States* (New York, Basic Books, 2000), 93–104.

The most useful general study of the Reconstruction Congresses is Michael Les Benedict, *A Compromise of Principle: Congressional Republicans and Reconstruction* (New York, 1975).

13. Conley, *Democracy in Decline*, 320–33.

14. *Congressional Globe*, 40th Cong. 3rd sess. (1869), s. p. 1640–41. When Vice President Wilson died suddenly in November 1875, Senate president pro tem Anthony delivered a moving eulogy.

15. Conley, *Democracy in Decline*, Joshua R. Rathbun of Tiverton, 321; Potter, 345.

16. Gillette, *Politics*, 84–85, 150–53; Laffey, "Suffrage Reform," 67–68; Conley and Smith, *Catholicism*, 100–01; James M. McPherson, *The Struggle for Equality: Abolitionists and the Negro in the Civil War and Reconstruction* (Princeton, N. J., 1964), 497, 560; *Providence Journal*, February 11, 1869, January 19, 1870; *Providence Morning Herald*, May 28, 1869; *Providence Evening News*, January 18–19, 1870. The political maneuvering and votes can be ascertained in the manuscript Journal of the Senate, 1868–71, and the Journal of the House of Representatives, 1869–71, at the Rhode Island State Archives. See also *The Message of Seth Padelford, Governor of Rhode Island to the General Assembly at its January Session, 1870* (Providence, 1870), 15.

17. Gorman, *Historical Statement*, 18–20; Laffey, "Suffrage Reform," 79–71; *The Rhode Island Lantern*, January 29, February 19, 26, 1870; *Congressional Globe*, 41st Cong., 2nd sess. (1870), 3605–6, 3649, 3828; and Senate Report No. 187.

18. Gorman, *Historical Statement*, 29; 83 U.S. 36 (1873). See also *Minor* v. *Happersett*, 88 U.S. 162 (1875), which reaffirmed the *Slaughter-House* decision in a case where a woman sought voting rights under the Privileges and Immunities Clause by challenging a state statute that limited the franchise to male citizens. On the current use of the Equal Protection Clause as it pertains to voting rights, see Congressional Reference Service, *The Constitution of the United States: Analysis and Interpretation* (Washington, GPO) in the section entitled "Fundamental Interests: The Political Process," and Ward E. Y. Elliott, *The Rise of Guardian Democracy: The Supreme Court's Role in Voting Rights Disputes, 1845–1969* (Cambridge, Mass., 1974).

19. Gorman, *Historical Statement*, 29; 92 U.S. 42 (1875); 92 U.S., 214 (1876).

20. Gorman, *Historical Statement*, 21–26; 46th Cong. 2nd sess. (1880), Senate Reports Nos. 427 and 572. In response to this criticism and because of the strength of the Equal Rights Movement in the 1880s, the General Assembly finally enacted a secret ballot statute in 1889.

21. Gorman, *Historical Statement*, 21, 26–27.

22. Ibid., 22–23; Laffey, "Suffrage Reform," 147.

23. Gorman, *Historical Statement*, 32–34. In figures from the Ninth Census (1870) upon which Gorman relied, the Irish numbered 31,534 in a total foreign-born population of 55,396; but the first figure did not include many immigrants of Irish ancestry who had migrated from England, Scotland, and British Canada. The number of Irish who followed this pattern of migration was considerable. See Conley and Smith, *Catholicism*, 117–19. The native population was 161,957, and it included many first- and second-generation Irish. The normal Republican majority in state elections was about 11,000 votes. See Bureau of the Census, *Ninth Census*, I, 320, 336–42, 370. A broader-based Fifteenth Amendment, or the modern interpretation of the Fourteenth, would have given Irish Catholic Democrats control over state government in 1870, except for the "rotten borough" senate.

24. *Congressional Record*, 46th Cong. 3rd sess. (February 13, 1881), 1490–99, separately published as *Defense of Rhode Island, Her Institutions and Her Right to Her Representatives in Congress* (Washington, 1881). For a compilation of Anthony's speeches, see Sidney S. Rider, "Anthony, H. B., Speeches in Congress and Other Papers (1861–1875)," Rider Collection, John Hay Library, Brown University.

25. Anthony, "Limited Suffrage." See earlier statements of this position in *Providence Journal*, October 6, 1871, and September 16, 1875.

26. Patrick T. Conley, *Rhode Island in Rhetoric and Reflection* (Providence, 2004), chap. 21, "The Constitution of 1843: A Sesquicentennial Obituary," 171–181, and chap. 49, "The Persistence of Political Nativism in Rhode Island, 1893–1915: The A. P. A. and Beyond," 465–73. See also Patrick T. Conley and Robert G. Flanders Jr., *The Rhode Island Constitution: A Reference Guide* (Westport, Conn., and London, 2007), Article II, "Of Suffrage," 121–28. For a perceptive contemporary assessment of the Bourn Amendment, see Sidney

S. Rider, "The End of a Great Political Struggle in Rhode Island," *Book Notes*: 5 (April 28, 1888): 53–58.

27. New Jersey's belated ratification on February 15, 1871, made it the thirty-first state to approve the Fifteenth Amendment. However, New York had rescinded its ratification on January 5, 1870, and four states (Virginia, Mississippi, Georgia, and Texas) ratified because Congress made such action required for restoration to the Union. Only twenty-six states of the twenty-eight that were necessary freely and unequivocally ratified the Fifteenth Amendment. Anthony's calculations were exactly correct! Gillette, *Fifteenth Amendment*, 84–85; Keyssar, *The Right to Vote*, 102–03.

28. The grandfather clause was a device in Southern state constitutions to circumvent the Fifteenth Amendment by granting an exemption from property-owning, tax-paying, or educational requirements to those who possessed the right to vote prior to the mid-1860s and to their lineal descendants. Since Negroes in the South could not vote at that time, they were excluded from the privilege granted to impoverished or illiterate whites. The clause was enacted by seven states, but declared unconstitutional in 1915 by the U.S. Supreme Court in *Guinn and Beal* v. *U.S.* (238 U.S. 347). The first southern grandfather clause was adopted in South Carolina in 1890. Ironically, and consistent with the theme of this essay, it was allegedly modeled on an 1857 Massachusetts statute passed by Know Nothing legislators to restrict the Irish immigrant vote. See Keyssar, *The Right to Vote*, 111–13.

29. Historian William Gillette, the author of the standard monograph on the framing of the Fifteenth Amendment, believes that many northern Republican moderates supported the Fifteenth Amendment in its final form mainly to enfranchise northern blacks in states where party strength was approximately equal, Gillette, *Politics*, pp. 85–91. Michael Les Benedict, the major authority on the Radical Congresses of this era, calls this belief "weak" and "naive." Citing remarks by Senators Wilson and Samuel C. Pomeroy of Kansas, both radicals, and House manager George S. Boutwell, Benedict concludes that "no Republican could discount the danger that by enfranchising northern blacks the party might alienate that minority of its white adherents who still opposed black politi-

cal participation in the North." Benedict, *Compromise of Principle*, 305–36. This view, that most Republicans acted from principle and "devotion to equal rights," is supported by LaWanda and John Cox, "Negro Suffrage and Republican Politics: The Problem of Motivation in Reconstruction Historiography," *Journal of Southern History* 33 (August, 1967): 303–30. On the initial legality of the South's campaign to limit the black vote, see Elliott, *Rise of Guardian Democracy*, 67–84.

The bicentennial commemoration of the Constitution and the Bill of Rights formally concluded in 1991 on December 15, the day when Virginia became the eleventh state to ratify the Bill of Rights. This action made the first ten amendments an integral part of the federal Constitution. That epochal event was marked by major ceremonies in Philadelphia and Richmond, Virginia.

At the Pennsylvania observance *Constitution Day* editor Patrick Conley of Rhode Island, president of the United States Constitution Council, delivered the major address (shown here) at Congress Hall, adjacent to the building where the Constitution was signed by thirty-nine delegates from twelve states (excluding Rhode Island) on September 17, 1787. During his oration Dr. Conley apologetically noted Rhode Island's absence from the Philadelphia Convention, while also noting that state's contributions to religious liberty, separation of church and state, democratic localism, federalism, and popular ratification of constitutional change.

Photo courtesy of Lou Notarianni

THE END